The Lisbon Lions

Celtic

The Lisbon Lions

Andy Dougan

Virgin

First published in Great Britain in 1997 by
Virgin Books
an imprint of Virgin Publishing Ltd
332 Ladbroke Grove
LONDON W10 5AH

A catalogue record for this book is available from the British Library.

ISBN 1 85227 602 9

Phototypeset by Intype London Ltd
Printed and bound by
Mackays of Chatham, Kent

To Christine, as always, and to Iain and Stuart who were born too late to see the Lions in their pomp.
And, of course, to the Lisbon Lions.

Acknowledgements

It seems self-evident, but this book would not have been possible were it not for the Celtic players who embarked on that grand European adventure with their first game against Zurich on 28 September 1966. I am enormously grateful to them for the privilege of having watched them in my childhood and in my youth, and I look forward in the fond hope of their modern counterparts enriching my middle years.

Anyone looking to find a blow-by-blow account of the 1967 campaign, with contributions from all those who took part, should look elsewhere. This is not a football book in that sense: it is an attempt to tell the story of a great adventure – an attempt to tell the story of how footballing virtue triumphed over crude cynicism. It was not my intention to speak to all of the Lisbon Lions. My choices were in many ways arbitrary and in many other ways quite logical. I know, however, that not everyone will agree with them.

I am, as always, so grateful to so many people, but especially to those Celtic players who took the time with unfailing good humour to relive the memories of 30 years ago. I would like to thank Steve Chalmers, Jim Craig, Tommy Gemmell and Bobby Lennox; but most of all, I would like to thank the greatest living Celt, Billy McNeill.

My thanks also to David Kells and Peter McClean at Celtic FC and to Andrew Smith of *The Celtic View* and, of course, to Tommy Burns. The contributions of the fans who took part in that glorious campaign should also not be overlooked. My thanks to Joe Connelly, Pat Monaghan, John McCabe and David Potter, as well as those who contributed anecdotes in various forms.

Many of the statistics in this book go beyond me, and I gratefully acknowledge the work of men like Pat Woods, Tom Campbell, Eugene MacBride, Martin O'Connor and George Sheridan, and their work in *The Celtic A–Z*, *An Alphabet of the Celts*, and *Celtic 1888–1995*. I am also extremely grateful for the patience of the staff at various libraries, but especially, The Glasgow Room at the Mitchell Library.

I should also like to thank Bob Crampsey, Hugh Keevins, Brian Dempsey and John Quinn for many things, and not just for their contributions to this book.

And finally, thanks, as always, to my agent Jane Judd, who is American, but still got the point of this book.

Author's Note

Anyone who felt so inclined could have seized complete control of Glasgow on the evening of 25 May 1967. For two hours – from around 5.15, until 7.15 – the city was completely deserted. A few moments after 7.15, the city felt like VE Day, New Year's Eve and the party round at your house the night you win the lottery, all rolled into one.

Only one thing could unite a city like Glasgow, no matter how briefly – football. Some 2000 miles away Glasgow Celtic were in the final of the European Cup. Not only were they in the final, but they had won it crushing the might of Inter Milan in the process. It was a great moment to be alive and to be a Celtic supporter. It was the night the Lisbon Lions were born.

There are two dates which every Glaswegian child of the sixties remembers. The first is 22 November 1963 when the city's huge Irish-Catholic community felt the death of John Kennedy almost as keenly as they did across the Atlantic. The second is 25 May 1967 when the city was united behind a team of young men, all of them born within 30 miles of each other, who were going out to show the world how football should be played.

I remember exactly what I was doing on both those days, but I suspect the Celtic game will live with me longer. It was a defining moment of my childhood, as it was for so many others. It was the first time that I realised why – even though I had never heard the phrase at that time – football is called 'The Beautiful Game'.

The Lisbon Lions were simply breathtaking. It was 30 years ago this year. This is the story of their adventure – a football fairy tale.

Chapter 1

EARLY IN THE EVENING of 25 May 1967, Billy McNeill made footballing history in Portugal. He was captain of a Glasgow Celtic side which had just beaten Inter Milan – the pride of Italy – in the European Cup final at the National Stadium in Lisbon. The Italians were such hot favourites you could scarcely find an Italian bookmaker who would take a bet. Celtic were a local team barely fit to lace the boots of the Italian maestros, so the argument went. Yet it was McNeill, and not his opposite number Giacinto Facchetti, who was the triumphant captain. Celtic beat Inter 2–1 and became the first British side to win the coveted trophy. They were also the first northern European side to win, ending eleven years of dominance by Spain, Portugal and Italy.

His fellow Celtic players called McNeill 'Caesar'. The nickname has its origins in the 1960 movie *Ocean's Eleven* which so impressed some of the young Celtic players that they formed their own Parkhead 'rat-pack'. McNeill was the only one with a car, and he was nicknamed after the character played by Cesar Romero, who did all the driving in the film. But, that day in Lisbon, his nickname took on more imperial connotations. His face a mask of confusion, disbelief and elation, sweat matting his hair to his forehead, he looked every inch the conquering hero as he lifted the trophy over his head.

He was the first British captain to get his hands on the world's leading club trophy. This moment of triumph completed an incredible journey for the then 27-year-old footballer. McNeill unashamedly talks about the 'fairy tale' which surrounds Celtic, but this was not a happy ending. This was only the beginning of the most remarkable period in the club's history, a period in which they would achieve an unprecedented domination of British football, as well as becoming one of the most feared footballing sides in the world.

The men who re-wrote the record books one afternoon in Lisbon became known as the Lisbon Lions. They were a carefree, happy-go-lucky bunch of young men whose adventurous and cavalier approach to their play swept away a style of football which threatened to choke the life out of 'The Beautiful Game'. But it was not all style without substance. They also contained some of the hardest players ever to set foot on the field, and a great many sides would discover that you crossed these men at your peril. They were mainly forged in the adversity and poverty of the Lanarkshire coalfields and the Glasgow housing estates, and they were magnificent in their pomp.

They owed their allegiance to two things. The first was to their club; these men lived and died for Celtic. The second was to their manager. Jock Stein was a man whose tactical reading and mastery of the game was second to none. He was the man who made the difference and the man who bullied, threatened, cajoled and nurtured eleven supremely talented players into the best club side in Europe, and possibly the world.

Like great plays, great films and great books, great football teams are not created overnight. Although Celtic took the foot-balling world by storm in 1967, their *annus mirabilis* was the culmination of a process which had begun more than ten years previously.

Celtic and Rangers – the 'Old Firm' of Scottish football – have dominated the game in Scotland almost since a ball was first kicked in anger. They have see-sawed in their pre-eminence – they are seldom great at the same time – but together they have collectively left every other club in Scotland choking on their dust. Fans of both sides will tell you there is no greater club game than the Old Firm derbies. This is not true. There may well be no greater rivalry – although fans of the rival teams in Manchester, Liverpool, Milan and Madrid would probably argue their case with some justification – but to be depressingly frank, the sectarian element of the enmity between the two sets of Glasgow supporters probably does give an Old Firm derby the edge over any other game in terms of sheer animal passion. That apart, the truth is that games between Celtic and Rangers are fierce, competitive and occasionally brutal, but rarely do they provide classic football.

The traditional New Year encounter in 1956 was one such game. Rangers won 1–0, but the game is only significant now for an injury to Jock Stein who was then the Celtic centre half and captain. Stein had been troubled by an ankle injury which he had picked up at the start of the season, but the recurrence of the injury in the Old Firm game was to effectively finish his career as a player. Despite a determined battle, he would play only three times more for Celtic and, after taking the advice of a Harley Street specialist, he was forced to hang up his boots at the end of the season.

Jock Stein was born in Burnbank, near the Lanarkshire town of Hamilton, on 5 October 1922. He was born 'John' and remained so in his youth, but by the time he started playing football, the Sunday name was reserved for close friends and family. Burnbank was a close-knit mining community, and like almost all of his contemporaries, Jock Stein's future was mapped out for him with numbing clarity. He would finish school at fourteen and go down the pit. Although Stein is remembered now as a great bear of a man, at that time his youth and his hard work meant that he was as lean as a whip. He toiled in the pits but, unlike others, he had been provided with an escape route through football. He played at amateur and juvenile level and briefly for one of Scotland's most famous junior football sides, Blantyre Victoria. The turning point for Stein came not long after his 21st birthday. It was 1942, and although football was continuing, it was badly hit by the Second World War. As a miner, Stein was exempt from military service and, with his junior football experience, he was invited for a trial with Albion Rovers. The Lanarkshire side were in desperate straits because wartime reorganisation had left them as a Second Division side well out of their depth in a reorganised First Division.

'They were then as they are now, everybody's chopping block,' says respected sports journalist and broadcaster Bob Crampsey.

Stein had three trials at centre half – the first, ironically, in a surprisingly creditable 4–4 draw with Celtic – and eventually signed for the Coatbridge club. Crampsey, a Stein biographer, believes that as a player Stein was much better than many people – including the player himself – gave him credit for.

'I saw him play quite a lot, and I can honestly say that I am one of the few people now who did see Jock Stein play a lot,' says Crampsey. 'When I first noticed him playing for Albion Rovers, the thing that struck me about him was that he was a great trier on behalf of a lost cause. Even a Martian going to a game and watching Albion Rovers for ten minutes would have worked that out. I think, though, that it was useful for him to have been with Albion Rovers because it gave him a genuine sympathy for smaller clubs. I don't think this was an assumed sympathy; I think there was a genuine fondness and understanding of the plight of the small side.'

Stein is generally regarded as one of the best signings Albion Rovers ever made and, lost cause or not, it was largely through his commanding presence on the field that Rovers won one of their rare honours when they were promoted from the Scottish Second Division in 1948. Then, as now, money was tight at Cliftonhill, and Stein found himself, not long afterwards, in an argument about wages. Throughout his career, Stein was a great believer that the labourer was worthy of his hire, and he was always determined to make sure that he got what he believed he was entitled to. When it was not forthcoming Stein was determined to move on. His next destination was a bizarre one.

Stein answered a newspaper ad placed by the Welsh non-League club Llanelli. The advertisement said that they were looking for 'players of proven ability. Transfer fees no detriment, only top players need apply.'

Having just had one row about money and possibly foreseeing more on the way, Stein signed for the Welsh club in a move which must have been inspired by financial reasons more than any serious career ambition. They were offering him £12 a week – twice what he was getting at Albion Rovers – and the chance of making a full-time living from football. So Stein duly headed for South Wales, leaving his wife and daughter at home in Hamilton.

'Non-League football in Wales really was the elephants' grave-yard,' recalls Bob Crampsey. 'I think he was always grateful to Celtic for bringing him back from Llanelli. The chap who did that and clearly remembered him playing for Albion Rovers was called Jimmy Gribben. As Stein became more and more successful for Celtic, the chairman, Bob Kelly, used to remember more and more about him, but it was really Gribben who should get the credit.'

Celtic were in dire straits at the end of 1951. The club was in the middle of an injury crisis, and it was indeed reserve-team trainer Jimmy Gribben who suggested Stein as a possible replace-ment who might tide them over. Stein at that time was so unhappy in South Wales – possibly due to homesickness as much as any-thing else – that he would have signed for anyone to get the chance to go back home. Stein was duly signed for a fee of £1200 and made his debut against Saint Mirren on 8 December 1951 in a game which Celtic won 2–1.

'Jock Stein wasn't really bought to play first team football,' explains Bob Crampsey. 'He was bought, at the time, as a useful second-eleven player and maybe someone who could teach the youngsters a thing or two.'

All the best stories require an element of luck, and providence took a hand almost as soon as Stein arrived at Celtic Park. The one thing which the Celtic side was actually overburdened with at that time was centre halves. There were three in the queue ahead of Stein, hence the feeling that he had only been bought to bring on the youngsters. However, first choice centre half Jimmy Mallan quickly aggravated a groin strain; Alec Boden injured his back; and Johnny McGrory was still recovering from a cartilage problem. Stein was barely in the door when this spate of injuries to the defence forced manager Jimmy McGrory to turn to his new signing. Stein seized the opportunity with both hands. Once he was in the side, he made the place his own and was never out again except through injury.

Fate once again took a hand to cement his place in the side. In those days the club captain was able to name his vice-captain and, by extension, his successor. The captain at that time was Sean Fallon, who had nominated Stein as his number two ahead of men like Bertie Peacock and Bobby Evans, who might have seemed more obvious choices. Just before the Christmas of 1952 Fallon broke his arm and was sidelined, so the captaincy then passed to Stein. Fallon plainly saw something in Stein which no-one else had at the stage when he nominated him. Fallon was one of the club's greatest servants, but he yielded to no-one in his admiration for Stein and, in later years, would set aside his own ambition to allow Stein to take over the managerial reins.

But together they formed a great partnership which was responsible for establishing the club's reputation. With the added authority and responsibility of the captaincy, Stein immediately set about stamping his mark on the Celtic side. He read the game superbly and organised his defence magnificently. In the space of three years he led them to a Coronation Cup win and a League and Cup double, as well as victories in the Glasgow Cup and the Charity Cup.

In football terms Jock Stein died a warrior's death. He collapsed at the track side with a massive heart attack during a World Cup qualifier between Scotland and Wales, at Ninian Park in Cardiff, on 10 September 1985. As Scotland manager, he had just sent on Davie Cooper, who scored the goal which gave Scotland the point they needed to be almost certain of qualifying for the World Cup finals the following year. Stein died 30 minutes later. One of the last interviews he gave before his death was an extended two-hour chat on stage with Crampsey. The occasion was part of the celebrations of the 100th anniversary of Dunfermline Athletic, a club which Stein had managed and injected with a renewed sense of self-belief, making the club a significant force in Scottish football in the sixties.

'He had been very friendly with Dunfermline, and he genuinely believed the club had done a lot for him,' explains Crampsey. 'It was a very relaxed discursive sort of interview, and at one point I said to him: "How would you describe yourself as a player?" He laughed, and then said: "A very average player". But he was better than that. He could pass that lunatic test that footballers impose on their managers. That ritual of "Show us your medals", which is the footballing equivalent of "What did you do in the war, Daddy?" He was good enough to have won a League Championship medal, a Scottish Cup medal, a Coronation Cup medal, and one Scottish League cap against the Football League. That's just about enough to shut up the boys in the dressing room.

'He was never a player about whom you would have said, "This man must play for Scotland." He was never even a semi-automatic pick; he was never in that category. But he worked very hard at his game. He was a good player and very good at utilising his own perceived weaknesses, such as a lack of pace, and being a bit one-sided.'

Despite his own assessment of his game, there is no doubt that the loss of Stein to injury at the end of 1956 was a devastating blow to Celtic. The half-back trinity of Bobby Evans, Jock Stein and Bertie Peacock was one of the finest the club has produced. The then manager, Jimmy McGrory, described Stein's injury in the Old Firm game as the turning point of Celtic's season. However, the Celtic side that Stein left was very quickly approaching its sell-by date. He himself was 35, and others, like Charlie Tully, Bertie Peacock and Bobby Evans were also on their way out. As a counter measure to their aging first team – who would incidentally have a glorious last hurrah by massacring Rangers 7–1 in the 1957 League Cup final – the club was setting great store by its youth policy. Critics maintained that it was simply a way for the side to avoid paying transfer fees, but chairman Robert Kelly insisted this was the way forward. They were known as 'the Kelly Kids' and the chairman believed they showed promise. However, they needed guidance; an old head who could settle them down and help them mature as players. Stein was the natural choice. He took over in the summer of 1957, and his brief was to take the youngsters from the school and juvenile ranks under his wing. In the club AGM of September 1957, an obviously delighted Kelly remarked that: 'The misfortune to Jock Stein has in a certain way been good fortune for us. Jock Stein is the ideal person to take on these boys and create a training school which could easily be the nucleus of our teams of the future.'

Stein took to his new task with relish and plainly enjoyed working with the youngsters. They were equally enamoured of him. Here was a man who was prepared to sit and talk with them and explain the game to them. Players never saw the notional manager, Jimmy McGrory, from Saturday to Saturday, unless it was in exceptional circumstances. In that respect Stein was a breath of fresh air which invigorated these young men. Perhaps he saw in them the nucleus of future Celtic sides which Kelly had spoken of. Whatever the reason, he was delighted to be working with young men who shared his enthusiasm, and whose talents he could harness. He was determined that if he was to do his job of bringing them on, then they would need improved facilities. One of his first moves was to persuade the club to buy a proper training ground and, under his prompting, Celtic acquired Barrowfield, which still serves as their training facility.

Stein was a forward-thinker, and he may well have seen, even then, that there was every chance that he would one day manage the club. He ran the reserves and the schoolboys his own way, resisting any interference from either Jimmy McGrory or the board. These youngsters could be the basis of his future at Celtic. If that was to be the case, then they would need someone to lead them on the pitch, as he would lead them from behind the scenes. Every great side needs an inspirational leader, and Stein believed he had found his.

Celtic Park had been used as the venue for a Scottish schoolboys' international in 1957, and one player in particular caught Stein's eye. Whether Stein knew it or not – and given his astonishing depth of knowledge of the game, it is unlikely that he did not – other clubs like Arsenal and Manchester United also had their eye on the player. Stein moved first. He had words with Kelly and McGrory. They already knew of the player because one of their Lanarkshire scouts, Eddie McArdle, had been recommending the young man for some time. Stein's endorsement tipped the scales, and so in 1957 at the age of 17 Billy McNeill signed for Celtic as a part-timer.

The fairy tale had begun.

Chapter 2

BILLY MCNEILL IS THE most successful captain in Celtic's history. His long career has been studded with national and international honours. He is, without doubt, in the hearts and minds of the Celtic faithful, 'the greatest living Celt'. He was an outstanding defender, a superb captain for club and country, and a marvellous ambassador for Scottish football. Once, on a European trip to France, the French hosts issued a gracious welcome to the Celtic side at a civic reception. After a moment, McNeill stood and issued an equally gracious reply in French. He is intelligent, articulate, and a deep thinker about the game. He has also been a successful manager at the highest level, including two spells at Parkhead. In short, he is a natural leader, and it is those qualities, more than anything else, which Jock Stein doubtless spotted when he saw the 17-year-old McNeill in that schoolboy game.

'I wouldn't have been at Parkhead if it wasn't for Jock Stein,' says McNeill, without equivocation. 'Jock Stein was impressed at that game, and it was basically his influence that brought me to Celtic Park. If it had not been for him, then I would have gone down south to either Arsenal or Manchester United. I had just sat my Highers, and there had been all sorts of offers – including some from other Scottish clubs – but my father never wanted me to do anything until I was absolutely sure about it. But Big Jock came out to the house with a man called Eddie McCardle who was a former provost of Motherwell, and did a wee bit of scouting. Eddie had been at the powers that be at Celtic to sign me for long and weary, but it wasn't until Big Jock saw me playing that it became a reality.'

McNeill kept on the day job after he had signed for Celtic and worked in a very understanding firm of insurance brokers who accommodated his requests for time off. It was obvious right from the start that there was an affinity between Stein and McNeill. For one thing, they both shared a position: they were both centre halves. But there was another, deeper bond – they were both from Lanarkshire. For all that it is located midway between, but still close to, the major cities of Glasgow and Edinburgh, that buffer-zone status produces a unique insularity about people from Lanarkshire. Their coalfield provided the raw material for Scotland's once vital manufacturing base, and there is a fierce shared pride and determination about their local identity. Although it is no more than 25 miles from Glasgow or Edinburgh, Lanarkshire is virtually a subculture founded on the twin virtues of hard labour and an innate sense of working-class fairness.

'With the possible exception of Sean Connery or Jackie Stewart, Jock Stein was probably the best-known Scotsman in the world,' argues Bob Crampsey. 'But he was really more than a Scotsman, he was a Lanarkshire man. He laughed when I told him once that one of the things that that entails is that he gets homesick going through the traffic lights at Baillieston, on the Glasgow boundary.'

Billy McNeill, too, believed that their shared geographical bond contributed to their working relationship. When Stein took over the Celtic reserves he was still living in Hamilton, while McNeill was nearby in Motherwell.

'Perhaps it was because he came from Lanarkshire,' McNeill concedes, 'or maybe, now, it just seems like that. There were three centre halves signed in the same year. There was me, a lad called George Gunn, and another lad called John Curran. But Big Jock, being a Lanarkshire man like myself, obviously had a big influence on me. He was the first one who took me and showed an interest in me – and not just me, but lots of the other lads who were there at the time.'

Travelling to Celtic Park, a couple of evenings a week, was a long and tedious journey for McNeill and his Lanarkshire cohort. After training, they would brave the winter chill or the driving rain for the long walk from Celtic Park up to the end of Tollcross Road to wait for their bus. The route on the twenty-mile trip back home was hardly what you would call scenic. But then fortune favoured McNeill – one of the first of the many times it would smile on him in a distinguished career.

'Celtic eventually got Jock a car,' recalls McNeill. 'Where we were fortunate was that, being from Lanarkshire, Jock used to give us a lift home after training. He used to take me, John Clark and Jim Conway, and drop us off at various stages along the route.'

During those car journeys, McNeill and his young cohorts learned huge amounts about the art of football, from one of the masters of the arcane craft. It is easy to dismiss Stein as a typical big man who had fallen into management by dint of having a career prematurely ended by injury. Anyone who did – and there were several Continental managers who did – were given a short, sharp reality check when they faced his Celtic side. Playing at centre half throughout his career had given Stein an unrivalled opportunity to read a game, to judge the ebb and flow of its playing patterns, and to acquire a tactical awareness and an intelligence which belied his bulk. And although many of the practices at Celtic Park in those days were archaic, there were others which were, with hindsight, astonishingly forward-thinking. Celtic officials, for example, were encouraged to go to England to watch the major European sides, who were frequent visitors for club and international friendlies. It was these high-profile club games which ultimately led to the foundation of the European Cup. This meant Stein saw at first-hand the magnificent Hungarian side which tore England apart at Wembley in 1953. He also saw, at first-hand, the 1954 World Cup in Switzerland, in which all of the British teams were thoroughly humiliated. Stein saw all of this, absorbed it, learned from it, and was now passing it on to his young charges on their journey home to Lanarkshire in his car. No-one, incidentally, was happier to see that car than McNeill, Clark and Conway.

'Before he got the car, Jock had to get the Lanarkshire bus as well,' McNeill remembers. 'If our bus came first, it was no go for us, we had to wait with him. His bus went by a different route, and his had to come first or we had to wait. But he was terrific with us, and the experience of those early days sort of set the standard for what to expect when he came back as manager.'

Glasgow Celtic Football and Athletic Club, to use its full and rather romantic title, has its origins in the crippling poverty of the East End of Glasgow in the late nineteenth century. The man largely responsible for the formation of the club was Brother Walfrid, the head teacher of the local Sacred Heart school. A sincere and good-hearted man, he saw his responsibilities as extending to more than simply providing spiritual platitudes for people who had neither food on their tables nor clothes on their backs and were singularly missing the means to remedy either situation. The club was formed as the very embodiment of muscular Christianity to provide a way of raising money for the poor of the East End. It was also intended to give the large Catholic community a sense of identity by giving them a team to rally round, much as the Irish community in Edinburgh had been doing with Hibernian. It was the Hibernian secretary John McFadden who suggested that a similar club be set up in the West of Scotland. Celtic duly and officially came into existence when they played their first game – against Rangers of all sides – on 28 May 1888. It was a friendly match in both name and spirit, since the sectarian aspect, which would taint future games, had not yet emerged. Celtic won 5–2, playing the kind of stylish football which has become their hallmark through the years.

The young reserve side which Stein took over in 1957 were the inheritors of a proud legacy. They included not only McNeill and Clark but others who would become first-team regulars in their time, like Frank Haffey, Pat Crerand and John Divers. But in the three years that he was in charge, he would also influence the careers of Steve Chalmers, Bertie Auld and John Hughes, who would all come under his guidance at one time or another. Five of those men would play crucial roles in the 1967 European campaign. Those who joined the club just after Stein had moved on for a legitimate taste of first-team management with Dunfermline, included Tommy Gemmell, Bobby Lennox, Bobby Murdoch and Jimmy Johnstone. Although they would not be directly influenced by Stein first time round, they would benefit from the systems he had left in place.

One other thing from which those in Stein's charge benefitted was a winning habit. He proved enormously successful with the youngsters who won the second eleven Cup in 1958, beating Rangers 8–2 on aggregate. They also won the reserve League title. On top of all this, the fans were starting to notice the difference.

'In those days Celtic used to play their reserve games on a Friday night,' recalls John McCabe, a Glasgow schoolteacher who has been watching Celtic for more than 40 years. 'A friend and I used to go along occasionally, and you could see what Stein was doing with them. You could see that they had a plan. You could see that they were playing as a team and that there were tactics at work there. He was very, very good with these young players.'

The idea behind a youth policy is to nurture young talent and provide it with a protected and protective environment in which to grow. Alex Ferguson's almost obsessive cosseting of young players like Ryan Giggs, and now David Beckham, at Manchester United, is a textbook example. Ferguson may appear to be an old woman at times, but he knows he is carrying precious cargo, and both players show every sign of flourishing under his stewardship. Doubtless that was Robert Kelly's thinking at Celtic, too, but it wasn't working out that way in practice. Even by their own recent low standards season 1959–60 was a dismal one for Celtic. They had failed to qualify from their League Cup section, they averaged less than a point a game in the League, they lost to Rangers in the Scottish Cup semi-final, and they came within six minutes of being beaten by non-League Elgin City.

The Kelly Kids, the alleged jewels in the crown of Celtic's future, were being used like cannon fodder. John Hughes, who had signed in 1959 as a 16-year-old, played 34 games in the 60–61 season and 43 the following year as a raw 18-year-old. McNeill had been playing regularly since making his debut in the 58–59 season. Other young players like Chalmers, Auld and Charlie Gallagher, were also being thrown into the breach in a desperate attempt to get some kind of success. The fact is that the club was in the middle of a run which would see them go eight years without winning a major trophy.

In the midst of all this, Celtic also managed to part company with the man who, even without the benefit of hindsight, was their best hope for the future. Stein's reserve side was winning trophies regularly, and it now seems glaringly obvious that since a lot of the youngsters he had worked with in the reserves were now in the first team, it would make sense to promote Stein. The moribund Celtic board, like their predecessors and successors, were never ones for doing the obvious. Instead, they persevered with the amiable and well-liked, but largely ineffectual, Jimmy McGrory.

Stein, meanwhile, had been talking to chairman Bob Kelly about his future. No matter who was in the manager's chair, no-one should be under the impression that anyone but Kelly ran Celtic at that time. His self-appointed responsibilities were awesome, and he claimed a dynastic right to virtually run every aspect of the club, even to the point of changing McGrory's team selection on an *ad hoc* basis. In an interview with the BBC some years later, Stein would reveal the gist of their conversation. One popular view among Celtic fans was that the club was looking to farm Stein out to another side to get a little managerial seasoning before bringing him back into the fold. That certainly doesn't appear to be Stein's recollection.

He told the BBC that, as far as Kelly was concerned, he had probably gone as far as he could at Celtic. There was a perception that, with the addition of Sean Fallon to the coaching staff, Stein's promotion chances had slipped somewhat. There was also another more sinister inference which Stein drew from his conversation with Kelly. Stein was a non-Catholic and Celtic, whose origins lie in a Catholic religious order, had never had a manager, or a board member, for that matter, who was not a Catholic.

'I was a non-Catholic,' Stein told the BBC, 'and maybe they felt that I wouldn't achieve the job as manager. But I moved out to try and prove that I could be a manager.'

Dunfermline Athletic were struggling against the prospect of relegation in 1960. Their board, which was plainly more forward-thinking than their counterparts at Celtic Park, saw Stein as their salvation and made an approach for his services as manager. Celtic tried to hold on to him by offering an extra £250 a year – the average working wage was less than £500 a year at this time – but Stein was adamant that he wanted the chance to manage his own side. He also asked that he be allowed to leave immediately to try to save Dunfermline from the drop. His players were distraught and despaired for their future if Stein was allowed to leave. But after their initial offer, Celtic did not stand in his way. Stein had been approached by Dunfermline on Sunday, 13 March 1960. The following Saturday he was in charge as manager for the first time. Ironically, they were playing Celtic, and the revitalised Dunfermline won 3–2 to begin a run of games which would see them successfully steer clear of relegation.

Having avoided the drop down to the old Second Division in his first season, Stein continued to thrive at Dunfermline. He took a provincial side and instilled in it a self-belief based on the basics of good football. One of their most significant results of his tenure was a Scottish Cup win in 1961. Again, Celtic provided the opposition for another managerial triumph. Celtic were fancied to win, but Stein organised his side superbly, and his goalkeeper Dennis Connaghan had the game of his life. The first game finished 0–0 and more than 115,000 spectators were at Hampden for the replay. Stein had made a couple of tactical changes from the first game, but, once again, Connaghan was in inspirational form. At the other end Frank Haffey was in goal for Celtic. Haffey had recently had the misfortune to be in goal for Scotland when they were hammered 9–3 by England. Another of his Celtic teammates – Billy McNeill – made his international debut against England that day, but McNeill had an outstanding game and was one of the few Scottish players to emerge with any credit.

Although he was now playing in a Scottish Cup final replay, the England debacle had affected Haffey, and it clearly still preyed on his mind. Dunfermline had already gone a goal up, but Haffey gifted them the game two minutes from time, by dropping the ball at the feet of Dickson who duly stuck it in the net. After his triumphs with Dunfermline, Stein then moved to Hibs, briefly, where his knack of winning trophies continued to flourish with a win in the now-forgotten Summer Cup, before the start of the 64–65 season. Celtic, for their part, continued to struggle, losing another Cup final, this time to Rangers. It was plain that something would have to be done and soon.

'Celtic, before 1965, were a shambles,' says Bob Crampsey. 'They would do things like win the first leg of a semi-final in the old Fairs Cup 3–0 here, and then go to Budapest and lose the away tie 4–0. They were going nowhere.'

Joe Connelly had seen Celtic play for the first time back in 1939 when he was a boy of seven. He genuinely despaired of them winning anything in those days. 'They were terrible,' he says simply. 'Nobody knew what they were doing, and Bob Kelly had far too much of a say in things. I think he was a straight man and an honest man, but he knew nothing about picking a football team.

'I remember when I was still a boy at school, and I'd come in from the match, and my mother would say: "How did they get on Joe?" I'd tell her: "Ma, we were all over them; we did this, we did that, we were great. We hit the post, we had penalties denied." Then she would say: "What was the score, Joe?" And I would say: "Rangers won 4–0." She said: "Joe, son, I think you're going off your head." '

If he was, then, Joe Connelly wouldn't have been the only one. The disaffection which was being voiced privately in the boardroom, and publicly among the fans, was also spreading to the players. Even the lion-hearted McNeill was looking to his future and considering his options after Stein had been allowed to leave. Pat Crerand, the immensely gifted midfielder who had signed on the same day as McNeill, had already been transferred to Manchester United. That was in 1963, but it looked like McNeill would be following him south.

'I was 25, and all of a sudden my career didn't seem to be heading any which way,' says McNeill, who by this time had the pressure of a wife and family to provide for, and a mortgage to pay. 'Celtic as a club were not being given any direction. To be quite honest I would probably have joined the drift of people away from the club. Celtic were heading nowhere. We had a whole lot of talented kids who had now got that bit older, but still didn't seem to be going anywhere.'

By 1965, Celtic had had only three managers in the club's

history. After the formation of the club in 1888, Willie Maley was appointed the first manager in 1897. He was succeeded by Jimmy McStay in 1940, and then Jimmy McGrory took over in 1945. McGrory was one of the best-loved players ever to pull on a Celtic jersey. As a centre forward he set, and continues to hold, all of the club's goal-scoring records. His job as a manager appears to have been largely titular. The autocratic chairman Robert Kelly picked the team and also had a large say in the tactics. McGrory was simply a figurehead. He was, however, revered by players and fans alike – even now Billy McNeill still refers to him as 'Mr McGrory' as a mark of respect – and if change were needed, then in his case it would have to be change with dignity.

The pressure for change was growing and, as is often the case at Celtic, it began with the fans. They could not help but notice how well Dunfermline and Hibs had done under Stein's steward-ship, and how poorly their own side was doing. They started to talk and chant openly about bringing Stein back to Celtic Park. After starting 1965 with three defeats, one of them against Rangers in the New Year's Day game, Celtic held an emergency board meeting. Stein had kept in regular touch with Kelly who, despite his own doubts about the suitability of the manager's religion, must have at least begun to see that he had made an awful mistake. Kelly was never one to admit his mistakes, but Stein tipped the scales when he let it be known that he was considering moving to England following tentative approaches from Wolves. Kelly spoke to the board and, after that emergency session, he was given permission to approach Stein. Naturally, Stein was more than receptive to the idea, but he was now also negotiating from a position of strength. He had managed two First Division teams without any of the sort of boardroom interference which had been the hallmark of the Celtic administration. If he was coming back, then he would want things done his way, or not at all.

However, the board were keen, and rightly so, to spare the feelings of Sean Fallon who was then McGrory's assistant. Although McGrory was the nominal manager, Fallon was the *de facto* manager, and his contribution to Celtic should not be overlooked. He was the one who was ultimately responsible for the signing of many of the players who would provide the club with its greatest success. Quietly spoken, and diffident to the point of shyness, in public, Fallon appears to have had no taste for the high-profile job of being a football manager. He and Stein met to discuss the situation, and Fallon assured the board that he would have no problem working with the man he had, after all, nominated to succeed him as club captain. Accordingly, a formula was worked out whereby it could be announced that Stein would be manager, but McGrory would take on the newly created post of public relations officer. Sean Fallon would stay on as Stein's assistant. The announcement of Stein's arrival was made in January of 1965, but he had been given dispensation by Kelly to remain at Hibs who had an outside chance of winning the League. He eventually took over at Celtic Park on 9 March.

The change from McGrory to Stein had immediate effects, and the first to feel the effects were the players. 'Mr McGrory was an old-style manager,' explains Billy McNeill, who by 1965 was team captain. He had taken over from Duncan MacKay at the start of the 1963–64 season. 'He had a trainer who did all the training, and Mr McGrory might come in and talk to you about the team. The training was different, too. There was a theory when I first went to Celtic Park that if you didn't see the ball all week it made you hungrier for it on the Saturday. That might well have been the case, but I used to think that you might well have been hungry for it but, if you hadn't seen it all week, you wouldn't know what to do with it. Big Jock changed all that. Obviously, there was still a lot of running; you can't eliminate that entirely, but it was done with a ball as much as possible.

'Mr McGrory was a lovely man, a real gentleman, but he was an old-style manager, and in his place we had this new modern image. I can't remember ever seeing Mr McGrory in a tracksuit, but it's hard to think of Big Jock out of one.'

The one other major change of the Stein regime was that the team manager now picked the team. Robert Kelly may not have liked it, and indeed there is every sign that he did not, at least to begin with, but the club was in such a state of crisis he could hardly object.

'I think when Jock came, it was going to be his team that

played, and not part of a team with somebody else's influence over it,' continues McNeill. 'That was very important to him, and I think Celtic realised that they had to do something dramatic. They accepted that, and from then on, it was just Jock Stein and us, the players. Directors didn't matter. Directors were just people who turned up at games and sat in a different seat from you. We were never really involved with them in any shape or form. Jock was the man you were involved with on a day-to-day basis.'

The last Celtic side in the pre-Stein era was the one which turned out against Aberdeen at Celtic Park on 30 January 1965, the day before it was announced that he would be re-joining the club as manager. John Hughes scored five goals, and Murdoch, Lennox and Auld scored one each as Aberdeen were hammered 8–0.

It is worth remembering that seven of that side would play and win in Lisbon two and a half years later. Three of the other members of the European Cup winning side – Simpson, Craig and Johnstone – were already on the Parkhead staff, but not playing that day.

Whether he knew it or not, Jock Stein had been given the tools to finish the job.

Chapter 3

BILLY MCNEILL'S DELIGHT AT Jock Stein's return to Parkhead is a well-documented part of the club's folklore. McNeill predicted to anyone who would listen to him that they would see some big changes.

Team-mate John Divers recalls McNeill announcing, when he heard the news, 'Oh, that's fantastic. Wait and see how things change now.' It's reasonable to assume, football dressing rooms being what they are, that McNeill, perhaps, phrased his observation more robustly. But he was right, of course; change was on the way. Not just on the training field, but in the dressing room, the board room and, more importantly for the players and fans, the trophy room. Within six weeks of Jock Stein arriving at Parkhead as manager, Celtic had ended their eight-year trophy drought. They won the Scottish Cup for the first time in eleven years and began an unprecedented run of success.

McNeill and Stein had kept in touch in the five years since Stein had left the post of reserve team manager at Parkhead. When he heard that Stein was coming back, his first reaction was to go to a phone and call him. Another member of the Parkhead squad wasn't quite so enthusiastic. Goalkeeper Ronnie Simpson had been snapped up from Hibs by Sean Fallon. He had been about to go to Berwick Rangers as player-manager when Fallon moved in and signed him from the Edinburgh club, who were then managed by Stein. The thinking by Celtic fans, especially those given to conspiracy theories, was that Stein had deliberately sold Simpson to Celtic as a sort of secret weapon, secure in the knowledge that he would soon be moving there. Stein's biographer, Bob

Crampsey, suggests that this is so much nonsense. Having been sold once by Stein, Simpson fully expected to be on the transfer list again.

'Stein didn't shed any tears over losing Ronnie Simpson,' says Crampsey emphatically. 'Ronnie would tell you that himself. In fact Ronnie's own reaction, when he heard the news of Stein's impending arrival at Celtic Park, on television, was to shout through from the dining room to the kitchen, "Pack your bags Jean, we're on the move again." '

Napoleon preferred his generals to be lucky above all else. Football chairmen prize the same virtue, equally highly. Successful football managers, like successful generals, often need luck more than skill, and Stein had indeed been lucky up till now, if only for being in the right place at the right time. According to Crampsey, who had been a promising goalkeeper himself, and was, in fact, Simpson's deputy in the Glasgow Schools side, Ronnie Simpson was one of Stein's biggest slices of luck.

Simpson was known to one and all at Celtic Park as 'Faither' in deference to his advanced years – he was 35 when he signed. He had had a remarkable career, and not just in terms of its longevity. He had played for Great Britain four times as an amateur, and had played twice in the 1948 Olympic Games. His club sides included Queen's Park, Third Lanark, Newcastle – in the same side as the great Jackie Milburn – Hibs, and now Celtic. He was a remarkably agile keeper possessed of great powers of concentration. He could be called upon to perform great saves after long periods of inactivity, a gift which would be a prerequisite of Celtic goalkeepers under Stein's managership.

'Stein had only one weakness, and that was that he was a very poor judge of goalkeepers,' argues Crampsey. 'Simpson was an accident. Who did he sign that was any good? Stein would sign people like Livingstone, who was a reserve goalkeeper for four years, and who never played. He signed people like Evan Williams and Alastair Hunter who were never quite there. Dennis Connaghan was probably about the best of the bunch. Jim Craig told me once that Jock thought goalkeepers were a bit weird because they picked the ball up. He said if Jock was designing the game from scratch he wouldn't have goalkeepers, and I think there's an element of truth in that.'

Crampsey's comments appear to be borne out by the fact that Stein was a particularly cruel taskmaster on the training field when it came to goalkeepers. One former Celtic player said: 'He could destroy goalkeepers.' John Fallon, in particular, suffered under the lash of Stein's tongue and, although he was popularly perceived to be weak in dealing with cross balls, it is more likely that his confidence had been eroded by his manager.

'But really,' Crampsey continues, 'Ronnie Simpson was an absolutely admirable goalkeeper for three years right at the beginning of Stein's time when they really needed a rock-solid goalkeeper. Before that, they had Frank Haffey who, I think, has been very harshly judged. It took a lot of people to let nine goals through,' says Crampsey of Haffey's role in Scotland's 9–3 defeat by England. 'John Fallon was technically an extremely good keeper, but I don't think he was suited to Stein's style of management. Stein, I think, made him nervous. So Stein needed a little bit of luck about him and, in his case, it was Ronnie Simpson.'

The Celtic supporters were as glad to see Stein back at Parkhead as the players were. 'As soon as Stein came, I knew we would win, and win a lot,' insists John McCabe. 'Before that, no, I never thought they would win anything under that set-up. As well as his success at Dunfermline, Stein had managed Hibs, and they had won the Summer Cup and put Rangers out of the Scottish Cup.

'He didn't have quality players there; in fact, he had players that other managers had found to be quite a handful, but he managed to control them. That, for me, was one of his greatest gifts. He could get the best out of players, even players who were allegedly difficult. There was one chap, who played for both Hibs and Hearts, called Willie Hamilton. He was a marvellous player, but he was a bit wild, and he wouldn't train. But Stein got hold of him and made him into something. He only played for just over an hour against Rangers, in that Cup game, but he destroyed them.'

Billy McNeill would agree that there was a certain amount of something in the air when Stein arrived at Parkhead. It may have been luck; it may have been predestination; or it may simply have been part of that Celtic fairy tale.

'When Jock came back it was just as if things seemed to happen,' says McNeill. 'I've often thought about it since then, and I think perhaps we would have won the Scottish Cup in any event in 1965. I think some things are predestined and meant to happen. But what happened after that would certainly not have occurred without his guidance. The whole thing just exploded. There was a nucleus of those of us who had known him previously – myself, John Clark, John Hughes, Stevie Chalmers and Bertie Auld – we knew him and respected him, but when he came back it was like a new wave at Parkhead.'

Stein's first game in charge was a Wednesday night fixture against Airdrie which Celtic won 6–0, with Bertie Auld scoring five goals. Stein had picked the team himself and the result made him almost bomb-proof when he went into the regular Thursday night board meeting at Parkhead 24 hours later. The four man board – Robert Kelly, Desmond White, James Farrell and Tom Devlin – had hired him, and now they had to back him. Team selection, so long the province of the chairman, was never mentioned, nor would it be again.

The players were delighted.

'It was very different in the days after I had just signed,' recalls winger Bobby Lennox, who joined Celtic in 1961, and was a first-team regular by the time Stein came back as manager. 'I stayed in Saltcoats, and I used to go to training at Parkhead. I would get the train from there and buy a paper to read. The team for the Saturday would always be in the Friday morning paper, because it had actually been picked at the Thursday night board meeting. That all stopped when Jock took charge.'

The immediate priority for Stein was winning the Scottish Cup. Celtic had made it through to the semi-finals before he arrived, and he shepherded them to a semi-final win over Motherwell, after a replay. In a neat touch of football irony, Stein found his new team facing his other footballing love, Dunfermline, in the Scottish Cup final on 24 April 1965.

In those days the Scottish Cup final was not the showpiece game that television has now made it. It was not the stand-alone fixture which was the climax of the season. That Saturday, 24 April 1965, was also the last day of the football season, and other fixtures were taking place. One fixture, in particular, demoted the Scottish Cup to second billing. Kilmarnock were playing Hearts at Tynecastle in what was the closest League Championship race on record. Hearts were leading by two points going into the last day. A win, or even a draw at home, would be enough for them to take the title, after leading for most of the season. The statisticians had been poring over their slide-rules and worked out that the Edinburgh side could even afford to lose 1–0 and still take the title. Both sides would have 50 points but Hearts would have a goal average of 1.87 compared with Kilmarnock's 1.84. A 2–0 win for Kilmarnock, however, would give them the title on goal average. So there was, literally, everything to play for.

Celtic were going into the final against Dunfermline as underdogs. They had done nothing in the League that season and had not won the Scottish Cup since 1954. They could not help but recall that on one of their more recent final appearances it was Dunfermline, managed by Jock Stein, who took the trophy after a disastrous mistake by Celtic keeper Frank Haffey in the replay. So, although newspaper pundits were divided, a reasonable number were siding with Dunfermline to repeat their earlier success.

'Dunfermline had a useful side,' allows Billy McNeill, looking back. 'It's astonishing how Scottish football has changed over the years. The Old Firm were always powerful, but they have become so powerful now that other teams almost don't exist. That wasn't the case then. I just think the drama of the occasion was such that it was going to be an absolutely brilliant final.'

Stein's arrival, too, had played a major part in Celtic's preparation. There was a spring in the step of the Celtic side for the first time in a long while. They were enjoying their football, and they had a sense of belief in themselves but, more importantly, they believed in Stein. No-one believed in him more fervently than his captain, and it was a belief which was reciprocated by Stein's belief in Billy McNeill. It would be simplistic to see the relationship between McNeill and Stein as one of surrogacy; that the manager who had been his mentor since McNeill was 17 years old was, in some way, also a father figure. Bob Crampsey argues, however, that there were may have been other factors involved.

'I think it went even deeper than that,' he suggests. 'I think McNeill was the centre half that Stein would like to have been. I saw both of them a great deal. I saw Stein quite a lot as a player, and I think you learn more about players when they're in adverse circumstances with small clubs. I wouldn't deprecate Stein as a player; he was a good First Division player, but McNeill was an outstanding player. Not only good but, to my mind, he fulfilled the real test of an outstanding player in that he was very good for a very long time. I think that there was an element of gratitude from McNeill. His career had been going nowhere up till then, even though he'd been playing for six or seven years, and he was a full international. So, you have this peculiar thing, where here is a chap who plays from 18 to 25 and, as far as his personal performance goes, he has nothing to show for it, then, suddenly, from 25 to 32, under Stein's management, his arms must have been dropping off from the weight of lifting up cups.'

There is no denying that Billy McNeill was an inspirational captain for Celtic. He was a gifted player and, more importantly, was not afraid of standing his ground against Stein when he had to. McNeill had his own ideas about the game and was capable of expressing them forcefully if need be. Stein respected this in his captain, as he did in others – like Tommy Gemmell and Bertie Auld – who were also given to voicing their opinions.

'McNeill looked like a captain,' says Bob Crampsey. 'If you went into the dressing room and didn't know who was captain, you would have made an informed guess at McNeill simply because of his bearing and the way he conducted himself. He was very good at cajoling and even bullying when he had to, to get the results on the pitch.

'There were, perhaps, others more technically suited to being captain, and Jim Craig comes to mind here,' continues Crampsey. 'This is conjecture, but I think the reason it suited Stein to have McNeill rather than Craig was that Jim is a "what if?" man. I think managers don't like that because it introduces a note of uncertainty. What you're really saying is, "Supposing Plan A is rubbish, what's Plan B?" In that event, the answer may very well be that there is no Plan B, and managers don't want to admit that.

'You can also think of players who were superbly skilful, but completely unsuited for captaincy, like Jimmy Johnstone, for example,' says Crampsey. 'Then there were others who were debarred, not because they weren't very good players, but because they were, perhaps, a touch over-modest, and Chalmers and Lennox come to mind in that category.'

'I think maybe Jock did try to hold me to a higher standard than the rest,' says McNeill. 'I think he felt that if he could get a responsible line from me, then the others would naturally gravitate and follow along. I think we just had a good relationship. To be honest it didn't really bother me whether people liked me or loved me so long as they respected me. I was hell-bent on winning. I had had long enough at Celtic Park with nothing, and winning became the most important thing.'

With a manager as gifted as Stein, and a captain as driven as McNeill, it was only a matter of time before things started to click at Parkhead. From Stein, there was a deliberate attempt to play down the build-up to the Scottish Cup final. The players spent the week at the seaside on the Ayrshire coast, training and relaxing, and then on the Friday they were sent home with instructions to have a long lie-in on the Saturday morning, and then report to a Glasgow hotel at lunchtime.

The fans were in no doubt that things were going to improve. In the few short weeks that Stein had been in charge, they had seen radical changes in the way their side was playing.

'I think there was just a general belief that they could do something,' says David Potter, who saw the 1965 Scottish Cup final as a teenager. 'They played with direction. They had always played with enthusiasm, but now they played with direction as well, and there was a bit of thought in their play.

'My impression was that Stein actually slowed them down,' says Potter. 'In the old days they would go at their game far too fast. You had people like Pat Crerand who could pass a ball better than anyone else, but the forwards were either too far forward or too far back. They didn't have any great thought or co-ordination about them.

'I remember there was a very special atmosphere in Glasgow that day. One of the evening papers had done a lunchtime souvenir special. There was a quote from that which always sticks in my mind. It said: "Even if by some unkind quirk of fate, the Scottish Cup is not wearing green and white tonight, nevertheless, changes will be made."

'I don't think there's any doubt that some of the Celtic side suspected they were playing for their places at the time,' he continues. 'There were certainly going to be changes, but there was a great feeling of destiny that afternoon. I was 17 at the time, and you can always kid yourself on about something which may or may not be about to happen, in retrospect, but I certainly felt this was a very, very important day in the team's life, and in my own life. I'm not sure that I would agree with Billy about some things being predestined,' Potter says. 'I think it needed Stein to think things out.'

Despite the competing attraction of a League decider in Edinburgh, there were 108,000 fans crammed into Hampden that day. Dunfermline were so keen to keep their side secret that manager Willie Cunningham marched his squad of sixteen straight off the bus and into the dressing room at Hampden, and promptly locked the door until it was time for kick-off. It was a windy day, which meant the notorious Hampden swirl – the vortex effect created by the shape of the national stadium which could render the best pinpoint cross absolutely useless – could play a part. Winning the toss was important, but McNeill called it right, and Dunfermline spent the first half attacking into the wind.

If the wind caused any problems, they were not obvious because Dunfermline took a 1–0 lead in sixteen minutes. Auld equalised for Celtic on the half-hour, but Dunfermline went back into the lead three minutes before half time. Again, Auld equalised for Celtic six minutes into the second half. Stein's advice to his players had always been to 'make a game of it', and that is certainly what they were doing in what was turning out to be a memorable final. And, according to McNeill, even though they were behind twice, it never occurred to him or his side that they might lose. This was the difference which Stein had wrought, even in those earliest days.

'I think it was just belief,' says McNeill. 'They wouldn't let go. A lot of the lads in that team had lost to Dunfermline when Jock was in charge there, and I think we were just so determined to get something out of the game, that we kept battering away and battering away and battering away at it. I don't think anyone ever said: "Come on, we're going to have to win this." It was just something that happened.'

There is no doubt that Billy McNeill was the most important player at Celtic Park in Jock Stein's reign. McNeill and Stein served as sword and shield to each other. McNeill's belief in the magic which surrounds his club is deeply held, and why shouldn't it be when he has had so much evidence of it? Evidence like the events of 4.31 on the afternoon of 24 April 1965.

'There are some things you never forget,' says McNeill quietly. 'To be honest, I hadn't scored many goals, because it wasn't the vogue, in those days, for centre halves to go up into the opposing penalty box, but this was something we had decided we would do if we got the chance. They had detailed a man called Alex Smith to baulk my runs. That doesn't mean he was trying to put me on the ground on every occasion, far from it. You don't need to do that. Sometimes it only takes a touch to distract you if you are that focussed, and he had been doing this very successfully.

'Charlie Gallagher and I had talked about this at half time. Charlie was a magnificent striker of the ball – a beautiful striker of the ball – and I knew he would put a good ball in. I told him to hit it as deep as he could, because it's my belief that if the ball is put into an area, then it is your responsibility to go and find it – defensively or offensively, it doesn't matter. For that particular corner, I kept myself well out of the box and, as I say, I had told Charlie to put it deep. If you ever see it on television or video, you'll see that I started my run well outside the box and stole a march on Alex Smith. He never really got to me, Charlie hit a great ball, and my timing was good.'

The moment has been frozen in time in one of the most memorable Scottish football pictures ever taken. There is the young McNeill, framed in the centre of the picture, head and shoulders above everyone else. The ball has left his head and is rocketing past the despairing form of Dunfermline goalkeeper Jim Herriot to the horror of the other Dunfermline players in the picture. The only other Celtic player there is the crouching form of Bobby Lennox who looks for all the world like he's giving his skipper a hand-up.

'The only thing about that picture is that I can't get Bobby Lennox out of it,' jokes McNeill.

'That picture really annoys him,' laughs winger Lennox. 'But there's no doubt that it was Billy's header that started it all off. Winning the Scottish Cup that day was the biggest thing that had happened to any of us.'

Regardless of his joking objections to Lennox's presence, McNeill points out that the drama of the moment was quite remarkable. That is something of an understatement. With nine minutes to go, McNeill had scored his only goal of the season and allowed his team to put one hand on the Scottish Cup. But even then, fate – or sheer blind luck – had played its part in the victory. John Fallon had kept Celtic in the game with two magnificent saves before McNeill had put Celtic in front. Then again, there was another slice of good fortune only minutes before McNeill got, what proved to be, the winner.

'John Clark saved one off the line,' McNeill remembers. 'It was an incredible thing, because he hit it with his knee or his thigh, and it flew upwards and just seemed to take forever. We were all wondering whether it was going to go over the bar or not, and it just seemed to hang there. Then it dropped over the bar. We rode our luck, but you always do in crunch games, and it led towards richer things.'

Celtic won the Scottish Cup final 3–2, and Stein would later admit that had they not won that game, then things would not have gone as well for the club. So, when fans thank Stein or McNeill, they might also spare a thought for John Clark's knee. Riding their luck or not, Celtic had lifted their first trophy in eleven years, and their fans were ecstatic.

'It was remarkable,' says McNeill, of the response. 'The Gorbals was still a real vibrant community in those days; the old tenements were still there, and it was a real hotbed of Celtic support. We were trying to get from Hampden into the Central Hotel for our celebration dinner, and I remember the bus having to dodge round street after street to avoid the crowds. They were all trying to stop the bus to wish us well, and the police outriders were going like hell to get us in. They did, eventually, and when we got there the whole city centre was thronged with people. Eventually, we had to go into a bedroom with a balcony, which overlooked the junction of Hope Street and Gordon Street, to let them see the Cup. It was incredible. I was 25 years old, and if Jock Stein hadn't come back, then I wouldn't have been part of that and what came after it.'

Given that the Celtic side had won the Scottish Cup after such a long interval, and given the style and tenacity they had shown in winning it, it's hardly surprising that their fans were ecstatic. This is something they had waited for, seemingly in vain, for a long time. Jimmy McGrory's annual reports to the board, in September, had, for the past eight years, spoken in sometimes embarrassingly apologetic terms of the team's failure to win any-thing. Not any more. If nothing else, at least Jock Stein would be able to start his first report on an upbeat note.

The importance of this first win to the fans cannot be under-stated. Fans like Pat Monaghan, then 22 years old and working in the Fruit Market in Glasgow, had begun to despair.

'I had honestly come to think they would never win anything,' he says, looking back. 'I grew up in a family tradition of sup-porting Celtic. My father was a supporter, and he took me to games when I was young. I remember going to see Celtic when I was a boy, and I remember the great atmosphere of games against Aberdeen and teams like that. But until Big Billy scored against Dunfermline, I never thought we were ever going to come back out of that period. I was absolutely delighted.'

With all of this drama taking place in Glasgow, the events of that afternoon in Edinburgh had been well and truly relegated to second place. But, like Celtic, Kilmarnock had also pulled off a remarkable result and had won 2–0. Hearts had lost the Scottish League title on goal average – by 0.04 of a goal.

'The scenes in our dressing room were incredible,' remembers Lennox. 'I had never been involved in anything like this. I don't think any of us had. Someone came in and said Kilmarnock had beaten Hearts and had won the League, and we all said, "Who cares?" '

Lennox was right. It may have been the closest-ever Scottish title race, but in the end it became academic. For the next nine years, only one Scottish club would be setting records.

Chapter 4

ITHIN SIX WEEKS OF arriving at Celtic Park, Jock Stein had what he wanted. He had a trophy in the cabinet and had immediately vindicated the board's decision to bring him in. However, he was also on the brink of discovering something which he probably didn't know he had – a team.

Before the Cup final, there had been suggestions in newspapers that Stein had come to Celtic Park with a view to having a clear-out. Whether this was going to be the equivalent of a wholesale fire sale, or whether it was simply judicious pruning, we shall never know. What is known is that only days after winning the Scottish Cup, he went to the weekly board meeting with a list of players he wanted to buy and, more importantly, with a list of those he wanted to sell. The list included John Hughes, Charlie Gallagher and Jimmy Johnstone.

Despite delivering the inch-perfect cross which had won them the trophy, Gallagher certainly would not figure greatly in Stein's plans from then on – although he would, on one more occasion, once again prove as vital to the club as he had on the afternoon of the Cup final, with yet another telling cross. Hughes's function was, thereafter, to provide Stein with flexibility in his forward line whenever the manager wanted to 'freshen up the side'. But Johnstone's contribution to the Celtic renaissance was incalculable, and the fans will be forever grateful that, for whatever reason, Stein did not go through with his plans.

'I think sometimes you can get managers' strong points wrong,' argues Bob Crampsey. 'Despite what others say, I always think that, for example, Graeme Souness's strongest point is that he is extremely quick to realise when he has made a bad signing, and moves him on. Other managers in that position spend the next two or three years trying to prove that the unfortunate player really was a good signing. I think Stein's great strength was not particularly tactical. He was not, for example, a great substituter – there's a certain irony in the fact that the last thing he ever did as a manager was to bring on Davie Cooper as a substitute against Wales, an act which led to Scotland qualifying for the 1986 World Cup. His great ability was as a discoverer of raw talent.

'His great strength was to say that so-and-so is a middling inside forward, "but if we move him back to wing half, I have a notion he would be good in there." I think he saw that he had good players, but that some of them were misplaced. The most obvious example was Murdoch at inside-right when he was never quite mobile enough to be an inside forward in the classic sense. Indeed, if you had him at inside-right, then you lost the value of his very good long-range passing. The other thing he didn't do very often, but when he did, it worked spectacularly, was to use John Hughes through the middle. Those would be the two most striking examples of Stein's changes.'

Steve Chalmers, who scored the goal which won Celtic the European Cup, was another who benefitted from Jock Stein's astute positional sense. Chalmers had been a Scottish junior international, but had come to the senior game late after a spell in the Army and a seriously debilitating bout of meningitis. Born in the north of Glasgow, he was the son of a professional footballer. His father, David, had caught the eye of Celtic but ended up playing for Clydebank in their previous incarnation as a senior side. He had, however, played alongside the great Jimmy McGrory when he was on loan to Clydebank. Although Steve was, notionally, an apprentice joiner, all he wanted to do was follow in his father's footsteps and play football.

'I had no real interest in doing anything other than playing professional football,' says Chalmers. 'But in all the football I played, whether it was for Brunswick Boys' Club or Ashfield Juniors, I was in, what we now call, the midfield. I was playing behind the strikers. But it was Jock who took a look and said he thought I would be better playing as a striker, and he moved me forward.'

The results were remarkable. Where previously Chalmers had been running to no purpose – fans used to joke that if you opened the gates while he was making a run, he would run right out onto London Road – Stein gave him a direction. Chalmers was a model professional and quickly became one of the most complete strikers in the game. He went on to score 158 goals – including that all-important one in Lisbon – in 260 games for Celtic: a formidable strike rate.

'There are very few players who come good relatively late in their careers,' says Bob Crampsey. 'But Steve Chalmers was exceptional. He's the only player I know who suddenly, in mid-career, got spectacularly better. He became a tremendous player, and he had great instincts.'

The newspapers, on the days after the Cup final, suggested that the Celtic side had played above themselves. However, when you consider that all but one of the European Cup-winning side were already on the Parkhead staff – and seven of them played against Dunfermline – it seems more likely that they were simply suf-ficiently motivated to play to their full potential for the first time in a long while.

'We were in complete disarray before Jock came along,' says Steve Chalmers. 'It was incredible the way he transformed a side that was going nowhere into the team it became. It was amazing the way he instilled a sense of self-belief into us.'

Skipper Billy McNeill admits that, whether the players voiced their concerns or not, there was a sense that some at least were playing for their places. 'I think a clear-out is always on the cards when a new manager comes in, because he is going to look at what he's got,' says McNeill who has himself been the new mana-gerial broom on a number of occasions. 'I'm quite sure that was in his mind, but what he eventually realised was the fact that he had an awful lot of very talented young players, and not-so-young players. So he had a nice blend of well-experienced players and also younger players, like Jimmy Johnstone and Bobby Lennox, who were real emerging talents. He recognised that, and he realised that they just hadn't been nurtured or brought on in the right way. The season before he arrived, for example, Bobby Lennox had been offered to Falkirk for a nominal fee. When you think about that now . . .' McNeill's voice tails away in disbelief.

What is even harder to believe is that the prodigious Lennox did not even know about this until much later. 'It was Jock who told me they were going to sell me,' says Lennox, who became the most loyal of the Lisbon Lions. 'He used to tease me by saying: "Aye, you'd have been away if it wasn't for me." I suppose when you think back it does make some sense that it was Falkirk that were in for me, because they tried to sign me when I first signed for Celtic from Ardeer Rec.'

But according to his biographer there was one other aspect of the Stein magic which was about to be brought to bear on Celtic's class of '65. 'I think, more than most managers in my experience, Stein got it right fairly quickly about who needed to be led and who needed to be driven,' says Bob Crampsey. 'I think he was always a better driver than a leader, by which I mean that the players who did best under him were the players who would spark if he said something to them. I think he suited very well the Bertie Aulds, the Tommy Gemmells and the Billy McNeills. I'm not so sure, though, that he was the ideal manager for some very gifted players who were there, like Charlie Gallagher and John Fallon. I think the introverts came off less well. I taught Charlie Gallagher when he was at school, and he was a very quiet boy. I think, in a footballing situation, if you criticised him, his tendency would be to withdraw a little bit. On the other hand, if you criticised Gemmell or Auld, you needed to be sure of your ground. I still think that John Fallon was a superb goalkeeper technically, but I happened to be at the training ground at Barrowfield one day when John was in goal. He was performing heroics, but then Stein came out onto the track from the dressing room, and Fallon just turned into a wreck.'

Those who knew Stein, and those who played under him, are in no doubt that his impact on Celtic was instantaneous and did not occur just because he had won a trophy. He, and his close friend Bill Shankly, at Liverpool, were the first of the modern breed of tracksuit managers: both Scots, both from mining communities, and each possessed of a formidable football brain. Some people, Billy McNeill among them, believe that Celtic would have been happy with the Scottish Cup win in 1965, content in the knowledge that they would pick up another trophy in a year or two. But Stein was having none of that. He may have known as early as the beginning of the next season just how good his side was. In those days the Scottish League Cup was effectively a curtain-raiser for the season. Most of the group games were played before the season started proper, and the final came in October, about eight weeks after the start of the League programme. That, according to McNeill, is when it all started to come right.

'Jock Stein's influence on everything at Parkhead was quite dramatic,' he says. 'Obviously, the 1965 Scottish Cup final started it all off, but we won the League Cup the following season, and that was the big turning point as far as I was concerned. What gave us belief and confidence in ourselves was the knowledge that it was Rangers that we beat in the final. It was a horrible game, as so many of these games turn out to be – two penalty kicks decided it for us and they got a late consolation goal – but it was a game in which we stood up to Rangers. They were the power-house of Scottish football at that time, and we matched them. We matched them first of all physically, but we also matched them in the sense of being able to put one over on them – to beat them. The fact that it was a Cup final meant that there was no holding back for us.

'You've got to win games like that,' McNeill continues. 'For a Celtic side to be successful, you have to be able to win crunch games against the Rangers. If you don't do that, then you are going to be second-best all your life, and it was a vitally important match for us. It was a desperate game because the League Cup final was played so early in the season in those days. I think it was entirely the wrong time to play a Cup final, but the result was the most important thing in that game. I have this belief that you can beat other teams – and you can win a Cup without ever meeting Rangers – but if you want to be successful, truly suc-cessful, you have to win crunch games against Rangers, and that was a crunch game.'

For McNeill, for the rest of the side, and for the fans, the League Cup win was indeed a touchstone. Things started to happen as

Stein grew in stature, and the players grew to respect him more and more. And having won the Scottish Cup in season 64–65, they won the League in 65–66.

Tactically, Stein had not wrought many changes at Parkhead, and the side was largely the same as the one which McGrory – or perhaps more correctly, Sean Fallon – had been responsible for before he arrived. What was different was the way the side played in the sense that they now had a belief in themselves which was entirely fresh. Whatever Stein was, he was an outsider. He was not tainted with the complacency which many of the playing staff he inherited believed pervaded the existing board. They had been every bit as unambitious as McNeill suggests, and would doubtless have been happy with the odd trophy every couple of years. Stein's appointment, however, should not be seen as one of ambition on their part. Instead, it was an appointment made out of sheer desperation. Stein's outsider status gave him the opportunity to change things. Those who had been there when he looked after the reserves looked up to him with something bordering on reverence. The mood was infectious, and those who had not been there under his previous tenure were prepared to give him the benefit of the doubt. This man was a winner with a proven track record and – footballers being superstitious by nature – they were prepared to let some of it rub off on them.

The self-belief on the training ground and in the dressing room was easily translated onto the pitch. This free-flowing Celtic side regularly scored barrowloads of goals. In that 65–66 season they scored 106 in 34 League matches – just over three a game. Aberdeen were hammered 7–1, Hearts 5–2, Morton 8–1, Falkirk 6–0 and Hamilton 5–0 and 7–1. Celtic played with an abandon which had seldom been seen before, and has seldom been seen since; their forwards swooped like raiders, their grace and skill matched only by the meanness and hardness of McNeill's superbly marshalled defence. Simpson kept a clean sheet in fourteen League games.

There was also a change in attitude which had been engendered by Stein.

'There has always been a certain amount of "Celtic against the world" at Parkhead, and Stein went some way to removing at least one of the chips from their shoulders,' observes Bob Crampsey. 'Coming in as an outsider he was able to do that.

'I remember, on one occasion, not exactly endearing myself to him when he said, "We get nothing" – "we" being Celtic of course – and I pointed out to him that when he was manager of Dunfermline he had become incandescent about a penalty kick that Celtic had been awarded, in a game against them. I suppose a lot depends on the point of view you have at a given moment.

'It's all a bit about psyche, and he had the advantage there of being an incredibly big man, physically. If you hadn't seen him for four or five months you forgot, actually, how big he was. One of the most daunting sights in Scottish football for a referee was coming up the tunnel at Parkhead and seeing a man who didn't allow so much as an inch and a half of daylight to appear between himself and the corners of the door. That must have been pretty intimidating.'

The other key ingredient Stein had added to the mixture was a new striker. When they had played Motherwell in the Scottish Cup semi-final the previous season, Celtic had twice had to come from behind in the first game. Both Motherwell goals were scored by Joe McBride. A little over a month after beating Dunfermline in the Scottish Cup, Stein had signed him for £22,500. Motherwell actually wanted McBride to sign for Dunfermline because they were offering a bigger fee which would have meant a larger share for the Lanarkshire club. But although Dunfermline offered a bigger fee, Celtic were offering a higher wage. Regardless of that, McBride wanted to play for Celtic, so he was prepared to lose money on the deal to sign for his first-choice club.

Joe McBride was that rarest of creatures, a natural goalscorer. He was a centre forward in the classically explosive mould, and it is mouth-watering to speculate what a player of his skills might fetch today. One of Stein's initial assessments of his new side was that they lacked punch up-front, and McBride was the man to do the job. Stein also had an eye on Europe since Celtic would now be playing in the European Cup-Winners Cup. Whatever his reasons, McBride galvanised the side. In his first season he established a post-war scoring record for the club with 43 goals – 31 of them in the League.

'The fact that we had beaten Rangers in the League Cup final so early in the season, set us up,' McNeill recalls of that first Championship season under Stein. 'The League wasn't easy at that time; it was hard fought. Our last game was against Motherwell – we would have had to have lost about 4–0 to lose the League – and we hammered and hammered away at them, but we couldn't get a breakthrough. It wasn't until late in the game that Bobby Lennox got the only goal.'

That goal from Lennox in the 89th minute gave Celtic the League by a two-point margin. It was their first League title since 1954, and the fans were again ecstatic. There was disappointment, however, when they failed to hold on to the Scottish Cup. They lost to Rangers in a replay, giving the Ibrox side some measure of revenge for their early season loss.

There was also a tantalising glimpse of European success. Celtic's earlier European endeavours had been marked with some catastrophic blunders, not least the debacle of two years previously when they lost 4–0 away to MTK Budapest after a 3–0 win at Parkhead. There would be no such carelessness under Stein. Celtic began the campaign with a hiss and a roar, beating the Dutch side Go Ahead 6–0 in Glasgow and 1–0 in Deventer. Then came the Danes from Aarhus who were despatched 3–0 on aggregate. Dinamo Kiev from the old Soviet Union were then disposed of 4–1 on aggregate in the quarter-final. The semi-final matched Celtic with Liverpool. Stein's team would take on the side built by his friend and admirer, Bill Shankly. Celtic dominated the first game and won 1–0 with a single goal from Bobby Lennox. At Anfield, however, Liverpool were in the ascendancy, and they won 2–0 to go into the final, 2–1 on aggregate. Even now, Celtic fans will tell you, almost unprompted, that they were robbed when a Lennox 'goal', two minutes from time, at Anfield – which would have taken them through on the away goals rule – was disallowed.

'To this day,' says Billy McNeill with the conviction of hindsight, 'to be quite frank with you, I believe that goal should have stood. Bobby Lennox was pulled back for offside, but everybody and their granny – everybody except the referee that is – admitted that it was a goal, and it should have stood. It's interesting, because looking back on it, the European Cup-Winners Cup final was played at Hampden that year, so we could have been in a European final in front of our own fans.'

Even now, no-one will be able to convince Bobby Lennox that it was not a goal. 'I can still see it clearly,' he says animatedly. 'The ball is kicked up the pitch, and I'm forward with Joe McBride, who jumps with Ron Yeats, and heads it down to me. I get the ball and run past the two of them – the full back is chasing me and the goalkeeper has come out – I'm passing the goalkeeper, and as the full back is sliding in, I put the ball in the net. I've run past two of them, so I have to be onside.

'The Liverpool boys are all standing there, and there are bottles and everything coming onto the pitch, but none of them thought it was offside. Still,' he says philosophically, 'the tie should have been won in Glasgow. All our good goalscorers – and they were good goalscorers – missed their chances that night.'

Jock Stein had been in charge at Celtic for a little over a year when they completed their impressive, but ultimately unsuccessful, European run. But whatever had happened on the field, off the field, he had won another important victory in his battle to do things his way, despite the intervention of the board. The Celtic board had been used to having things their own way until Stein turned up. But having won the all-important initial skirmish on team selection when he took over, Stein won the final battle during that European run. With a 3–0 win in the first game against Dinamo Kiev at Celtic Park under their belts, the return seemed little more than a formality. In fact, it was a nightmare. The wintry conditions in Kiev, in January, meant the game had to be switched to Tblisi, which is warmer – relatively speaking. The game was delayed by a week because the Celtic visas had not been cleared in time by the Russian authorities. Then the plane had to make an emergency stop in Copenhagen on its way to the Soviet Union. Finally, after the 1–1 draw, the Celtic party were delayed, on their homeward leg, by being snowbound at Stockholm – to where they had been diverted. Eventually, they arrived back in Scotland on a Friday evening, facing an away game against Hearts which was scheduled to take place in a little more than twelve hours. There was no offer of a postponement from the

Scottish League and, despite a spirited performance given the circumstances, Celtic lost 3–2.

There were other ramifications from the Soviet trip which were felt in that match against Hearts. Defender Jim Craig had been sent off following a clash with Khmelnitsky of Kiev. Club policy dictated that – regardless of any punishment inflicted by any other authority – the player would have to apologise to the chairman, and be suspended by the club.

'Big Jock told me about all of this, some time later, on a trip back from Seamill,' recalls Craig. 'He told me: "You're the man who got me a free hand at Celtic Park." And then he told me the story.

'I remember he had said, a couple of times, while we were held over in Stockholm, that I would have to apologise to the chairman for being sent off. He told me it was club policy, but I told him there was no way I was going to apologise. He kept mentioning it, and eventually I said: "Let me make it quite plain, boss. Apologies mean you've done something wrong, and I have done nothing wrong. I have nothing to apologise for."

'What had happened was that the winger and myself were having a bit of needle throughout the game. He had sold me a dummy and I had sort of half-bought it. Then I realised at the last minute what he was trying to do, so I stepped across and blocked him. He pushed me and shouted something in Russian. I shouted back then, suddenly, somebody had punched me, and the referee sent the pair of us off. We got back to Glasgow at eleven o'clock on the Friday night and went to Hearts the next day. As usual, at half-past two, Jock read out the team, and my name wasn't on it. I had been dropped. It was one of those horrible moments when everybody is looking at me and looking around and generally not knowing where to put themselves. But I wasn't playing – he played Big Billy at full back and John Cushley at centre half, if I recall – and I just took my passes and went up to the stand.'

Stein would doubtless have fought his player's corner, but with no apology forthcoming, the autocratic chairman Bob Kelly could stand on club policy and demand that the player be dropped. On his way to the stand, Craig met Celtic board member Desmond

White, who would eventually become chairman of the club. Given that it was now only twenty minutes before kickoff, White, not unnaturally, asked Craig why he wasn't playing. Craig emphatically pointed out that he had been dropped because he had refused to apologise to the chairman for being sent off. White, a sober and distinguished man who could be quite splendid in his wrath, was livid. At the following week's board meeting, his wrath was still unabated. Pointing out that Celtic had been forced to change a winning side and lose 3–2 because of archaic practices – and adding that Craig was quite right not to apologise in the circumstances – he demanded, and got, a change in club policy.

To be sure, this may have been a dispute which was escalated by White for political reasons: to establish his ascendancy in the four-man board. Also, he may have recalled that it was similar boardroom interference with disciplinary matters which had lost them Pat Crerand, one of the great right halves, to Manchester United in 1963. But whatever the reason, in future, Stein's team selection would never again be hampered by the interference of the board, or the policies of previous administrations.

Despite what Billy McNeill says, there are those who will argue – and they include players as well as fans – that Celtic were naive in not beating Liverpool out of sight in the first game at Celtic Park. They won 1–0, but it could have been four or five. There should never have been any question of playing 'what if?' about a dodgy offside decision more than 30 years on. Celtic lost to Liverpool in the second leg at Anfield on the Tuesday; on the Saturday they drew 0–0 with Rangers in the Scottish Cup final; the following Wednesday the Ibrox side won the replay 2–1. Two major prizes had been lost in just over a week but, on the plus side, Celtic had finally won the League title and qualified for the European Cup for the first time in their history. The players were delighted and looking forward to great things, but there was a section of the support who remained to be convinced.

'I'm not sure that first League Championship was actually as significant as it has become,' maintains Bob Crampsey. 'I'm not sure that certain sectors of the Celtic support didn't go away from that Cup final replay thinking: "It's very nice to have won the League, but here's a situation in which we are odds-on favourites to win the Scottish Cup final, and we have lost again to Rangers, as we did in 1963." I think perhaps some of them thought this was getting to be a habit.'

If it was a habit, then it was a habit that would soon be broken. Celtic were about to be transformed. Within twelve months these young men would become the Lisbon Lions, and they would pass into the football record books. But there were two final pieces to fit in the jigsaw, and one of them would be found thousands of miles away as Celtic headed way out West.

Chapter 5

THE LAST TIME CELTIC had won the Scottish League was in the season 1953–54. They also went on to do a rare double that year, winning the Scottish Cup as well. Jock Stein was captain of that side, and now, as manager, he was in charge of the first Celtic team to win a League title in twelve years. They had also won the Scottish Cup and the League Cup, giving them three trophies in twelve months, and the team and the manager had grown in stature on, and off, the pitch.

'There's no doubt that Jock Stein was the first manager to challenge the power of the board,' recalls Billy McNeill. In his previous tenure in charge of the reserve team, Stein would frequently lobby the board for an extra £1 or £2 a week for his young charges, and occasionally for himself. His background had left him with an abiding memory of what it was like to work hard, and he believed sincerely that players deserved to be paid well and treated fairly. Stein, after all, as captain of Albion Rovers, had led a sit-in in the dressing room, at Falkirk, only moments before a Scottish Cup tie, because the board would not increase their win bonus. So he was a man who could thrive on confrontation.

'From that point of view – the idea of challenging the board – there is no doubt that he did change things dramatically,' recalls McNeill. 'His early success obviously gave him the power to combat any challenges from that direction, but he was still an interesting man. He had this reputation of being a strict disciplinarian which he was and he wasn't. He used this aura and reputation he had of being a tyrant to intimidate, but he really wasn't that bad. He was quite soft in many ways, but he was perfectly capable of coming down on top of you like a ton of bricks, if he felt it was necessary. But there's no doubt that those early days were absolutely magnificent.

'You could maybe argue that it was a wee bit of good fortune on Jock's behalf that we won the Scottish Cup in 1965. But having won it, the next season was absolutely brilliant. We were all good trainers but, the following season, we couldn't wait to get onto the training ground. Every day was like a gala day. There were tactics, there was ball work, everything seemed to be done with a smile on your face, and a laugh and a joke. Obviously, there was still some heavy running – you can't eliminate that entirely – but as much as possible, from pre-season onwards, everything was done with a ball. It was a dramatic change.'

Certainly, Stein's training methods, while far from revolutionary by the standards of some other clubs, were positively innovative at Parkhead. Tommy Gemmell had signed for Celtic just after Stein had moved on to manage Dunfermline. He signed for the club on the same night as Jimmy Johnstone, and the two of them, along with other young players, would travel out to Celtic Park two or three nights a week for training.

'I was an apprentice electrician at the time,' recalls Gemmell. 'I would be up at seven in the morning and heading out to Celtic Park, by tram, straight from work most nights. There was maybe only time for a wash and a sandwich, and away you went. Many a time I was so tired I fell asleep on the tram and had to walk back to the ground from Glasgow Cross.'

Bearing in mind the ages of these young players, and the fact that they were all part-timers who had all done a day's work – generally dirty, thankless work as apprentices or labourers – the training regime seems positively barbaric. It sounds now like a schedule devised by Torquemada. Hardship tends to ingrain itself into the soul, and even now Gemmell can recite the training routine as if it were a litany.

'I can remember it as vividly as if it was yesterday,' says Gemmell wryly. 'I was training two nights a week, maybe three. The schedule was an easy lap, two easy laps, a fast lap, two fast laps, ten 220-yard runs, ten 100-yard sprints, ten 50-yard dashes, then it was, "Right lads, go and have a bath." We never ever saw a ball. The only time we saw a ball was in the summertime when the nights were light enough. Then we would all turn up half an hour early to see if we could get a kick-about before training started.

'Tactical awareness was the same inasmuch as it was virtually non-existent,' recalls the defender. 'If there was any at all, it was to get the ball from back to front as quickly as possible, A to B, route-one stuff. There was a wee bit of encouragement for the full backs to swivel round and protect the central defenders, but that was about it. There were no tactics at all to speak of.'

Jim Craig, who would become Gemmell's defensive partner in the European Cup-winning side, was equally appalled with what he saw. Craig is a qualified dentist and, in his first two years at university, he had taken time out from football. He had been playing for Scottish schools and continued to train at university where he was a cross-country runner. At Glasgow University, Craig was training with the cream of Scotland's athletes under experts from Jordanhill College – in the west end of the city – which has become a centre of excellence for physical fitness. Despite his burgeoning athletics career, Craig's first love was football and, as he was still on Celtic's books, he had a standing invitation to come along to Celtic Park and train any night he wanted to.

'It was unbelievable,' says Craig, of his visits to Celtic's training sessions. 'We were training at university with these guys from Jordanhill in a scientific and structured fashion, and then you would get out to Celtic Park – a professional football club – and they'd be running laps. I remember one occasion when the pitch was covered in straw. They used to do that in those days to keep the frost off. Somebody decided to run across the pitch through the straw, and a pitchfork whipped up in the air. Someone had stood on it, and it flew into the air. It could have killed someone. It was pathetic. But Big Jock changed all that. From the moment he arrived it was all ballwork and talking tactics. The players went daft for it.'

In fact, the Celtic players played like children who had suddenly discovered that they were being let out of school a week early.

They revelled in their new-found freedom, and every other team in the League bore the brunt as they notched up more than 100 League goals to win the title. However, despite their prodigious efforts, the League was not won at a canter. As McNeill recalled, it was a tough season, and it did go down to the last day. It was always mathematically possible for Celtic to lose the title until Lennox got that late winner against Motherwell.

'That was on the Saturday,' recalls McNeill, 'and four days after that we were off to America. It was astonishing; we were away to America for five and a half weeks. You wouldn't contemplate taking a professional team away for that length of time now. They'd all be complaining about how tired they were. We didn't know what tiredness was – we were a winning side. When you're successful, you don't think about anything else.'

Taking a football team away for that length of time was, as McNeill points out, unprecedented. These were young men who had all been born within 30 miles of Glasgow. They were steeped in the traditions and culture of West Central Scotland. A few of them had never been out of the country before except to play football, and now they were going on holiday to a place which only existed, for most of them, in the movies. But it was this tour, where Celtic lived and worked together for five and a half weeks, that created the Lisbon Lions. It was this tour which created the almost uncanny ability for any Celtic player in trouble on the field to find another green-and-white-hooped jersey, almost without thinking.

In the summer of 1966 when Celtic went to America, football was in the process of evolution. That was the summer when Alf Ramsey's so-called 'wingless wonders' would win the World Cup for England. The old traditional line-up of goalkeeper, two full backs, three half backs, and five forwards was called the 'W' formation because of the way they formed up on the park. This was now giving way to a more flexible 4–2–4 system with four defenders, two midfielders, and four forwards. The accent now was on skill and retaining possession. It was about exploiting space rather than simply hoofing the ball upfield and hoping some preternaturally tall centre forward would be able to bundle it, and the goalkeeper – if necessary – over the line.

'Jock was very keen on having us run into space,' explains Steve Chalmers. 'He believed that you could do as much damage without a ball as you could with one. If, for example, we're playing the ball out of defence, and I'm out on the right, then, in the set-up we played, I would quite often shout for the ball and run inside. I had no intention of getting the ball, and the defenders knew that as well but, what I could do, was draw one of their players to me and leave space for the wingers, or the overlapping full backs, to exploit.

'That's an aspect of the British game that seems to have gone now. Players want the ball played to their feet too often, and they spend too much time chasing the ball. Bobby Lennox and I would practice diagonal runs – decoy runs – day in and day out, in training. It was all about adding variety to our game and making it harder to play against us.'

Lennox, who was similarly encouraged to make decoy runs, says, in that respect, Stein was well ahead of his time. 'He knew that you didn't need to have the ball to be effective,' he says. 'I've seen him come up and say, "Well played", when I haven't kicked the ball for the whole game. But I had been doing a lot of running off the ball.'

Jock Stein used the American tour to change Celtic's style of play completely. He knew which players were out of position and he knew where they would do best. On that tour he put his theories into practice.

'When Stein arrived, Bertie Auld was playing as an orthodox left winger, and Bobby Murdoch was playing like an old-fashioned inside forward,' recalls Tommy Gemmell. 'So on that tour we shoved Bertie back into midfield and brought Bobby back in there as well, and we switched to 4–2–4.'

The results were electrifying. Murdoch's precision passing could lay the ball into the path of pacy strikers like Hughes, Chalmers and Lennox, with unerring accuracy. Auld was equally effective on the left-hand side of the field. Both had the added advantage of being extremely hard men and, when they were forced to defend, no-one got past them without a struggle. Stein also harnessed Gemmell's natural buccaneering style of play as an attacking full back and encouraged him to go forward whenever he could. Jim Craig had missed the tour because he was staying in Glasgow to sit his dentistry finals, but he, too, would slot into that system and go forward whenever he could. The rule was, however, that when Craig went forward, Gemmell stayed back, or vice versa. Happily for everyone concerned, a few months later, in Lisbon, Gemmell – not for the first time in his life – would decide that rules are there to be broken.

The North American tour was intended as something of a break for the players, and it did start that way with an idyllic stop-over in Bermuda. But there was also hard work to be done, and the Celtic squad would play eleven games in their five-and-a-half-week stay, and emerge undefeated. These were not games against sides of local stiffs. They were matched against some of the leading clubs in Europe who were similarly engaged on missionary work in the colonies. They played Tottenham Hotspur three times, winning twice and drawing once, they also drew with Bologna and Bayern Munich, and played the Mexican Champions, Atlas, who they beat.

'You had a whole load of lads in that squad who were hungry for success,' recalls Billy McNeill. 'They all wanted to play for Celtic and be successful for Celtic. They were really tough games – especially the three against Tottenham – and the game against Bayern was a bit of a brawl. That was all Gerd Muller's fault.'

It was still some years before Muller would become the most lethal striker in the world, and when Celtic played Bayern in that match in San Francisco, he was actually playing in defence. Not only did he get into a fight, but he got into a fight with Steve Chalmers, one of the most gentlemanly players ever to pull on a jersey.

'It really was something to see,' says McNeill with a broad grin. 'Stevie went in and challenged the goalkeeper. It was perfectly fair, but it was taboo as far as they were concerned, and Muller had a go at him. Muller thought that would have been the end of it, but Stevie wasn't having any of that – I should also say that Stevie was so far forward, he was on his own – so Muller started to run. Stevie started chasing him, and half the German team started chasing Stevie, by which time we had come forward, and we started chasing the Germans. The referee had lost the place altogether, and it ended up looking like something out of *Monty Python*.'

Looking back some thirty years later, Chalmers recalls the incident with some chagrin. 'It is quite embarrassing to think back on it,' he says. 'Muller was a really strong, stockily built wee man and, possibly, the last man you'd choose to pick a fight with. It all started quite innocently. There was a bit of a scrimmage and Muller and I, and the goalkeeper, all went up for the ball. I must have barged into the keeper but, when I came down, Muller punched me in the mouth. It was one of those things where I actually turned onto his punch and met it with my chin, and he just stiffened me. The next thing I knew was that my mouth was split and bleeding.'

At that point, the red mist descended on Chalmers who, like many of the Celtic players, was much more capable of handling himself than he might have looked.

'It was just temper,' he continues. 'At least if you get a kick, then you go down, and you have a couple of seconds to compose yourself, but I just lost the place. I started to run after him, and he took off. I eventually caught up with him behind the goal. I had him on the ground and then I felt this pair of hands grabbing my shoulders. It turned out to be a Celtic fan who'd come out onto the pitch to get Muller for me. He pulled me out of the way; then the German players arrived, and then the rest of our boys arrived.

'The referee had lost the place entirely. He took one look at what was going on and blew his whistle for full-time even though we hadn't played the ninety minutes.'

For the record, the score was 1–1, and for Celtic it was another good result against the then German Cup-holders and future winners of the European Cup-Winners Cup. The Chalmers–Muller confrontation was undoubtedly a bizarre and ultimately pointless incident as so many of these things are, but it does serve to illustrate the team spirit which was now building up among the squad. Chalmers, for example, remains convinced that it was the American tour which, more than anything, created the European Cup-winning side. Also, he believes that Stein arranged it deliberately, because he knew it would be the key factor in turning eleven players into a team.

'He was very keen on us looking the part,' says Chalmers. 'He was very keen on good professional attitudes. We were always neat and smartly dressed because we were ambassadors of the club. He was, also – perhaps surprisingly for a man who grew up in a mining community – very much against bad language. He could curse up a streak himself when he had to, but he didn't like to hear it from others, and there was more than one person pulled up by him for their language.'

The players delighted in their American experience. Jimmy Johnstone did his best to become a born-again American. Bobby Lennox recalls that Johnstone discovered pancakes on that tour and insisted on a stack of them every morning for breakfast.

'It was the best tour ever,' says the winger. 'We all wanted to come back, and Sir Robert Kelly said that, if we won the European Cup, then we could come back the following year, and he was as good as his word.'

'That tour definitely did cement relationships,' Billy McNeill agrees. 'I'm not saying everybody was the best of pals, because we weren't,' he continues. 'We had the occasional argument, of course we did, but that's only to be expected so when you have a group that contains so many strong-minded individuals. It reminded me of the old Labour Party. They used to keep their arguments among themselves, and so did we. But when we came out to face anyone, it was with a united front as, I think, Gerd Muller and a few others found out to their cost. Jock Stein probably encouraged that.'

Tommy Gemmell's view of the American tour is a little rosier than that of his former skipper. He remembers it as being 'one big happy family', and the man responsible for uniting the side was Jock Stein. Although, to be fair to both Gemmell and Stein, the familial bonds are probably closer to *The Three Musketeers* than *The Waltons*.

'He had a great love for Celtic of course, having been there before,' says Gemmell, of Stein. 'But he also captained the 1954 double-winning side, and they were pretty much one big happy family. They had their jokers and their characters, but that's what he wanted for us. I think he wanted the same attitude in our side that he had in his. The important thing about that tour, though, was that we all got to know each other very very well, players and management alike.'

On paper, the Celtic squad was a volatile bunch, but Stein was able to mould their differing temperaments. Religion played a part, but in a healthy, positive manner, rather than the foul sectarianism which blights the Scottish game. Although Celtic is a club of Catholic traditions, it did not maintain the sectarian signing policy which Rangers enforced up until the arrival of Graeme Souness. There were Catholics and Protestants in the side, and the players themselves played on their differences. In the sixties, for example, Catholics were still instructed, under pain of sin, not to eat meat on Fridays. If Celtic were away, like that six-week trip to America, the non-Catholics would have a field day. Players like Gemmell and Auld would make great sport of tucking into the footballer's favourite meal – thick, juicy steaks – while Catholics like Chalmers, Craig and McNeill grudgingly sat down to fish. Rather than splitting the side, the good-natured joking about religious differences strengthened the team.

Although he was a tactical genius, Stein's man-management skills often left something to be desired. He would, as one of his players has said, destroy goalkeepers. He did not have a lot of time for those who shrank from his criticism. Stein treated the whole team in the same gruff, boisterous manner when perhaps there were talents – like Fallon and Charlie Gallagher – who required more individual handling to bring the best out of them.

'One of the things that made Stein laugh,' remembers Bob Crampsey, 'was a quote from Bob Paisley to the effect that the secret of football management was keeping the five who hated you from getting together with the six who hadn't made up their minds about you yet.

'I don't know that there were five who hated him, but I think relations with Tommy Gemmell and Bertie Auld were always a bit strained, though hate is too strong a word. There were also the fringe players to consider, and John Cushley, I suspect, was not a great Stein fan. I think, by any standard, he would have to concede that Billy McNeill was the better centre half, even though John was himself a very good centre half.

'This is always the difficulty. How do you accommodate the really good reserve who is that much below the chap that you've got, but that much above everyone else in the Scottish League. I think there was a resentment there.'

Stein, in fact, appeared at times to go out of his way to get Cushley to leave. He frequently told him, in front of others, that he had no future at Celtic as long as McNeill had the centre-half position. Cushley, for reasons best known to himself, but possibly out of sheer stubbornness, would not be budged until the summer of 1967 when he went to West Ham.

'Tommy Gemmell wasn't afraid of him,' Crampsey continues. 'I think Jim Craig, too, had his differences from time to time. It wasn't always as marvellous as it looked from the outside. But I think on the big questions – how to play the game, what tactics to employ – he was almost always right.'

If his man-management was flawed in some areas, in others areas it could be positively inspired. Football clubs can be notoriously clannish places, and cliques can easily form to poison the most good-natured dressing room. Stein went out of his way to make sure that didn't happen.

'He used to change the rooming arrangements around all the time,' remembers Steve Chalmers. 'There were some players who always seemed to room together – Jimmy Johnstone and Bobby Lennox, for example – but Jock would rotate the room-sharing. I shared with Tommy Gemmell for a time, and then John Fallon, and it was just moved around to make sure everyone knew each other really well and there was no bad feeling.'

When the tour was planned, no-one except perhaps Stein and his lieutenants – Sean Fallon and Neilly Mochan – could have known that it would be one of the elements in preparing for a European Cup run. But there is no doubt that the psychological boost the players received on that break, set them up and sustained them in the season ahead of them. Their most rapturous reception was in Kearney, New Jersey, an area which looks like a green-and-white hybrid of Glasgow and Dublin. It was packed with expatriate Scots and Irish, all of them Celtic supporters. When these people had emigrated from Scotland and Ireland in the great emigration boom of the early sixties, Celtic were in the middle of a trophyless trough, with no end in sight. Now, they found that the players they had invited all those months ago were coming to them with three trophies under their belt, including the League Championship. The reception the players received was like an American equivalent of a Roman triumph. It was infectious, and even Stein got into the act. On one evening at a social club in Kearney, he took the microphone and regaled the full house with his version of a particularly maudlin Scottish song, 'Auld Scots Mither Mine', a dirge which is guaranteed to bring blood from an expatriate stone.

'This is going to cost these guys a fortune,' said the club secretary to Billy McNeill, gesturing round the room.

'Why?' asked McNeill, not unreasonably.

'Because there's no way you'll be able to stop them going home for a visit after they've heard that,' he replied.

The community singing would become an integral part of Celtic on tour in the Stein years. So important was it that some of the players joked that if you couldn't sing you had no chance of getting into the team.

'Some of the boys were very good singers,' says Bobby Lennox, who was an international class winger but, on his own admission, no better than a backing vocalist. 'The boss was a good singer. He also sang "Only A Bird In A Gilded Cage" as well as "Auld Scots Mither Mine". Joe McBride was good as well, and so was wee Jimmy, and Bertie Auld too.

'They all had their party pieces,' Lennox remembers. 'Ronnie Simpson sang "The Star O' Rabbie Burns"; Big Tam would do "From Russia With Love" or "Anything Goes"; Bobby Murdoch did "Little Ol' Wine Drinker Me"; Billy gave us "Will You Still Love Me Tomorrow"; and from John Clark it was always "St Theresa Of The Roses".

'Wee Jimmy was great – he could sing anything – but "Maggie May" was a favourite. Willie Wallace did "When I Fall In Love" and Bertie was great at "On The Street Where You Live". Jim Craig, Stevie and myself would usually just join in.'

Bolstered by community singing and practical jokes – someone discovered that the patch pockets of the Celtic blazer were just the right size and shape for hiding an opened tub of mustard – the Celtic bandwagon kept rolling on.

'We were like conquering heroes to those people,' says McNeill. 'It was the same in Bermuda with the Caledonian Society, then in New York, then in St Louis, San Francisco, Los Angeles, Toronto and Vancouver. Everywhere we went. I don't want to give the impression that we were a bunch of altar boys – we played hard and we lived life to the full – but at the end of that tour we really felt we could challenge anyone and everyone.'

By the end of the season stretching before them, McNeill's premonition was proved staggeringly accurate.

Chapter 6

I T IS DEBATABLE WHETHER any team has been in better shape to start a season than Celtic were when the 1966–67 Scottish League season officially kicked off. Physically, they were at the peak of their fitness thanks to eleven games in just under six weeks; psychologically they were a winning side, and they were brimful of confidence. They were unbeaten in those eleven games and finished off their pre-season preparations with a warm-up against Manchester United who, despite the presence of Denis Law, George Best and Bobby Charlton, were unceremoniously dumped 4–1. The fans loved it. They had never seen anything like it, and Celtic Park was regularly full to bursting.

'You could see the quality of the side when they beat Manchester United,' insists John McCabe. 'Even though it was a friendly, I found myself thinking that this was not just a good Celtic side, this was something quite different. I had a notion, even then, that they would go quite far in Europe. I didn't think they would win but I thought they would go far. It was obvious that it was Stein who had planned everything and who had made all these players believe in themselves.'

The Scottish season, in those days, kicked off with the League Cup. It was played in sections of four teams who played each other – home and away – in six ties before the start of the League Championship. Celtic were drawn in the same section as Hearts, Clyde and St Mirren, and quickly served notice that they were going to be every bit as effective as they had been the previous season. In their first three games they scored sixteen goals, beating Hearts 2–0, Clyde 6–0 and St Mirren 8–2. In fact, by the end of the qualifying section, they had scored twenty-three goals in six games and conceded only two. Their form continued in the League proper, and they started the season with a 3–0 win against Clyde. You have to feel some sympathy for Clyde, one of Scottish football's best-loved sides. They had played Celtic three times in three weeks, losing each time, conceding twelve goals in total, and only managing to get one back. Celtic and their fans would have felt no such sympathy for their opponents in their second League match of the season in which Rangers were comprehensively beaten at Celtic Park with goals from McBride and Auld.

Domestic football was not providing much of a challenge for Celtic at that stage. They were winning, and winning comfortably. It would be November before they dropped a point, and New Year's Eve before they lost a game – one of only two League defeats that season. The players were revelling in their success and, at times, could not believe it. Stein, however, had his eye on other things. He knew that then, as now, domestic honours are not enough. If a side was to seek a true measure of its worth, then it would have to be done in Europe and not at home. His thoughts, after winning the League title in 1965–66, give a very clear picture of his intention.

'It is up to us,' he told one sports journalist, 'to everyone at Celtic Park now, to build our own legends. We don't want to live with history, to be compared with legends of the past; we must make new legends, and our League Championship win is the first step towards doing that. The greatness of a club in modern football will be judged on performances in Europe. It is only in the major European tournaments that you can really get a chance to rate yourself alongside the great teams.'

It is obvious that, from the moment Celtic won the League on 7 May 1966, Stein's intention was to win the European Cup. He, like his managerial compatriots Bill Shankly and Matt Busby, was a visionary. While the club and the board may have been content with domestic success, his horizons were much wider. The European Cup had been set up in season 1955–56 largely at the instigation of journalists from the French newspaper *L'Equipe*. It had been dominated by the Spanish side, Real Madrid. They won the first five tournaments and would win the competition six times in its first eleven years. Apart from Real, the tournament had been dominated by Portuguese and Italian sides. Benfica followed Real by winning the trophy twice in succession; then it was AC Milan, and then Inter Milan, who won it twice in 1964 and 1965, before Real notched up their sixth win in 1966.

British football had been traditionally insular and, as such, was reluctant to get involved in the early days of the tournament. European football, however, had caught the imagination of the fans and clubs alike, and the idea quickly caught on. By the end of its first decade, the European Cup had become the Holy Grail for any manager with a spark of ambition or innovation.

The tournament was contested by the champions of the countries making up what is now UEFA – the Union of European Football Associations. In the sixties the world was a much smaller place in geo-political terms. The Soviet Union was still the Soviet Union; Yugoslavia was still Yugoslavia; Czechoslovakia was still Czechoslovakia. Germany, of course, was not still Germany, and both East and West Germany had representatives in European football. All in all there were 32 member countries, and the League champions of each country would contest the premier tournament, the European Cup.

Celtic's first foray in the tournament came in the preliminary round when they were drawn against Zurich of Switzerland. The first leg would be at Celtic Park on 28 September 1966. The fixture calendar was much less crowded in those days, and the return leg would be in Switzerland the following week. These days there are two weeks between European ties. Zurich were a part-time side but still reasonably well-considered among the European hierarchy. The tie would be a significant if not crucial test of Celtic's ability to compete at the highest level in Europe. Certainly their domestic record suggested that they should have no real concern about playing anyone at Celtic Park. Before meeting Zurich they had played eleven games, winning them all, and scoring thirty-nine goals in the process for the loss of only eight – and three of them had come in a bizarre League Cup quarter-final against Dunfermline which Celtic won 6–3.

Celtic had been naive in Europe in the past. They should never have given up a three-goal lead against MTK in 1964, and they should have put their semi-final against Liverpool beyond doubt in the home leg the previous year. But they had learned their lesson.

'That goal that was disallowed against Liverpool should have been academic,' says full back Tommy Gemmell. 'We should have finished them off at Celtic Park. But at the same time, Bill Shankly had made Liverpool a great side. When you look back at the players they had, they were, more or less, all internationals, and I think that gave us an insight into our own ability. We knew we could go up against those sides and have every chance of beating them without any problems, and that was eventually proved very forcefully. But the games against Liverpool gave us a lot of confidence in our own ability, and let us know that we were there.'

Gemmell wasn't alone in his belief. Billy McNeill, too, was convinced, going into the season, that it might be a bit special; that things might finally have fallen into place. Call it magic, call it a fairy tale, call it footballer's superstition, but McNeill was a born leader. Confidence radiated from him on the field, and when the club captain believes the future is so bright he has to wear shades, then that will spread throughout the team as a sustaining, supportive force.

'They were making *The Celtic Story*, which was a film about the history of the club up to that season,' recalls McNeill. 'The director was Jimmy Gordon, who was then with Scottish Television, and I remember asking him, at the start of the season, how he thought it might all finish up. "Billy," he said to me, "I just have this feeling that everything is going to finish up fantastically well, because there is a fairy tale about Celtic which hasn't yet been told, and I think it might just unfold." You wouldn't believe the luck of a team doing a film like that,' McNeill continues. 'All they were doing was trying to trace the history of the club to the present day, and bingo! the club wins the European Cup – the first British side to do it – and they have captured it all on film. Astonishing.

'I always remember, though, the belief we had in ourselves. We were never frightened of anyone. We didn't know what fear was, and we had supreme confidence in our ability to beat anyone on our day. Not false bravado, but an attitude of mind, a state of mind. I think we had a whole lot of aggressive people, even nasty people in some cases, with marvellous skills and strong personalities, and, of course, we had a master tactician. But we had people in that side who would sell their souls to win.'

Stein appeared to have only one problem going into the home leg with the Swiss, and it was the sort of dilemma managers would sell their children to have. He had twelve fit players and only eleven places. Joe McBride had been bought by Stein with an eye to winning the European Cup. He knew that he needed additional firepower in his front line, and McBride was a magnificent striker. However, on the Saturday before they were due to play Zurich, McBride wrenched his knee in the 2–1 win against Dundee and had to be substituted by Steve Chalmers. But on the Monday morning no-one was more pleased than Stein when McBride told him he felt fine, he was keen to train, and he wanted to play against Zurich. McBride went straight into the normal Celtic training routine and came through with flying colours and without the slightest reaction to his injury. This left Stein with six forwards vying for five spaces. It was a problem he had frequently, and his defenders smile as they recall his frequent announcements about 'freshening up the team'.

'That always meant problems for one of the forwards,' says McNeill, smiling. 'He never changed the defence or the midfield, it was always the forwards.'

Again, Stein's man-management skills came into their own.

'You'd see it at Barrowfield on the Thursday before a Saturday game,' remembers Tommy Gemmell, with amusement. 'It was a standing joke with Stevie Chalmers that the boss would go up to him and throw an arm round his shoulder, and as soon as you saw that, you knew he wasn't playing. That was the kiss of death, the absolute kiss of death. It was like a manager being told he has the full confidence of his board.'

'It was bizarre,' remembers Chalmers, taking up the story. 'He'd come up, and he'd be laughing and joking and saying things like, "God, you're fair buzzing today, Stevie," and just keep telling you how great you were. I soon got wise and realised that meant I was going to be on the bench.

'But what was worse was that, while you were sitting there next to him on the bench, he'd be tearing strips off whoever had replaced you and asking you why you weren't out there.'

Stein had an embarrassment of riches in his front line. He had the pace of Lennox and Johnstone on the wings, the sharpness of Chalmers, the guile of Auld, the explosiveness of McBride, and the strength and versatility of Hughes, who could lead the line when called on or, just as easily, stretch a side with his play on the left wing. However, Stein wasn't going to concede any advantage to Ladislav Kubala, his opposite number at Zurich and a well-respected figure in European coaching circles. There were few craftier managers than Stein, so that even when he was keeping his team secret, he could appear to be doing it for the purest of motives.

'The only reason I am not giving a definite line-up is because, at the moment, I do not know myself who will be playing where,' he told journalists, presumably with a straight face, on the morning of the match. 'The selection will depend on the weather tonight, and the pitch itself. The grass was soaking wet yesterday, and I will wait and see what it is like tonight, and whether the night is wet or dry.'

Plainly, Stein must have known he wasn't kidding anyone. To be fair there may just have been a suspicion about McBride possibly wrenching his knee again on wet turf, but Stein knew in his own mind who would take the field. There was never any real chance of McBride being left out, as he had been bought with the specific purpose of scoring goals in Europe, especially since the player himself admitted he was fit and raring to play. In the end, as any halfway-intelligent observer might have speculated – and that certainly would include Kubala – Stein maximised his options by playing both McBride and Chalmers. McBride came in for Lennox at inside-right with Chalmers leading the line.

This psychological warfare was a well-established part of the pre-match ritual which precedes any European tie. Kubala, who had been around the track a few times himself, was at it as well. When the Swiss arrived in Scotland, Kubala was publicly offering very little for their chances of survival.

'We will lose this European Cup tie,' he said on the eve of the match. 'Not only will we lose it over the two games, we will lose it here tomorrow night. We know we have no chance. The players know we have no chance, and there is no point in trying to blind ourselves to the facts.'

Any manager who makes that sort of public comment, and believes it, deserves to be beheaded on the spot by his players. Of course, Kubala did not believe it. He also insisted, before leaving Zurich, that his star striker Stuermer, and his key midfielder Kuhn, were injured. However, at their eve-of-game training session, both men were seen running like deer and delivering and withstanding some reasonably robust tackles. As a parting shot, Kubala also offered an indication of how his players would play the following evening.

'We consider we have nothing to lose by attack,' he told reporters. 'If we defend, and we are heavily defeated, we will lose our prestige. If we try for goals, we may surprise ourselves, and maybe leave a good impression with Scottish football supporters.'

In the end, the only impressions that Kubala's men left on Scotland were on Celtic players. The match, played in front of 50,000 spectators, was a bruising affair in which Zurich defended their goal at all costs. They had come looking for an early goal and gave Simpson a fright in the first minute but, after a goalless quarter of an hour, they duly filed back into defence. They packed their penalty area and stifled the Celtic forwards who, it has to be said, in the first half at least, were not making much of an impression with a nervy, uninspired performance.

'They had done their homework,' says Tommy Gemmell ruefully. 'They didn't come to play. They had, obviously, picked the players that needed sorting out and tried to nullify them. Basically, we knew if we were allowed to play there wouldn't be a problem, but they put man-markers on players and set out to stop us playing.'

The Swiss tactics in the second half were brutal. They were determined that the game should remain goalless, and Hughes and Johnstone were chopped down at every opportunity. Toes were trodden on to stop forwards jumping for the ball, players were obstructed, and the Swiss – who had ten men in their penalty box for much of the game – wasted time at every opportunity.

Celtic, of course, were no shrinking violets and gave as good as they got. Johnstone, for example, exacted a measure of revenge against one of his worst tormentors when he 'sorted out' left back Stuerli in an off-the-ball incident. Gemmell, who was playing behind Johnstone, went to lend a hand, and the game erupted in a brawl. Referee Fred Hansen had, by this time, lost the place completely, and the game was close to anarchy. Stuerli was eventually booked along with left-winger Meyer and Murdoch of Celtic.

'We could all look after ourselves,' says Tommy Gemmell matter-of-factly. 'Bertie could handle himself, and all the guys at the back could look after themselves. Stevie was a lot harder than he looked, as a few people found out to their cost. Nobody would ever ask Bobby Lennox to kick anyone but, if anybody needed sorting out in regard to him, then one of us would take care of it.

'Big Jock would never tell you to do that; we were out there to play football,' Gemmell continues. 'But occasionally, if things were getting bad as far as Jimmy was concerned, he might say: "Joe Bloggs is giving the wee man a hard time, if you get the chance in a tackle then let him know you're there." He would never tell you to kick anyone. But there were definitely some players around who needed to be sorted out, because they knew if they let us play football, we would be all over them.'

Tommy Gemmell was one of the more flamboyant members of the Celtic side. He was a charismatic full back who made up for what he lacked in tackling skills by making his swashbuckling runs down the wing. He could also play at either left or right back, which gave Stein some versatility, and was well able to look after himself, and others, if the occasion demanded. But Gemmell, who had a shot which was perfectly capable of bursting nets, liked nothing more than to attack.

'When I heard that Jock Stein was coming to Celtic, I thought I might improve my chances a wee bit,' says Gemmell, recalling his early days at the club. 'There were a few weeks between his appointment and his actually taking over, so I thought I would do a wee bit of showing off with some forward runs whenever I got the chance. I was told by one of the coaching staff at that time that – and I quote – "If you cross that fucking halfway line again, you won't be playing in this team." That was the extent of tactical awareness before Big Jock arrived.'

Stein, however, knew the value of having a full back overlap and put pressure on the other side, especially on the winger he's supposed to be marking. In the second half, Gemmell was encouraged to overlap to give the attack extra width. He was playing at right back with Willie O'Neill on the left. O'Neill was always more inclined to hang back, and since Zurich hadn't threatened Simpson all night, there was very little danger in encouraging Gemmell to go forward. Eventually, it paid off. In the light of what had happened in the previous hour, Gemmell had, probably wisely, decided that going into the penalty box was inviting serious injury. However, in the 64th minute, John Clark squared the ball into the path of the full back, who had been lurking about 35 yards from goal. Gemmell scarcely broke stride as he hit it and watched it smack off the underside of the bar and into the net for Celtic's first goal in the European Cup.

Zurich, like so many others, had come to stifle Celtic. There was no plan B and, once it had been successfully breached, the defence simply fell apart. McBride had missed a number of chances earlier in the game but, five minutes after Gemmell scored, he got his name on the scoresheet with a fierce, low drive from the edge of the area. Purists might argue that it took a deflection on the way past goalkeeper Iten, but that is academic. The final act, of what had been a farcical display by the referee, was still to come however. In the very last minute of the game McBride scored what appeared to be a perfectly good goal, with a close-range header. Referee Hansen blew for full time and disallowed the goal, claiming he had blown his whistle before the ball had crossed the line. Celtic were right to feel aggrieved. For one thing, the ball appeared to be over the line before the whistle blew and, for another, the referee had gone back on his threat to the Swiss to add on extra time for their cynical time-wasting. Celtic won 2–0 but felt they should have been going to Zurich the following week with a three-goal cushion. But given the circumstances of an extremely ugly game and a desperately poor referee, they could not, in the end, have been unhappy to come off when they did.

After the match, referee Hansen did what no-one else could; he united both teams, if only in their criticism of his performance, and insisted that he had blown his whistle 'seconds' before McBride's header crossed the line. He also said that he had never refereed a more difficult game in his life.

For all his pre-match humility, Kubala was full of bravado when he left Scotland with his players. He was especially pleased that Celtic had not scored an early goal.

'A goal for Celtic then could possibly have led to a four- or five-goal defeat for us,' he told reporters at the airport. 'Now we are only two down and we have ground advantage next week.'

One other unnamed Zurich official offered a more prescient analysis of the result. The morning after the game he told journalists that no team in Europe – including Real Madrid – could beat Celtic, at Celtic Park, on that performance.

Chapter 7

ELTIC HAD MADE AN auspicious start to their European Cup campaign. The 2–0 win against Zurich gave them a comfortable cushion for the away leg, in Zurich, but the cynicism of the Swiss side – who had been regarded as a decent outside bet for the trophy – had been disturbing. If they were prepared to play like that away from home, what would they be like in front of their own fans? Would they be even more physical, or could they, instead, play football? And what were Celtic's chances if there was another referee like Hansen?

Both camps were publicly talking-up their sides' chances, but privately, both sides felt that the game could end in a 2–2 stalemate. Of course, away goals would have counted for double in the event of a tie, but if both sides won 2–0 at home, there would be no away goals. In that instance, and without extra time, a third match would be needed to separate the sides. Neither team was keen to play such an important fixture in a neutral country in front of a handful of disinterested spectators, so it had been agreed that, in the event of a tie, they would toss a coin – a Swiss franc – to decide whether a third match would be in Scotland or Switzerland.

All of that was still in front of them when the Swiss party left Glasgow on the wrong end of a 2–0 scoreline. They left to a chorus of disapproval from the Scottish press, who were unanimous in their condemnation of the thuggish tactics of the Swiss. The Swiss, like others before and since, were stoic in the face of such criticism.

'We have been reading reports in the newspapers that last night's game was the roughest ever seen at Celtic Park,' said a club official, as he was preparing to board the plane. 'That is European Cup football, as Scots fans will find out if Celtic experience other games in the competition.'

Although this may appear to be a dismissive statement, its meaning would not have been lost on Jock Stein, especially the use of the word 'if' in the last sentence. Not only were the Swiss suggesting that the Glasgow side was naive, they were also effectively discounting Celtic's chances of going through to the next round. Stein took it all on board and made his plans accordingly.

There was only a week between European matches in those days, so Celtic would be flying to Switzerland just a few days after the Swiss flew out of Glasgow. There was, however, a League game against Hibs, in Edinburgh, to take care of before that. This game, always a difficult fixture, especially with the Easter Road slope, proved to be no exception. Celtic found themselves trailing 3–2, and they could have been forgiven if their minds were elsewhere. But they rallied superbly to win 5–3, with McBride scoring four of the five goals.

The last-minute rally has become a Celtic tradition. They have won trophies and titles when all seemed lost. Part of that has to do with a will to win, but the other fact that has to be taken into account is that the Celtic side of 1966–67, in particular, was a superbly fit team. Few teams could match their level of fitness for any sustained period of time.

'Apart from Bertie Auld, everyone of us was a great trainer,' says Tommy Gemmell. 'Bertie was a lazy so-and-so, but he'd tell you that himself. Our fitness probably won us more games in the last twenty minutes than anything else. We just went forward whenever possible. If we could go forward for ninety minutes, then we would go forward for ninety minutes, that was our style of play. And when we were up against sides who tried to stop us playing, then we generally took them in the last twenty minutes.'

That had certainly been the case with Zurich, in the first leg, and with Hibs at Easter Road. But it's not just about fitness. You can be fit enough to run all day and all night, but if you don't have any ability, there's no point. Gemmell concedes that Celtic's superior skill level also gave them an advantage:

'Jock Stein had the knack of sticking people into a position where they could do most damage,' he recalls. 'His philosophy in football was, basically, that if you have the ball, then you won't lose matches. Basically, it was a case of getting the ball and knocking it around to keep possession, and we had a great ability to hold onto the ball and knock it around. We had folk chasing us all over the place. You could give the ball to wee Jinky, and he'd give it back to you when he felt like it. He would do his wee bit of jinking on one side and, on the other side, Bobby Lennox's pace was incredible. We created so much ammunition for the guys up front, that they would have been hard pressed not to score goals.'

Stein wanted his players to play in a particular way, but to do that he required them to have the confidence to express themselves as individuals while having the discipline to remain part of a team.

'Big Jock's attitude to the game gave us so much confidence in ourselves,' says Bobby Lennox. 'I had never played at outside-right in my life before, but that's where Celtic played me when I signed, at first. It was Jock who played me through the middle. He was able to tell you what you were best at. He wasn't that keen on forwards tracking back too far, and he would tell you that you were no good to him back there. He was very strong on you conserving your energy and taking your time.

'Morale was great in those days. When we started winning, everybody was desperate to stay together. I remember we were coming back from an away game – I think it was Dunfermline – and Billy came up to the back of the bus and started telling us how we could really go places if we all stuck together. I don't know whether Jock had sent him or not, but it wouldn't have occurred to anybody to leave at that time – we were all having too much fun.'

Celtic's style of play was maturing under Stein. They still played at a terrific pace, but there was none of the madcap desire to get the ball from back to front. The 'route one' approach had been well and truly laid to rest, and the more flexible formation which he had introduced on the American tour was starting to pay dividends. Stein believed that possession was the key to the modern game, possession, and the denial of space to the opposition. With Murdoch and Auld being switched to midfield roles from the more conventional inside forward positions, Stein had men who could dictate the flow and pace of the game.

'He never asked you to do something you weren't capable of,' says Tommy Gemmell. 'That was probably his strength. He had a great saying which was: "Play to your strengths and disguise your weaknesses." To give you an example, Billy McNeill would be the first to admit that he wasn't the greatest player of a ball on the deck, but he was magnificent in the air. John Clark, who played beside him, was terrible in the air, but he read everything on the deck. So the two of them complemented each other. I wasn't the greatest tackler in the world, for a full back, but I would charge forward and do things that other full backs wouldn't do.

'We could also read each other like a book,' says Gemmell, describing one of the prime benefits of the American sojourn. 'Even years later, after that side had been broken up, and the bulk of them had stopped playing, we would get together for charity matches. Even then we played as if we were still playing as "The Lions" and could still read what the others would do. Every time I got the ball, I always had three outlets – which was the same as when we were playing – I could knock it to a front player, I could knock it to a midfield player, or I could knock it to a back player. You always had outlets, this is something that you never lose. That only comes from working together, working well together, and being able to read each other. We could do that so well it was unbelievable. That was one of our greatest strengths.'

In the mid-sixties, the pre-eminent coach in Europe was Helenio Herrera who was, at that time, in charge of Inter Milan. European ties were ultra-defensive affairs, and the accepted wisdom which flowed from Herrera was that you attacked cautiously at home and defended resolutely away. Stein had made a close study of Herrera's methods, and while he thought they had some merit, he was not entirely convinced. Within a few months, he would get the chance to pit his own theories against the Italian maestro in a head-to-head contest. But, for the time being at least, he decided that resolute defence was not the way to approach the Zurich game.

He reasoned that Zurich could not play the way they had at Parkhead. What would be the point of packing their own eighteen-yard box when they needed to score at least two goals? Stein felt that surrounding Ronnie Simpson with a ring of green and white jerseys would be suicide, it would invite the Swiss to lay siege to the Celtic goal for the whole of the game.

'That would be a gamble, and one that might succeed,' he told reporters at his training camp just outside Zurich. 'But if they get a goal within half an hour, the strain would be off them, and tied tightly around us. That is the position I am trying to avoid, and that is why we will do our share of the attacking. We will not be foolhardy or stupid,' he continued. 'We know the Zurich players must come to us this time, and we will be making certain that they do not get too far, too often. When they attack they must be much more vulnerable than they were in Glasgow, and that is the basis on which our plans will be built. We will strike when and where we think it is right.'

Obviously, Kubala would have been paying as much attention to this as Stein had paid to the Swiss coach's 'we will lose this in one night' homily at Parkhead. But, chauvinism aside, Stein was, in fact, telling the truth. He had served Kubala with notice that he had every intention of throwing aside the accepted practice, and getting his retaliation in first. Whether Kubala believed him or not, we don't know, but he must have been heartened when Celtic then took the extraordinary step of leaving out Joe McBride. This would be unthinkable to a foreign coach, but Stein was a believer in horses for courses, and would pick sides to suit circumstances, and not just on the basis of fitness and form.

McBride had been the only player who appeared to be immune from Stein's constant fussing with his forward line to 'freshen up the side'. He had played in every game, up till then, partnered with either Steve Chalmers or Bobby Lennox. This time round, Stein let it be known that Lennox was the one who was certain to start, and the uncertainty would be over Chalmers and McBride. Stein had reckoned that, with Zurich having to come forward, there would be gaps at the back, and those gaps could be exploited by someone with the incredible pace and agility of Lennox. Signed from the Ayrshire junior club, Ardeer Recreation in 1961 – not long after Stein had left to manage Dunfermline – he was capable of blistering runs, leaving defenders trailing in his wake. But Lennox was also one of the most composed finishers in the game, and required little more than a sight of the net to score. He was also a tireless runner who would run all day if it meant the difference between winning and losing. Frequently, it did. A number of games, notably the League deciders in 1966 and 1968, were won with Lennox goals in the final minute. He played 348 games for Celtic, from 1961 to 1980, and scored 168 times – that's as near to a goal every two games as makes no difference, and it is a phenomenal strike rate for a forward.

'People don't appreciate what an accomplished finisher Bobby was,' says Billy McNeill. 'He used to put the ball in the net, and he would ask, "Did it cross the line?" He didn't care whether it burst the net or even hit the back of the net, as long as it crossed the line, that was all that mattered to him. His runs behind defences were breathtaking, and he used to do it all the time. His belief was that, unlike modern strikers, you didn't have to make one or two runs, you had to make 102, and if only one of them came off, then you would score. Bobby thinks modern players are lazy, and I have to say, I tend to agree with him.'

Celtic had left behind some fairly dismal late autumn weather in Glasgow, but October in Zurich was a different proposition. The temperature was in the 80s, and the players were actually warned to stay out of the sun for fear of heat exhaustion. The climate may have played some part in Stein's decision to go with Lennox and Chalmers, two pacy front men who could exploit a nervous Swiss defence on a mild October night. He conceded before the game that it was unusual to play Lennox and Chalmers in the same side. But he had his reasons.

'Their styles are very similar,' he agreed, only a few hours before kickoff. 'They are both experts at racing through the middle and scoring goals. In Scotland it frequently doesn't pay to have two players who are almost identical twins in their approach to the game. Tonight, however, it is different. We are leading by two goals and, although we will be attacking, we will be paying a lot of attention to defence. This time, Zurich cannot play the game they played in Glasgow. They have to come to us and they have to open out. They will have to attack constantly, and I cannot think of better men to exploit the gaps that will be left than Chalmers and Lennox.'

Stein's game plan had been formulated in much the same way as a general planning a military campaign. He had pinpointed the enemy weakness and had taken steps to exploit it. Only one note of sentiment crept into the proceedings. The game took place on Stein's 43rd birthday. One newspaper reported that he had breached etiquette and asked his players for a gift.

'Nothing made of solid gold from the vaults of the banks of Zurich,' he was quoted as saying. 'One goal and one European Cup victory will do.' This, it has to be said, does not have the ring of truth about it. This is a quote far too florid to have passed the lips of any Lanarkshire miner, and one suspects that more than a little journalistic embellishment has been involved. His reply to his players when they asked – at the pre-match lunch – what he wanted for his birthday seems more credible.

'Give me a quick goal and I will be happy for the rest of the year,' he told them simply.

Stein's battle plan was to take no chances at all for the first twenty minutes. However, the idea was also to soak up the Swiss pressure, silence the 25,000 crowd, and then start to probe the gaps which had to be exposed, as the increasingly anxious Swiss pressed forward. He had a huge slice of luck in the Swiss team selection. Although Kubala had been expecting his whole squad to be fit, two key players cried off at the last minute. The twin strikers Mattinelli and Meyer were ruled out. Mattinelli had not recovered from an injury he had picked up the previous weekend and Meyer, who had been one of the few Swiss to cause any problems in a playing sense at Celtic Park, came down with flu on the morning of the match. Zurich were so depleted that Kubala, whose triumphs as one of the great Hungarian players were all behind him, had to name himself for the game. He was just two years younger than Stein.

Stein almost got his birthday present earlier than he had anticipated. He had been prepared to wait twenty minutes, but Celtic had the ball in the net even quicker. Johnstone had smacked the ball past Iten after one of his trademark mazy runs, but the referee had spotted Chalmers loitering with intent on the goal-line and disallowed the goal for offside. The authorities were taking no chances after the ineffectual performance of Hansen in the first game, and had appointed Italian referee Concetto LoBello, a strict disciplinarian, to be in charge of the second leg.

However, five minutes after LoBello had chalked off Johnstone's goal, Celtic were legitimately in front when Gemmell scored after another of his hallmark forays up the field. Before half time, Chalmers had repaid Stein's faith in his selection by opening his European account and making it 2–0. Chalmers would go on to be Celtic's leading scorer in that season's European campaign, with Gemmell only one goal behind him.

At the interval, Celtic were 2–0 ahead on the night and 4–0 ahead on aggregate. The tie was clearly beyond the Swiss, and an element of niggle crept back into their play. Signor LoBello was standing for no nonsense, but he did appear to be, at the least, insensitive to some fairly legitimate claims by the Celtic players in the first half. However, even he must have realised that Zurich were beyond saving, and only a few minutes after the re-start he awarded Celtic a penalty when Lennox was brought down in the box by Neumann. In the end, it was the only way the Swiss could contend with his pace. Gemmell did the honours from the spot, giving Celtic a 5–0 aggregate win.

The game was well and truly dead, but Celtic refused to retreat into defence. They turned the second half into an exhibition with their passing and possession skills. The local supporters had seen very little to match them, and by the end of the game they had abandoned their own side and started to applaud the Glasgow team.

Celtic's first excursion in the European Cup had been an unalloyed triumph. They had met a fancied side, and beaten them home and away. They had served notice that they themselves were going to be no push-overs, and they had also served notice that they were bringing with them a style of football which could change the way the game was played.

Although he could be demonstrative with his players, and often forcefully so, Stein rarely allowed himself the privilege of showing emotion in public. But there was no concealing his delight on the journey home from Switzerland.

'I'm not worrying about our next opponents,' he said confidently. 'If the boys do as well, no-one inside Parkhead, or on the terracing, will blush with shame.'

Chapter 8

CELTIC WOULD HAVE A few weeks to wait to find out who they would face in the next round of the European Cup. It would have been perfectly understandable if the Glasgow side had been hoping for one of the tournament minnows – a nice draw against the Irish side Linfield, for example – to ease their passage into the quarter-finals. But Stein would have none of it. He was barely off the plane before he started telling people that he was hoping to be drawn against one of the big sides in the next round. And with the likes of Liverpool, Atlético Madrid and Inter Milan all comfortably through to the next round with Celtic, there were plenty of big names to choose from.

Obviously, Stein and his players were brimful of confidence after their dazzling start to the League season, and their swift despatch of Zurich. But a tie against the likes of Inter Milan, at this early stage of the season, might not have been the best thing for them. Better for them to acquire a bit more seasoning yet before they stepped up a class. In the end, the European Cup draw paired Celtic with Nantes from France. The French side were not the pushovers that, say, Linfield might have been, but it was a game which was well within Celtic's compass.

There was domestic business to be taken care of first. A little more than a week after returning from Zurich, Celtic found themselves facing Dunfermline Athletic in the League Cup quarter-finals. The two sides found themselves drawn against each other very frequently in the sixties and seventies, and the games threw up some rare tussles. This, however, was not going to be one of them. It was a two-legged affair, and Celtic won the first leg 6–3 at Celtic Park, before travelling to East End Park and winning 3–1, thus maintaining their prolific scoring record in the tournament. Airdrie were their semi-final opponents and the Lanarkshire side were beaten 2–0.

This put Celtic into the final, where they would face their old enemies Rangers. Celtic had beaten the Ibrox side 2–1 in the previous year's final, which Billy McNeill cites as the real beginning of the Parkhead renaissance. However, Rangers had gained some measure of revenge by winning the previous year's Scottish Cup final, after a replay. There is no doubt, though, that Celtic were going into this game with the upper hand. They had already beaten Rangers 2–0 in the League and 4–0 in the Glasgow Cup.

However, from the moment the referee blew his whistle to start the 1966 League Cup final, it was all Rangers. Celtic's so-called psychological edge seemed to do nothing more than fire up the Ibrox side, who dominated the game. Celtic had very few chances in the match, and even though Rangers were not taking theirs, the old Celtic side would have wilted under the pressure. But the self-belief which now ran through this side meant that it only needed one real chance to win a game. The chance came after nineteen minutes in a move which involved Auld, McBride and Lennox. Auld got the ball and fired a clever lob to the edge of the Rangers' penalty box. McBride got his head to it and flicked the ball into the path of the onrushing Lennox, a precision finisher. Lennox steadied himself momentarily before firing a fierce shot past Bent Martin in the Rangers' goal. Lennox's strike was the only goal of the game and, although there were anxious moments for the fans in a crowd of almost 100, 000, McNeill organised the defence, and Celtic stroked the ball around to retain possession, and with it, the League Cup.

It was a good time to be a Celtic player. Men like Tommy Gemmell, who had been at the club for more than six years, simply could not believe the situation in which they found themselves. He and Jimmy Johnstone – who had signed for the club on the same day – became close friends, and they were both revelling in their new-found winning run.

'I was a wild, unmarried boy at the time, and the first toy I decided to buy myself was a car,' says Gemmell. 'Having got the car, I used to pick up Jimmy Johnstone and John Clark in the morning to go to training. As the season progressed, we would have the same conversation every Monday morning. We would invariably have won on the Saturday, and maybe we'd be saying, "That's us top of the League" or, "That's us six games undefeated." Then we'd get through the League Cup section and we'd win the League Cup. And we'd make more progress in the League, so the Monday morning chat got to be along the lines of, "There's every chance we can win the League here." It was the same in Europe. After we'd won the first two rounds we were saying: "There's every chance we can get to the semis." And as the season progressed further, then we started thinking we could maybe go all the way. You could actually feel the buzz about the place. Everybody wanted to be involved in training, and everybody wanted to play.'

Such was the confidence which was spreading through the side that Gemmell remembers one or two Celtic players would actually start to predict the scores before the games: 'We'd sit there and say, "What do you think today? 3–0, 4–1, 4–0?" We were so confident of beating teams – without being over-confident – that some of us actually talked about it in the dressing room.'

The footballer's dressing room is a holy of holies on match days. It is purely and simply the province of the eleven men who are going out onto the field, and their manager. A chairman may enter, but he would be advised to do nothing more than stick his head round the door with a quick "All the best, lads", before retreating to the directors' box.

The Celtic dressing room in that season was a very particular place.

'We were all really shy when we first got to Celtic Park,' says Bobby Lennox. 'Willie O'Neill, Charlie Gallagher and myself would hardly speak to each other, never mind anyone else. But that year it became the greatest dressing room in the world. When directors came in they were always viewed with suspicion. It was always a case of, "What are they doing in here?" There were the players, Big Jock, Sean Fallon, the trainers Bob Rooney and Neilly Mochan, and Jim Steele, the physio. Once that door was shut it was just us. The Big Man regularly put people out, and that's how it should be. If a director wants to speak to a manager, then there's a time and place to do it. After two o'clock on a Saturday afternoon the manager is in charge.'

Superstitions abound in the dressing room. Stein, for example, would pick a tie and wear it until his side lost, and then he would change it. On that basis he would only have got through four ties in the whole of that season. Tommy Gemmell, on the other hand, had no dress phobias but always went out third in the tunnel. Billy McNeill was particular about his route to the ground on match days. Some players, like Jim Craig, would never dream of mentioning the possibility of winning something, for fear of jinxing their prospects. Gemmell, Johnstone, and a few others, had no such qualms.

There was, as there always is, a price to be paid for such hubris. On 5 November, Celtic faced St Mirren at Parkhead in a game which they should have won at a canter. But despite dressing-room predictions of what would doubtless have been a big win, the Paisley side hung on for a 1–1 draw. Celtic had dropped their first League point of the season, and with Rangers snapping at their heels and making equally short work of everyone else in Scotland, the loss of a point could be vital. Stein was furious and lambasted his players in public for allowing confidence to become over-confidence. Two weeks later, there was another scare when Celtic found themselves trailing to their old adversaries Dunfermline but, obviously, Stein's public criticism had the desired effect, and they fought back to win 5–4.

By the time Celtic were due to face Nantes in their European Cup tie at the end of the month, the ship had been steadied. After hiccups against St Mirren and Dunfermline, Celtic were back on course with a 3–0 demolition job against Hearts on the Saturday before the first leg of the European tie. Conventional wisdom is split on how European ties should be played. Against a big club you would obviously want the first leg at home to give you the chance of building up a lead rather than trying to come back from a drubbing. Against one of the smaller sides, or one from the old Eastern Bloc, where travel is a nightmare, you might prefer to play away first, getting a useful result, and then turning it on at home. Against a team like Nantes, a worthy if unspectacular team from a country with no major travel difficulties, it really makes no odds which way round the ties are played.

In the event, Celtic were drawn away first, but the Celtic party was in a relaxed mood when they turned up in France for the game, which was to be played on St Andrew's Day, 30 November. The air of bonhomie spread from the top, with Stein admitting he wouldn't be too bothered if his side even lost by a couple of goals.

'We are not thinking of defeat at the Malakoff Stadium tomorrow night,' he said, in Nantes, on the eve of the game. 'We are thinking only in terms of victory. But strange things can happen in the European Cup, especially when you are playing on foreign soil. If we do happen to lose by one goal, I am completely confident that we will score often enough to win the tie in Glasgow next week.'

Once again, Stein flew in the face of accepted practice. It was normal for the coach of the away side to come into town, promise to attack, and then turn his eighteen-yard box into a reasonable facsimile of a redwood grove by packing it with the biggest, hardest defenders available. This time, not only was Stein saying he wasn't too fussed if they lost, but he also went so far as to reveal his side, 36 hours before kickoff. Normally, nothing short of sodium pentathol would get a manager to release details of his side until the mandatory half-hour deadline, and even then only under duress, in some cases.

Stein said that, barring any training injuries, the team which took the field against Nantes on the Wednesday night would be the one which took Hearts apart the previous Saturday. That meant it was a case of as you were in defence, with the forward line comprising Johnstone, Chalmers, McBride, Lennox and Auld.

In truth, Stein had no need to avail himself of the weasel words normally beloved of the visiting coach in a European tie. Playing attacking football was as natural as breathing to his side and, in the traditions of the great Brazilian teams, the notion of defence often came down to simply scoring more goals than the other team. The presence of Johnstone, Chalmers and Lennox made it blindingly obvious how Celtic would play, and Nantes must have been well aware of this.

'You have seen them in action,' Stein told journalists, of the three forwards. 'It is just not in their make-up to play deep in their own half of the field. They are so fast, and Chalmers and Lennox so direct, that either they are used in attack or we lose their full value.'

The orders of the day for the game against Nantes were the same as they had been for the last game against Zurich. Hold your ground for twenty minutes, soak up the punishment, then take the chances if they present themselves.

'We are not going to be stupid enough to leave ourselves wide open at any time, and certainly not at the beginning of the game,' said Stein. 'But I think we can win, both in France and in Scotland.'

Stein's relaxed atmosphere may simply have been a front to unnerve the French, or it may be that, after the scares against St Mirren and Dunfermline, he knew his players had learned the difference between taking their game seriously and taking themselves seriously. Either way, the French resolutely refused to be lulled into any false sense of security, and produced their own little psychological ploys to make life difficult for Celtic. When the Glasgow side turned up to train at the Malakoff Stadium, they were refused permission to train on the pitch – a common enough tactic to prevent the opposition getting a feel for the turf. Nantes officials, full of the most profuse apologies, explained that the ground had been used for a very important rugby match on the Sunday, and the groundsmen were still repairing turf, which had been cut up in the rainy conditions.

Celtic were ordered to a smaller training ground, but when they got there they found that the French side were there before them. The French had been ordered to get to the ground at the crack of dawn so they could get in a training session of their own, and then watch Celtic as Stein, Sean Fallon and coach Neilly Mochan put them through their paces. It's debatable whether they would have learned much, because Celtic, under orders not to risk anything before the game, went on to play a practice match which was so lacking in resolve it was virtually meaningless.

Stein, however, refused to be put out by any of the French spoiling tactics. In fact, he even went so far as to say he was quite glad they had been refused permission to use the Malakoff pitch.

'It does not matter where we train,' he said. 'Any football pitch will be good enough, providing it is not dangerous. As a matter of fact, this decision suits us perfectly. When Nantes come to Glasgow next week – and if Celtic Park turns out to be soft – then we will be able to direct them to our training ground at Barrowfield without any bickering or unpleasantness.'

On the day of the match, the Celtic squad were having a lie-in, on Stein's instructions, when the first waves of what would turn out to be a green and white invasion hit the shores of Europe. The fans shared the feelings of Gemmell and Johnstone that their side could go all the way, and they were determined to be there to see it. Around 500 Celtic supporters made the trip to Nantes for that game. These were the relatively prosperous who could afford the then luxury of Continental travel. As the tournament progressed, their numbers would grow fifty-fold, and they would come, from all walks of life, to support the 'Hoops'. The strength and fervour of their support meant that, frequently, Celtic were effectively playing with twelve men at home and abroad.

Stein's final team talk came on the Wednesday evening. He was a simple man who liked to keep things simple. His players respected his analysis of their opposition, and they trusted his advice – he had yet to let them down, after all. Stein had gone to see Nantes' game against Nice, and he was convinced he knew how they would play. His team talk was brief and to the point. 'I want a victory, and we are going to play for one from the word go,' he told his players.

Things didn't go quite the way Stein had planned. His game plan was almost thrown into disarray when his star striker, Joe McBride, turned up without his boots.

'We all had a wee green bag like an airline carry-on bag,' explains Billy McNeill. 'It was just big enough for two pairs of boots, a pair of shinguards, and that kind of thing. For whatever reason, Joe had ended up without his.

'It was quite funny in a way, because once we found out, we were all scared to tell the Big Man,' says McNeill, who was not inclined to believe that his role as captain extended to breaking this kind of bad news to the boss.

Forgetting your boots flew in the face of the professionalism and self-respect that Stein had been trying to drill into the team. Eventually, the news was broken to him, and he was, as expected, less than pleased.

'He was raging, absolutely raging,' remembers Lennox. 'It was understandable because Joe had been scoring right, left and centre, and there he was without his boots. The boss ordered Joe and Sean Fallon back to the hotel in a taxi, and they got the boots and made it back to the ground before the kickoff'

Even with boots for McBride, the game still was not going quite the way Stein had planned. For one thing, the target of holding them for twenty minutes went by the wayside when Nantes went a goal up in seventeen minutes. The centre forward Magny, far and away the best of the French players on the night, put his side ahead. Indeed, Nantes might have scored three by half time had it not been for the sharpness of Simpson in the Celtic goal. Celtic, however, continued to press. Before the game, the French said they were concerned because they had heard great things about Joe McBride. In the 24th minute their fears proved well-founded. McBride got the ball from a pass by Lennox and almost burst the net to bring Celtic level.

'I hate to think what would have happened if Joe hadn't scored,' says Lennox.

There is no doubt that, technically, Nantes were a very good side, but they were unable to match Celtic either for fitness or skill. Johnstone was having a terrific game. He frustrated the French defence constantly with his mesmerising runs. Although it appeared that he was indulging himself by beating man after man, after man – only to lose the ball to a French defender – Johnstone was actually playing to instructions. Stein did not want the ball delivered into the box; he wanted Johnstone to wear down the defence. The French supporters were entranced by his performance. It's debatable whether their enthusiasm was shared by the unfortunate French left back, Robin, who saw more of Johnstone that night than he would have cared to. With Simpson and Johnstone both performing heroics, and Auld constantly driving the midfield on, it was only a matter of time before Celtic's better discipline and fitness prevailed.

Murdoch hadn't had the best game of his life in a Celtic jersey that night. He and Gemmell had been out of position in Nantes territory, when they lost the ball between them, allowing Magny to put the French ahead in the first half. He redeemed himself, however, with another of his trademark precision passes, in the second half, which found Lennox. The winger shook off the attentions of two French defenders before taking the ball into the box and beating Castel from close range. Late in the game, the Nantes centre half Budzinski was guilty of a similar defensive error to that of Murdoch and Gemmell. Like them, he was punished for it when Chalmers nipped in to tap the ball past Castel.

It was not a great Celtic performance. They had been naive at times, and had been fortunate not to be punished. If Stein had got his wish – to be drawn against one of the bigger sides in the tournament – there is no telling what might have happened. A better-organised side than Nantes might have exposed Celtic's shortcomings fatally. After all, while Celtic were winning in France, one of those bigger sides – Liverpool – were losing 5–1 to Ajax, in Amsterdam. Nonetheless, for all their faults, they had won, and won well, and, with three away goals in the bag, it seemed unlikely that anything could stop them heading for the quarter-finals.

'We said we would attack here, and we did,' said Stein after the game. 'The strain is now off. We played well, and that is not boasting. Next Wednesday, we will try to make it a festival of football for our own supporters. We will be out to score a lot of goals even though we are 3–1 in front.'

Stein was obviously pleased with the result, but he was not yet entirely happy. His team still lacked one ingredient. The jigsaw was one piece short. Within a week, he would find the missing piece.

Chapter 9

THERE'S AN OLD FOOTBALL saying which suggests that strikers win matches but defenders win titles. Old sayings only get to be old sayings because they are true, and, certainly, that particular adage could sum up Jock Stein's approach with his Celtic side. His defence was rock solid and, barring injury, it was seldom changed. However, his forward line was chopped and changed to suit the occasion. And, as he contemplated his side towards the end of 1966, Stein realised he was still short of a match-winning striker.

There was no doubt of Joe McBride's quality as a centre forward. As Celtic were preparing for the return leg of their European tie against Nantes, he was only two short of his 150th goal in just under three and a half seasons. Given that the First Division was then a 34-game season, that meant he was averaging around a goal a game when Cup matches were taken into account. Stein, however, felt his side still lacked weight up front. They were capable, as they still are, of playing attractive football without being able to finish well. Despite winning the League and the League Cup in Stein's first full season, there was also a long barren spell where goals were in short supply. Celtic statistician *par excellence*, Pat Woods, worked out that, between Bobby Lennox scoring against Liverpool in the Cup-Winners Cup at Parkhead on 14 April 1966 and Jimmy Johnstone scoring on the stroke of half time against Morton on 30 April, Celtic actually went 445 minutes without scoring a goal. That's almost five matches between goals. Clearly, by the time Celtic were about to face Nantes in the second leg, Stein must have known that his team could have a reasonable European run. But, as the quality of opposition improved, so too would their defences, and there could be no more goal droughts.

Goalkeepers apart, the one thing Jock Stein could do was judge a player, and he had an encyclopaedic mental reference of their strengths and weaknesses. His biographer, Bob Crampsey, can testify to the lengths Stein went to, in order to check on players. Crampsey, one of the few men left in Britain still possessed of the Corinthian ethic, is one of those men who – when he's not broadcasting – will go and see a game for no other reason than that it looks like it might be a good match.

'Jock Stein was a tremendous worker, a prodigious worker,' recalls Crampsey. 'I used to go on a whim to see the most bizarre matches, like Stranraer against Alloa for example, or East Stirling versus Stirling Albion. And the number of times you would bump into Jock Stein at a game like that was quite extraordinary. I feel that if you said to a modern manager, in conversation, that you had been to see Stranraer and Alloa, his first reaction, these days, would be to say: "Is there anybody any good?" And if you told him, he would agree with you without ever having seen them play. But in a similar conversation, Jock Stein would immediately tell you, not only what the player looked like, but also what his strengths and weaknesses were. Unless,' adds Crampsey 'he thought the player was any good, in which case, he would invariably ask, "Who else did you see?" I think he did that for two reasons. The first was not to tip his hand, and the second was not to give you the satisfaction of having him agree with you on what constituted a good player.'

For most of 1966, Willie Wallace had been desperately unhappy with his lot at Hearts. He felt that, at Tynecastle, he wasn't getting anything like the wages he should have been getting. By the end of the year, Wallace's discontent had reached the point where he was actually on the verge of quitting Scottish football altogether. He and his wife had already talked things over, and had decided to emigrate to Australia. Wallace had even gone so far as to contact Australia House and complete all the formalities. All he needed to do was pick a date and go.

Wallace had played for Stenhousemuir, Raith Rovers and

Hearts, but had never really settled. Stein was aware of his qualities and equally aware of the fact that he was unhappy in Scotland, and was contemplating a move to Australia. He was also aware of one other thing – Rangers were equally interested in signing him. At a board meeting on 2 December 1966 – just two days after returning from Nantes – Stein told the Celtic directors that he wanted to buy Wallace. The board, who had also – presumably – been made aware of the interest from Ibrox, agreed that the deal should be done, in Stein's words, 'as soon as possible'. Only four days later, and on the eve of the return match with Nantes, Wallace signed for Celtic for a club record £30,000.

Stein had had his eye on the striker for some time and might have signed him earlier had it not been for the shyness of his left back Willie O'Neill.

'We played Hearts in the Scottish Cup, and we had drawn at Tynecastle and taken them back to Celtic Park for the replay,' remembers Bobby Lennox. 'Big Jock said to Willie O'Neill, who was playing at left back, "If you get a chance, tell Willie Wallace the Big Man would like a word with him." O'Neill was such a shy guy then, much more than he is now. So at the end of the game, Jock said, "Did you speak to Willie Wallace?" and O'Neill said, "Sorry boss, I never got the chance."

'He'd been out on the park standing next to Wallace for an hour and half, but he stood there, with a straight face, and told the boss he never got a chance to talk to him.'

Wallace became known to his new team-mates as 'Wispy'. There are two schools of thought on the nickname. One suggests it came from his first three initials – WSB for William Semple Brown – and the other suggests it came from his quiet-speaking voice. Either way, there is no argument about his qualities as a player.

'Get the ball in the box and Joe would score for you. Joe was an amazing striker, but Willie Wallace was a smashing football player,' says Bobby Lennox, who played alongside both men. 'Willie could play midfield – he played at right half a lot of times when Bobby was out of the team – but Joe was an out-and-out striker. The two of them were actually both super strikers, but you wonder if they would have linked up as such. It's one of those things we'll never know. They were both fine players, but maybe

Billy McNeill just two days before the start of Celtic's European Cup campaign on 26 September 1966 *(Hulton Getty)*

Right Ronnie Simpson, the Celtic keeper, comes out to collect the ball during the European Cup final against Inter Milan *(Hulton Getty)*

Left and below McNeill battling for Celtic on their way to the final *(msi)*

Top left Sarti, Inter Milan's keeper, protests after Tommy Gemmell's equaliser *(Hulton Getty)*

Bottom left Steve Chalmers wheels away from Sarti having scored the winning goal *(msi)*

Above Scenes of jubilation in Lisbon as the final whistle blows *(msi)*

Right McNeill receives the European Cup *(Hulton Getty)*

Left McNeill fights his way across the pitch in an attempt to get to his team mates *(msi)*

Above and right Tommy Gemmell and Billy McNeill lift the Scottish FA Cup having beaten Rangers in 1969 *(Colorsport)*

Above McNeill
celebrates Celtic's win
over Rangers *(Colorsport)*

Left Bertie Auld in 1969
(Colorsport)

just a wee bit similar. Joe and Wispy would both have liked Stevie playing beside them to make the runs and just get into the box so they could score goals.'

Stein had told Billy McNeill that he thought the combination of Wallace and McBride could become the greatest striking partnership Scotland had ever seen. He also fancied that they could even be the best in Europe.

'I think when Jock took over as manager, he knew that he had potential there, but it probably wasn't until the following season that he started to think, Yeah, maybe I have got something here. Obviously, though, he knew that he needed a better quota of goals from the side that he took over so, first, Joe McBride came in and then, latterly, Willie Wallace.'

Stein's astuteness in the transfer market had been highlighted by the League fixture which fell between the two Nantes games. Celtic were held 0–0 by Kilmarnock at Rugby Park, one of only two League games all season in which Celtic would fail to score. By that stage, of course, the moves to bring Wallace to Celtic Park were already in train.

Wallace was delighted to have been thrown a lifeline by Stein. As he turned up at Tynecastle for the last time to collect his boots, he told waiting reporters that he hoped his wandering days were now behind him. He also said that signing for Celtic was the greatest event of his football career. One reporter asked Wallace which position he wanted to play for the Glasgow side. 'Any position Mr Stein decides,' replied Wallace, with undisguised gratitude. 'I am a happy man to be a Celtic player.'

While Wallace was picking up his boots in Edinburgh, his new team-mates were preparing to face the French side in what everyone expected to be little more than a formality. Wallace himself said that he was looking forward to being in the crowd at Celtic Park and enjoying the spectacle. The French side had arrived in Glasgow on the Tuesday, 36 hours before the match. They could not have been any worse prepared if they had tried. Not only were they trailing 3–1 from the first leg, but they had also lost five League games in a row in France, and had been deposed from the top of the French League. No wonder that, when one reporter asked the arriving French officials what they thought of their chances for the game against Celtic, he was greeted with a typically Gallic, but undeniably eloquent, shrug of the shoulders.

Celtic, as Stein had promised in France, had indeed offered the use of their training pitch at Barrowfield rather than Celtic Park itself. The French, who after all had started the war of nerves, had no option but to comply. As it was, they had a rather lack-lustre training session before heading for Loch Lomond for some sightseeing. What the French did not know, indeed what no-one outside Celtic Park knew, was that Celtic had one very serious injury worry. Joe McBride, the star striker and one half of their newly purchased strike force, had a knee injury which would ultimately keep him out of the match. Stein let journalists believe that he would be fielding an unchanged side from the one which had beaten Nantes 3–1 in France, but it was never likely that McBride would play. On the day of the game he actually named a pool of fifteen players, the largest he would name in the European campaign. McBride's injury was disguised by the smokescreen of the four extra players. Stein preferred, instead, to talk about the possibility of John Hughes making his European Cup debut. Hughes had been injured in the League Cup win against Rangers, in October, and hadn't played since. Stein continued to leave open the possibility of Hughes playing against the French even though the player still had a dressing on his injured knee. The rarely used Charlie Gallagher was another of the additional players in the squad as forward cover. The other two named by Stein, were keeper John Fallon – only goalkeepers could be substituted in the event of injury in the European Cup – and full back Davie Cattanach. All the same, the pundits were still betting on the same eleven players taking the field, later that night, against Nantes.

In the end, Stein made two changes – one in personnel, the other tactical. The injury to McBride meant that Chalmers moved into the traditional centre-forward role, with Gallagher getting one of his infrequent outings at inside-right. If the Celtic fans were surprised by the team, when it was announced before the kickoff, they would still not have been worried. They, like many of the players, were beginning to feel that eleven men in green and white hoops – no matter who they were – were a match for almost anyone.

The French side were known as 'The Canaries' because of their distinctive yellow jerseys, but Celtic made sure they had nothing to sing about that night. The game became a triumph for Jimmy Johnstone who frequently shone on the European stage where his talents would be appreciated by the widest possible audience. Johnstone, who had been in rare form in the away leg, more or less started where he had left off. Full back De Michele, who had been tormented by the winger in the first game, was given more of the same in the second leg, and must have regretted passing his late fitness test.

Johnstone put Celtic 1–0 ahead with a fierce shot, after a dazzling run. There were only thirteen minutes on the clock and Nantes were now 4–1 behind on aggregate. The Parkhead faithful scented blood and settled in for the anticipated rout. The French unsportingly refused to collapse and – perhaps for the first time over the two legs – made life difficult for Celtic. The French striker Georgin made the scores level on the night when he got on the end of a great pass from the Yugoslavian international Kovacevic, and swept the ball past Simpson. A few minutes later Georgin again brought a fine save out of Simpson, who was forced to scramble the ball away on the goal-line. Had that one gone in, the French would have pegged it back to 4–3 on aggregate and, doubtless, would have attacked with renewed vigour. Celtic, for their part, were showing some signs of naivety at this level. Almost every time their forwards mounted an attack, the French defenders would step up, spring their offside trap, and the attack would break down. It was cynical, it wasn't pretty, but it was certainly effective.

The sides went in at the interval tied at 1–1, and there was still the remote possibility that the French might get a result. Johnstone took things into his own hands in the second half. Offside traps only work against a side which is playing a long-passing game. Johnstone simply ran at the French defence time after time, pulling them all over the park. It wasn't long before one of those runs gave him the space to deliver a cross onto the head of Steve Chalmers who, obligingly, put Celtic 2–1 ahead. A few minutes later, Johnstone repeated his mazy run and cross, and this time it was Lennox who was on hand to tap the ball in and give Celtic a 3–1 lead.

To their credit, Nantes continued to make a game of it. Their football was attractive but, when you're staring down the wrong end of a 6–2 hammering, no-one can blame you if your heart isn't in it.

It was a good result for Celtic under straitened circumstances. Johnstone had given one of his best performances in a European game, but it was still a team effort, even if the defence had rarely been troubled. Also, Stein must have been encouraged by the fact that even without three of his front-line strikers – McBride, Hughes and the newly signed Wallace – his side were still more than good enough to win.

The French officials and the French media were unanimous in their verdict when their team left for home. Celtic were in the quarter-finals of the European Cup, and it was going to take an exceptionally good side to prevent them going further. 'There is no question of belittling this Scottish victory,' said the national sports daily *L'Equipe*. 'Celtic, by their own qualities, showed what a fine footballing side they are.' *L'Equipe*, however, like many of the other French papers, took heart at Nantes' dignified and skilful display. *L'Equipe* said: 'It is a pity that Nantes were not at their best in the first leg, for this could have considerably changed the face of things.' The biggest national newspaper, *France-Soir*, agreed, but given the recent devastating poor run of form by the French champions, took heart, the day after the game, in a Pyrrhic victory. 'Last night's defeat for Nantes was as good as a draw, almost a victory,' the paper argued. 'This really was Nantes' rehabilitation.'

Stein was pleased. His side was in the quarter-finals of the European Cup which, to allow for the severity of the winter in many parts of Europe, would be played in March of the following year. By that time, his new striking partnership would have bedded in to become the most feared duo in Scotland, and would be ready to take on the best that Europe had to offer. However, it didn't work out that way.

McBride's knee injury was much more serious than anyone had

first suspected. Years of hard knocks, and putting himself in harm's way as a centre forward, were taking their toll on his knee joint. The kneecap was actually eroding and producing flakes of bone which could then, effectively, roam around in the knee joint causing excruciating pain and potentially career-threatening damage. Joe McBride and Willie Wallace were supposed to plunder defences the length and breadth of the country that season. In fact, they only played together twice. Wallace made his debut against Motherwell on the Saturday after he had signed. Celtic won 4–2, but it was Wallace's striking partner, Steve Chalmers, who grabbed the headlines with a hat-trick, while Wallace didn't get his name on the score sheet. The following week, McBride and Wallace did play together in a 6–2 rout of Partick Thistle, getting three of the Celtic goals – one to McBride, while Wallace scored his first two goals for the club.

On Christmas Eve, 1966, Celtic played Aberdeen at Pittodrie. It was a 1–1 draw and again Wallace and McBride were playing up front. However, McBride damaged his knee again and, it was only after this game, that the real extent of the damage became apparent. Despite various attempts at a comeback, McBride would play no further part in Celtic's *annus mirabilis*, and it was only through the skill of a surgeon in a pioneering operation that he would ever be able to play again.

'I think Jock always had it in his mind to sign Willie once Joe had joined us,' Billy McNeill suggests. 'It was always in his mind that he needed one or two good front players. He always talked about freshening up the side, and what he meant was juggling the front players. At that time, we had Joe and Willie, Steve Chalmers, John Hughes, Bobby Lennox and Jimmy Johnstone, so there was no shortage of talent.'

Also, Stein may have been looking to sign Wallace as a long-term replacement for the ageing Chalmers, who would not have many seasons left in him at the highest level, no matter how hard he trained.

The point about whether Wallace and McBride would have formed the kind of unbeatable partnership that Stein had in mind is largely moot now. McNeill, for one, believes it would have been an interesting combination.

'Joe was an explosive player who played almost exclusively within the penalty area,' he says. 'If you were ever looking for a pass from Joe inside the penalty box, you could forget it, because it was never going to come. But he was such a complete finisher that, if you put the ball into the area, then he was sure to get on the end of it. That was the way he played the game, and it was great.

'He wasn't the quickest player in the world, but he made up for that by being as brave as a lion. He was superb in the air and a great striker of a ball. Joe was also very single-minded. Once he got the ball inside the box, then he considered it was his mandate to try and score a goal. Stevie would have complemented him because he was quick and sharp-running, and would run off the striker.

'Willie was an interesting player because he could play in any position. He could play anywhere from right across the midfield to right up front. He was a good midfield player, and he was sharp and quick-thinking. I honestly think that he and Joe would have been successful together.'

It looked, for the first time, that the happy chance which had blessed Celtic over the eighteen months of Stein's reign had, perhaps, deserted them. The club had spent an unprecedented £50,000-plus on two strikers, and they had played only two games together. However, it's an ill wind, and the injury to McBride forced Stein to make changes in his forward line. Rather than go out and buy someone else, he was convinced that he could achieve what he wanted with the players on his staff. Steve Chalmers, who had been one of the more expendable fixtures in the Celtic forward line, now made the number nine shirt his own for the rest of the season. That enforced positional change would pay big dividends five months later in Lisbon.

'It's ironic,' says McNeill, reflecting on the way things turned out, 'but if Willie and Joe had played together, then Stevie would have been relegated to the supporting cast. But it was Stevie who ended up as the top scorer in the European campaign that year as well as scoring the winner in the final.'

Chapter 10

CELTIC ENDED 1966 ON a low note. Having gone from the start of the season to 5 November without dropping a point, they saw out the Old Year with their first defeat. Dundee United beat them 3–2, at Tannadice, on New Year's Eve, in what was to be the first leg of a unique double for the Dundee side. They would be the only team to beat Celtic home and away that season, notching up another 3–2 win at Parkhead the following May. As Billy McNeill points out, that game was virtually meaningless, but the first defeat was something of a set-back.

Celtic were now looking at going into the traditional New Year fixture against Rangers on the back of a draw at Aberdeen and a defeat by Dundee United. Hardly the best preparation for a match against your fiercest rivals and nearest challengers in the League. But, again, providence smiled on Celtic. The New Year fixture was postponed because of the weather, and would not be played until the end of the season. Despite two poor results, Celtic were still in front in the Championship race, but Stein plainly felt that changes would have to be made.

While all this was going on, Jim Craig must have been rueing his choice of career. Craig was a dentist and, while he had played 22 games in Celtic's Championship-winning season, he had missed out on the tour to the United States.

'I had to stay behind because of my final exams,' says Craig. 'It was some decision. I missed one tour, and I stayed out of the side for six months.'

Jim Craig was unusual in that he was the only member of the

Celtic squad with a profession. Regardless of what happened on the field, he was first and foremost a dentist, so it would have been no surprise when he chose to take his finals rather than go on tour. Stein, frankly, found this baffling, but that was one of several areas where he and his defender did not see eye to eye.

Craig's absence meant that there was a re-shuffle in the Celtic defensive line-up. Tommy Gemmell moved across to play at right back, with Willie O'Neill playing at left back. Gemmell's overlapping runs and his constant desire to go forward had paid off handsomely, especially in Europe. And if Celtic were doing well with one overlapping fullback, how much better would they do with two?

Physically, Craig was tall and strong. He was a gifted natural athlete and had also excelled at the long jump – once, in competition, coming a close second to Olympic gold medallist, Lynn Davies. He was an aggressive full back who was a fierce tackler, but he could also distribute the ball, spraying passes the length of the field if need be. He also liked to go forward, whereas Willie O'Neill, who was a fine defensive full back, preferred to stay in his own half.

Stein took the decision to bring Craig in at right back, switching the naturally right-footed Gemmell to the left-back slot, and relegating O'Neill back to the reserves.

'Jock told me I had been knocking on the door for a while, so now it was time I got my chance,' says Craig, of his Celtic call-up in the first game of 1967. Dundee were the opposition and, since Celtic scored five and only conceded one, then the positional switch obviously paid off. Craig gave the side more balance, but switching Gemmell to the other side of the park also paid dividends.

'The thing is, when you're a right-footed player playing at right back, your tendency is to hit the by-line and cut the ball right back,' explains Craig. 'When you're a right-footed player playing at left back, as Tommy was, then you're inclined to slip inside and score. Tommy wasn't scoring all that often up till then but, after he switched wings, his scoring rate picked up again. As a left back who was right-footed, his instinct was to go towards goal, whereas my instinct as a right-footed right back was to cut the ball back. That's one of the things I became known for – laying on a good pass. I think, at the time we changed, the team was starting to stutter a wee bit. But the main thing about having two attacking full backs, at that time, was that it meant everything got compressed towards the opposition goal, which puts them under more pressure.'

The switch worked for Celtic and for Tommy Gemmell. Playing at right back, he had scored more goals in Europe than he had at home in the first half of the season. But once he switched to the left-hand side of the field, he went on to score six goals in the second half of the season.

Celtic's first two games of the New Year had both ended up in 5–1 victories, against Dundee and Clyde. Stein had been using Gallagher in the midfield instead of the injured Auld but, when Auld came back, Gallagher dropped back into the reserves. The next game was against St Johnstone at Muirton Park – their home, in those days – on 14 January 1967. Celtic were back to their normal form and won at a canter 4–0. The Celtic team that day is worth noting. It was:

Simpson, Craig, Gemmell, Murdoch, McNeill, Clark, Johnstone, Wallace, Chalmers, Auld and Lennox.

To anyone at Muirton Park that day it may have seemed like just another demolition job as Celtic got back on the rails on their journey to the title. But looking back from five months later, anyone in the crowd at Perth, that Saturday in January, would have realised they had seen footballing history being made. The Lisbon Lions had played together for the first time.

It is an event which, to be fair, is significant only in hindsight. It would be too good to be true if Stein had watched his side win 4–0 and suddenly realised, like Saint Paul on the road to Damascus, that this is where his salvation lay. Naturally, it didn't happen like that. That incarnation of the Lisbon Lions was a brief and shining moment and, the following Saturday, Stein brought in Hughes for Lennox, and the side had changed again. The results did not suffer, because Hibs were despatched 2–0 with goals from McBride and Chalmers.

Jock Stein was notorious for fussing with his forward line. The fact that he chose to change what had been a settled defence, at the turn of the year, is an indication of how seriously he took Celtic's relatively poor form. He would chop and change his strikers, sometimes to freshen up the side, sometimes to teach a lesson to a player he felt was not performing as well as Stein felt he should, and sometimes just because the occasion demanded it. Hughes, for example, was a magnificent sight in the rain, and was invariably preferred on heavy ground where his speed and strength could be telling. There was also one other, more interesting, reason for the changes.

'I just don't know if Jock knew what his best side was,' says Steve Chalmers. 'He had such a wealth of talent available to him, that it's hard to know if anyone could have picked the best Celtic side out of that squad. The reserves in those days had players like John Fallon, Willie O'Neill, Davie Cattanach, John Cushley, George Connelly, Charlie Gallagher and David Hay, with young-sters like Kenny Dalglish, Danny McGrain, Lou Macari and Victor Davidson coming through. It was an exceptional pool of talent for any manager to choose from, and if one of us was injured or suspended, then one of them could easily step up without any difficulty. We used to regularly play training games where the first team would take on the reserves, and they beat us as often as we beat them.'

Defensively, Stein certainly knew his best side. The pairing of Gemmell and O'Neill had conceded twenty-four goals in sixteen games. Gemmell and Craig together would concede only nine, in a similar number of games, as Celtic drove towards the title. Gemmell's improved scoring rate from the new position was an added bonus. The other defensive pairing of McNeill and Clark was inviolate, barring injury or suspension. The quiet Clark was one of the unsung heroes of the Celtic side. He was a ferocious tackler, and his ability to read a game was unsurpassed. With Clark majestic on the ground, and the inspirational McNeill domi-nant in the air, the Celtic defence was beginning to take on the air of an impregnable redoubt.

Murdoch and Auld were Stein's preferred choices for the midfield. He had seen their potential in America and had converted them from their former duties on the wing. Auld, in particular, thrived in his new role, and became a midfield general long before the term had any real currency. Murdoch may not have been the most mobile man on the field, but he could deliver a ball onto a sixpence, and had a ferocious shot.

That left four spaces for five players. Johnstone, Lennox, Wallace, Chalmers and Hughes took their positions at the whim of Stein and his assessment of the suitability of the opponents and the pitch. Wallace had been bought specifically to score goals and to complement the now-injured Joe McBride. In McBride's absence, he had scored enough important goals to justify his position, and was never out the side from the moment he was eligible. Lennox and Chalmers were equally important for their uncanny instincts in front of goal, coupled with their selfless running off the ball which stretched and confused defences. Looking back, Hughes was always likely to be the one to be left out. He was, after all, the man who Stein had wanted to sell almost from the moment he came in the door. Hughes, also, did not fit in to a team pattern as well as the others. The fans loved him for the very thing that made him so frustrating for his team-mates. He was gloriously unpredictable. He could, and often did, beat four or five players and then lost the ball to the sixth, or ran it out of play altogether while the other forwards waited in scoring positions in the middle. When Hughes was on form, Celtic were always likely to win; but it was more likely to be an individual performance by Hughes, rather than a team performance by Celtic.

Johnstone, on the other hand, could generally be relied on to take the ball, beat five or six men, and then do something constructive with it, even if it was only denying possession to the opposition.

'Jinky was marvellous when you were under pressure,' recalls Steve Chalmers. 'You could give him the ball and he would just hold onto it. I don't think he knew himself what he was going to do with it but, once he had it, no-one was getting it off him until he was good and ready.'

Jimmy Johnstone had signed for Celtic on the same day as Tommy Gemmell, back in 1960. Both players arrived at Parkhead just too late to gain the benefit of Stein's influence, first time round. Johnstone, however, was a natural-born footballer. He had learned his skills playing under street-lights with a ball not much bigger than a tennis ball. His temperament was as fiery as his red hair, but he was the darling of the die-hard fans in 'the jungle' at Celtic Park. His temper meant that he was often prone to retaliate when he was scythed to the ground but, when he chose to rise beyond temptation, Johnstone's tenacity on the ball was an invaluable weapon in the Celtic arsenal.

'Wee Jimmy could look after himself,' says Tommy Gemmell, with undisguised admiration. 'He was hard as nails and strong as an ox. He was a great trainer, and he could look after himself, whatever the problem. Jim Craig played behind him more often than I did that season, but I had played behind him often enough in the past to realise how he played. The only way to get the ball off him most of the time was to put him up in the air, and that gave us a free kick. But every time he got up-ended he would ask for the ball to be played to his feet again. He knew he had the upper hand over the guy who had fouled him because, if he did it again, then he was either going to have his name taken or be sent off. So Jinky just asked for the ball back, and he was off again.'

Stein, also, was well aware of Johnstone's ability to put a defence under pressure.

'It's just like Tommy says,' agreed Steve Chalmers. 'Any time Jinky got fouled, Jock would be out of the dug-out urging him on, and telling him to go back at the same guy again. He knew there was always the chance we would get something out of it.'

Celtic were definitely on a roll now. From the moment Stein changed the defence around and provided the added impetus of another attacking full back, the side swept over almost everyone they met. In seven League matches in the January and February of 1967, they scored twenty-five goals for the loss of only three. In the first two rounds of the Scottish Cup, Arbroath had been despatched 4–0 and Elgin City were trounced 7–0.

Celtic were in rare form as they headed into the quarter-final of the European Cup – which is just as well. Their opponents were Vojvodina of Novi Sad, in the former Yugoslavia. They were described by Jock Stein when the draw was announced as 'physically strong and technically excellent'. He was not wrong, and his side, which was growing in ambition and aspiration, was about to be put through its sternest test of skill, strength and character.

Chapter 11

As ever, Jock Stein had done his homework for Celtic's quarter-final against Vojvodina. The Yugoslavian side had qualified for the quarter-final stages by beating Atlético Madrid in one of the epic European encounters. With the teams deadlocked after the first two games, it required a third match to separate them. The Spaniards appeared to be coasting at 2–0 up, but were being kicked off the park in the process by the extremely physical Yugoslavians. With what they thought was a sensible cushion, the Spaniards started to give as good as they had been getting and mixed it up with the Slavs. This suited the Yugoslavians perfectly and, once they had encouraged the Spaniards to lose the place entirely, they went back to playing their extremely skilful brand of football. Vojvodina then pegged the score back to 2–2, which took the tie to extra time, before they eventually won 3–2. They had, however, paid a price in having two men sent off which would make them ineligible for the quarter-final.

Stein had been in Madrid to see the Yugoslavs at their cynical best and had a good idea what to expect should his team be drawn against them. When they did come out of the hat together, Stein persuaded his directors to arrange a friendly against another Yugoslavian side, Dinamo Zagreb. The game took place in February, just a few weeks ahead of the first leg in Novi Sad. Stein's ostensible reason to his directors was to gauge the strength of Yugoslavian football. But, in fact, it allowed him to try a number of tactical experiments. Celtic dominated the game, but the forwards were in poor form, missing chance after chance and, in the end, Zagreb won 1–0 with a late goal.

The pattern of play against Zagreb would be repeated in their last League match before flying out to Yugoslavia for the first leg of the quarter-final. In what was arguably their worst result of the season, Celtic drew 1–1 with Stirling Albion. The game was played in dreadful conditions. Lashing rain had turned Stirling's Annfield ground into a sea of mud and, even though Stirling keeper Murray was in inspired form, again the Celtic forwards just could not find the net. Despite Stirling being reduced to ten men, Celtic were 1–0 down at half time, and only a second-half header from John Hughes spared their blushes.

Billy McNeill was plainly furious with all around him as he barged his way into the tunnel at the end of the game. And not just because he had had a penalty claim turned down and a goal disallowed – or because Rangers were now within two points of Celtic in the League. McNeill knew that a performance like that against Vojvodina would leave Celtic in dire straits, and the European bubble could be well and truly burst in Yugoslavia. On the plus side, he was able to communicate to his colleagues, in no uncertain terms, that they could not afford to take it easy against a team who were, by common consent, one of the top four in Europe, and fancied to go all the way themselves.

Vojvodina were managed by Vujadin Boskov, a small, pugnacious character who would stand a fair chance of success in any James Cagney look-alike competition. He had his problems for the game with two of his players suspended from the previous round, but he was every bit as crafty and cunning as Stein could be in handling the psychological battle which takes place before a ball is ever kicked.

Stein, for his part, had the sort of headache that every manager dreads. He was going up against one of the top sides in Europe, looking for a goal or two away from home, and he had no established striking partnership. Since his knee gave way against Aberdeen on Christmas Eve, Joe McBride had been struggling courageously to get fit, but it was a losing battle. He had made one appearance since then, in a second eleven Scottish Cup tie again Hearts, at the end of January, but the knee had broken down again. McBride was attempting another comeback against Dundee reserves the week before the Vojvodina match. The plan was that McBride, who had been resting for a fortnight with no ill-effects from the knee, would play against Dundee reserves on the Tuesday, Stirling Albion on the Saturday, and then be fit for the crucial game against the Yugoslavians. It turned out to be another false dawn, and McBride broke down again and had to stay in Glasgow for intensive treatment while his team-mates went off to Yugoslavia. His notional striking partner, Willie Wallace, flew out with the Celtic party, but he wasn't eligible to play since he had been signed from Hearts after the deadline for the quarter-finals.

'I suppose, in a lot of ways, not having Joe or Willie put a bit more pressure on us,' says Billy McNeill. 'We had capable deputies in men like John Hughes. Big Yogi was great going through the middle and preferred playing there as opposed to the wide position, so we had some cover as far as that aspect was concerned. I think, going out there, we were less concerned about winning away from home than we were about coming back with a result. I think when you had the second leg at home you always wanted to be in touch. A 1–0 defeat was the box-office scoreline because it meant you had to win 2–0 at home.'

There were serious question marks about the Celtic line-up as the team flew out of Glasgow on Monday morning. To add to Stein's worries, the harsh tackling of Stirling Albion on the Saturday had also taken its toll.

'Jimmy Johnstone took a couple of nasty knocks on the leg at Annfield,' Stein told newsmen at the airport. 'It's too early to say whether he will be able to play against Vojvodina. He will be having treatment from the moment we arrive in Novi Sad. We have also had a few other minor injuries, but all the players should be fit by Wednesday. No man will play unless he is completely fit,' Stein cautioned.

One of the first priorities on arriving at any European venue is to check out the stadium where the match will take place. Players need to get as good a feel as possible for the new, and invariably hostile, environment. There was an added urgency about checking out the stadium at Novi Sad. Stein was particularly concerned about the quality of the floodlights. The Yugoslavians had only had them installed a few days before the game. Stein had been told they consisted of two diametrically opposite pylons. He was genuinely concerned that they might not be up to the job and feared that his side might be playing one of the most important games in their history in half-dark conditions. Celtic had given serious thought to refusing to play if, in their opinion, the lights were not up to standard.

'The one thing I really remember about the game is that they had the most magnificent set of floodlights I have ever seen,' remembers Jim Craig. 'Novi Sad was the most primitive town; a lot of the streets weren't even paved, which was a bit of a surprise for many of us. But there was this remarkable set of floodlights, in a primitive town, in the middle of what is now Croatia. The great concern beforehand was whether there would be any lights at all, but they were really astonishingly good.'

Craig was making his European Cup debut against Vojvodina. Even though he and Gemmell were now the established full-back pairing, football writers were backing Stein to give the nod to Willie O'Neill for this game, because of his size, his strength and his European experience. O'Neill had played in Celtic's four previous ties.

'To be fair to Willie, I think Jock was stuck on the idea of playing two full backs who wanted to attack,' recalls Craig. 'Although he was a very good full back, Willie was never very comfortable going forward, so that was how I got my first game in the European Cup.'

The game against Vojvodina was Celtic's toughest test in Europe thus far. The only side they had met of similar calibre was Dinamo Kiev at the same stage of the previous season's European Cup-Winner's Cup. Celtic won that one 4–1 on aggregate but had the advantage of playing the first leg at home, and building up a three-goal lead. This time they were on foreign soil and, despite their previous victories against Zurich and Nantes, they were stepping up a class. This time it was Vojvodina who would be expected to build a cushion for the second leg.

'In those days, you didn't have the advantage of television as you do now,' recalls Billy McNeill. 'Vojvodina was a trip into the unknown for us, but I do remember that they were a really big, powerful side. All we knew was that they played in a city called Novi Sad, but that didn't mean much. We didn't have a clue where we were going when we went to play in Europe, particularly with that one.'

Boskov paid Celtic a compliment by travelling 30 miles to watch them go through an intensive training session the day before the game. Obviously, he was sufficiently impressed with the reputation that had preceded the Glasgow side from their results in Switzerland and France. Boskov stood and watched and made copious notes as the sixteen-man Celtic squad went through their paces. With him was another of his spies, who identified each of the Celtic players, by name, for the coach's benefit. After watching the Scottish side, Boskov calmly announced that his side would beat Celtic by two goals.

Stein was plainly taken aback by his rival's presumption and could only manage a terse, 'We'll see,' when the news was relayed to him. Nonetheless, Boskov was getting under Stein's skin. The Celtic manager had told the Scottish media that he would name a team after that Tuesday training session. That was still his intention until he discovered that Boskov had been watching his players go through their paces. After the news was broken to him, Stein simply announced that the team was not set yet. However, he did let it be known that he would be choosing from a squad of thirteen. There was speculation that Johnstone's injury was not fully healed, but it seems likely that Stein already knew who would play, and he was simply trying to unsettle Boskov.

'The team will not be announced until we reach the stadium,' he said. 'We are ready. We know the importance of the job we have to do, and we will not lose by doing stupid things on the field.'

Billy McNeill showed similar resolve a few hours before the game. 'Everybody knows that this is one of the most important matches in Celtic's history,' he said tersely. 'We know what victory means to the club and to the players, and each man knows the job he has to do tonight. We have promised the boss that we will not fail, and we do not intend to let him down.'

Stein's original assessment of the Vojvodina side as being physically tough and technically perfect had been drilled into his players ever since the draw was made. He knew that they knew the importance of the job at hand, but he was sensible enough not to overburden them.

'Vojvodina were, possibly, the best side we met in the tournament,' recalls Jim Craig. 'They were physically very strong, and they had a great touch on the ball. But Jock wasn't much for giving a man-for-man breakdown. He was a crafty old bugger, and he would know that, sometimes, if you build some of their players up too much beforehand, panic can set in. Unlike Dukla Prague or Inter Milan, there wasn't really a single star name in the Vojvodina team. But Jock certainly left us under no misapprehensions about their quality.'

In the end, Stein dropped Willie O'Neill and Charlie Gallagher from his thirteen-man squad, which meant that Craig retained his usual right-back slot while Lennox was paired with Steve Chalmers in place of the ineligible Wallace. Stein would be relying on his side to dig in under pressure and hoping that the tireless running of Chalmers and Lennox up front might yet bring them a result.

'Naturally, we will be looking to score a goal or two, but we will take the minimum of risks in defence,' he said, before the game. 'We have lost very few goals since the beginning of the year, and that is the way we mean to keep it. We have no complaints about the ground or the pitch. Everything is better than we expected, and it is up to us now to produce a good result for Scotland.'

Stein knew that his side would be up against it. Boskov had promised Vojvodina's fans that his side would attack from the first whistle – and they would have 25,000 supporters in the ground to cheer them on. Celtic would not be packing their eighteen-yard box but, equally, they would be taking no risks.

The Yugoslavians did indeed start the game as Boskov had predicted by swarming forward against the Celtic defence. They quickly showed that Stein's assessment had been absolutely spot on as they built attack after attack. However, like Celtic against Zagreb a month previously, they had enormous problems getting a shot on target. Simpson barely had a save worthy of the name in the first half. Stein had accurately predicted how Vojvodina would play, and he deliberately set out a strategy that would stop them. McNeill was in magnificent form at the heart of the defence. He won everything in the air that evening, and he was equally impressive on the ground. His example inspired the rest of the Celtic defence, who harried and tackled tigerishly to make sure that Vojvodina never came within sight of Simpson's goal. Murdoch, Clark, Craig and Gemmell played superbly, and they were occasionally joined in defence by Auld and even by Johnstone, who would come back to take possession and give the others a breather. The Yugoslavs were forced to shoot from so far out that the Celtic keeper was comfortably able to deal with anything that came his way. In the course of the evening, Simpson was only called on to make one save, although there were a number of occasions when he would watch as yet another long-range shot sailed past the post or over the crossbar.

Having held them for 45 minutes, Stein plainly felt that his side could manage to sneak a goal in the second half. He made a number of tactical changes. Defenders were instructed to play long, wide balls to Johnstone and Lennox, or to play them long through the middle to Chalmers. Gemmell was also told to go forward whenever he could. Stein was gambling on the Yugoslavs pushing forward and leaving gaps at the back. The tactics looked like paying off early when both Lennox and McNeill squandered good chances.

Billy McNeill was Celtic's ace in the hole at set pieces on many occasions, but in the 53rd minute the Celtic captain made a rare excursion into opposition territory during open play. McNeill had the ball at his feet and beat his Yugoslavian opposite number for pace before shooting narrowly wide. A few minutes earlier, Bobby Lennox, an established striker with a phenomenal strike rate, came close. Auld found him with a through ball, but the attacker shot too early, and Pantelic was able to gather the ball after another marvellous save. The keeper didn't know it, but he made an enemy that night.

'I really hated him,' says Lennox of Pantelic. 'The one thing I remember most about that game is the big goalkeeper dragging me up by the hair. I was on the ground, and it looked as if he was helping me up, but he had a handful of my hair, and he was pulling me to my feet. I hated him.'

Lennox would have his revenge, but not that night.

The one Celtic failure in Yugoslavia was Hughes, who was not having his best game in a green and white shirt. Consequently, Gemmell found himself constantly tracking up and down the left wing as Celtic pressed forward. This, actually, gave Vojvodina the edge because Gemmell was plainly exhausted, and in the 68th minute he tried to pass the ball back to Clark rather than face another sapping run up the wing. Clark, normally excellent at reading the game, was taken by surprise and failed to control the ball, allowing Stanic to step in and give Vojvodina a 1–0 lead.

'As we had anticipated, they knew how to look after themselves on the park,' says McNeill, of the bruising encounter. 'Good quality teams are always able to sort things out for themselves. I remember playing well, and I remember they had an attack, and Tommy Gemmell cleaned it up nicely. But he had somebody on his tail, so he showed him a wee bit of a dummy and he thought the boy had come with him. But when Tommy had shown him the dummy, the lad had stopped playing, and when Tommy back-heeled it, Stanic was on to it.'

That was Celtic's only mistake in a heroic performance, and they held on to the end to lose by only that single goal. The players were delighted. They knew they had taken on one of the best sides in Europe, and had acquitted themselves well. They also knew that, if they had their way, there would be a different story at Parkhead the following week.

The scoreline was the one which had been in Billy McNeill's mind as they flew out to Yugoslavia. 'I'm not saying that we went out there thinking we could lose 1–0,' he insists, 'but it certainly wasn't the end of the world for us. I do remember that in that game we played really well, and as a defensive unit we played brilliantly.'

Vujadin Boskov obviously agreed with the sentiments of the Celtic party. He faced the assembled press after the game looking like a bulldog who's swallowed a wasp. 'I demanded from my players a lead of two goals and I got only one,' he said gruffly. 'My forwards will get no medals for shooting, and I do not know if a 1–0 victory in Yugoslavia over Celtic will be enough to get us into the semi-final of the European Cup.'

The Yugoslavian media were similarly perplexed by the failure of their side to brush aside this presumptuous challenge from the Scottish upstarts, and establish their European pedigree. They were unanimous in their agreement that Boskov should not be making plans for the semi-final just yet. They also felt that in the previous night's cautious display they had not seen the best of the Celtic side.

The Belgrade daily newspaper *Borba* said: 'Celtic were so mean in expressing their true values that they remained a mystery throughout. The stories about them are not exaggerated, but they are not invulnerable either. The Celtic players were faultlessly prepared. They are a team of athletes who never slow down, either in defence or attack.' *Borba* went on to single out Johnstone, Lennox and Chalmers for particular praise, on the previous night's display.

'The Scots remain a riddle,' claimed another Belgrade daily, *Vecernje Novosti*. 'We have only seen their defensive qualities. Vojvodina cannot be calm. They should play much better in Glasgow than they played last night – even though they dominated most of the game.'

The Yugoslavian media were plainly not over-enthusiastic about their team's chances. But Jock Stein was more than willing to answer Boskov's queries about whether one goal would be enough.

'We shouldn't have lost,' he said, after the game. 'But we know we're a better team than Vojvodina, and there's no reason why we shouldn't win next week.'

Chapter 12

THERE WERE FEW MORE impressive sights in football than Celtic Park enjoying a midweek European fixture in the sixties. The stadium would be packed to capacity, the floodlights blazing, and the eastern sky over Glasgow illuminated to a dazzling electric whiteness. And on top of that, there was the noise. The unabated roaring of over 70,000 Celtic fans is a sound which beggars both description and belief.

That was pretty much the sight that met Vojvodina when they came to Glasgow for the second leg of their European Cup quarter-final. Whatever doubts they might have had before the game about the suitability of a single-goal cushion must have turned into portents of doom the moment they arrived at the ground.

'That was my first European night at Parkhead, and I can recall it clearly and vividly even now,' remembers Jim Craig. 'The crowd at Celtic Park was unbelievable that night; it was absolutely fantastic. When you look back on it, some people remember great nights and great games, but I remember other things. The first thing I remember is when the police escort picked up the team bus out at Barrhead. There was a definite quickening of the pulse and, suddenly, you'd be blasting through Glasgow with these guys riding in front of you with their lights flashing. Suddenly you thought, Hey, this really means something. I can't speak for how the other guys felt but, for me, a Saturday game was okay, but in a floodlit game you are on a real stage. I always imagine it must be like that for an actor playing *Hamlet*. You step out there and suddenly you are the centre of attention. There would be people who had arrived early, and you'd go out for your warm up in front of about twenty or thirty thousand people. It was just incredible.'

Craig was very definitely a big occasion player. One of his great strengths was his inability to be affected by the pressure of a night such as this. Conversely, he often found it difficult to raise his game in lesser matches. He could be relied on to live up to the demands of the evening. So, too, could Steve Chalmers who was, by this stage, a veteran of 23 previous competitive European matches for Celtic, plus one for Glentoran, when he was on loan there in 1965. He was one of the club's most experienced players, but even he knew that the atmosphere on this night was something special.

'I remember the noise when we came off the park at about quarter to eight,' says Chalmers. 'It was incredible. We all came down the tunnel into the dressing room and we just couldn't wait to get back out onto the field to get at them.'

Chalmers had been fighting to be fit for the game and was only able to take the field after days of intensive treatment. He had badly bruised a shoulder in the first leg, and there was genuine concern that with Wallace still ineligible, Celtic would be without a recognised centre forward in a game where they had to score at least two goals. Once again there had been hope that McBride would be fit, and once again the hopes were dashed. Stein had returned with the team from Yugoslavia firmly hoping that McBride would be able to take part in the Saturday fixture, against St Mirren, which came between the two European ties. It was not to be. McBride, although able to train, could not stand up to the rigours of a game. On the day that Celtic were preparing for the most important game in their history, McBride finally accepted the inevitable and was preparing to go into hospital for major surgery. The surgery would enable him to play again, but not for some time. He never figured in Stein's plans again, to any great extent, and the following year he was sold to Hibernian. It's a measure of McBride's explosive striking qualities that even though he only played up until Christmas Eve – a little less than half the season – he still finished up as top scorer in Scotland with 33 League goals.

Celtic had played St Mirren without McBride and the injured Chalmers. Wallace, of course, was able to play in League games, and he contributed two of the goals in a 5–0 win in mud-bath conditions. Dennis Connaghan, the goalkeeper who had defied Celtic in the Scottish Cup final of 1961, again played another great game, but not even he could keep out a rampant Celtic forward line which showed no signs of weariness from the European trip. Jimmy Johnstone had been rested for the game in Paisley, and John Hughes played on the right wing in his place. His performance attracted glowing praise from the match reporters, and there was speculation that Hughes could be Stein's trump card the following Wednesday. Stein, more than ever, was playing his cards close to his chest. He was a gambler by nature and inclination, and would frequently lose his last shilling – but only at the racetrack. Stein was not one for taking risks when he didn't have to, and especially not on a football field. He had pinned his hopes on two things – a quick goal, and a fit Chalmers.

There was another worry for Stein when Chalmers turned up for treatment at Celtic Park on the Monday before the game. Bertie Auld was with him. Auld had to leave the park a few minutes before the end of the St Mirren game after picking up a leg injury. Stein was sanguine about Auld, but his reaction to Chalmers's injury is a clear indication of how important the player was to his game plan. Chalmers was never one of Stein's favourites, but the manager suspected that he could not win without him.

'Auld's injury is not as bad as it might have been,' said Stein on the Monday morning. 'He is coming on well, and we are banking on him being fit. Everything that is possible will be done,' said Stein, of Chalmers. 'Without McBride and Willie Wallace, Chalmers is a must for this match.'

Stein let it be known that, if necessary, Chalmers would receive treatment in the dressing room right up to the kickoff, but nothing short of a life-threatening injury – and possibly not even that – would prevent him from playing.

Whether he knew it or not, the other part of Stein's game plan – the quick goal – had not been a feature of their play lately. Against St Mirren they took half an hour to score, although they went on to win comfortably. Elgin City held on for 44 minutes before they let in the first of seven, and it took Celtic 40 minutes to go in front against Ayr. Vujadin Boskov must have taken some heart from this and, perhaps, realised that if he could hold Celtic as long as possible without scoring, their frustration would increase.

Boskov had arrived in Glasgow with his Vojvodina side on Monday morning. The week between the games had clearly improved his outlook, and he was in much more bullish mood coming off the plane than he had been at the end of the first leg. Having first wondered whether the single goal lead would be enough, he was now predicting that his side would beat Celtic home *and* away to go through to the semi-final. Boskov also pointed out that the side which had beaten Celtic a week ago was not his first-choice team. Trivic and Pusibrik, the two men who were sent off against Atlético Madrid and suspended for the first game against Celtic, were now available. Boskov had a full-strength squad to draw on and would be able to leave out Stanic, the man who scored the goal in Novi Sad. Boskov obviously felt that bringing in two mystery men and discarding the star striker who had given them their valuable lead would strike a significant blow in the psychological tussle between the managers.

Stein, in unusually expansive mood, let it be known that he was giving his team and his game plan much serious thought. 'Boskov is nobody's fool,' he said before the match. 'He knows that I am trying to read his mind, and I know that he is trying to read mine. Boskov may well think it out this way: "Celtic will throw every man bar their goalkeeper at us for the first five minutes to try and make the breakthrough – so instead of our having ten men in our goalmouth we will turn the tables on Celtic. When their defenders are up, pushing forward in attack, we will try and make a burst and get a goal of our own."

'I can't remember any game that required so much thought, so much careful planning, and so much preparation for any sudden happening on the field,' said Stein.

The day before the game, the battle of the managerial psyches was stepped up a gear, and almost escalated into full-scale war when Stein banned the Yugoslavs from Celtic Park. Boskov had given his players the day off after they had arrived in Glasgow late on Monday night. After a day's relaxation, with the inevitable stocking up on tartan souvenirs, he was keen for them to train on Celtic Park, under lights, exactly 24 hours before the kick-off. Stein took firm and decisive action when he heard what his opponents were planning.

He immediately told Boskov that the pitch was far too soft, after weekend rain, to allow the Yugoslavs to train on it. Stein told them they could train under lights if they wanted to, but at Celtic's training ground at Barrowfield, not Parkhead. He also let it be known that there was no point in appealing to a higher authority because, in this case, there was none. It was his decision, and it could not be countermanded. A stunned Boskov had no option but to agree.

All things considered, it wasn't a bad day for Stein. He had put Boskov on the back foot and, just to put the icing on the cake, Chalmers, a naturally fit player and a quick healer, was making good progress and responding well to treatment. It now looked as though the eleventh-hour measures, which had been contemplated earlier in the week, would not be necessary.

On Tuesday night, Stein gave Chalmers 'a good chance' of playing. By Wednesday, he was able to announce that his centre forward had made a good recovery and would be on from the start.

'You can take it from me that the bruised shoulder has healed completely,' said a much more relaxed Stein, to reporters. 'If there had been the slightest possibility of his not being able to jump and move freely for the full ninety minutes, he would not have been considered for a game which is unquestionably one of the most important in Celtic's history.'

With all the attention being focused on Chalmers, the injury to Auld had gone largely unreported. This was a deliberate move by Stein, who knew that the injury was worse than originally feared, and that Auld had little chance of making the game. He did not, however, want Boskov to have the advantage of knowing that his influential midfield commander would not be available for such an important match.

Any team which plays an important game against Celtic, at

Celtic Park, will acknowledge the effect the crowd can have on the side. Few sets of supporters are so fervent and so capable of lifting a team as the Parkhead support in full cry. They are frequently, and with good cause, referred to as Celtic's 'twelfth man'.

'You're never aware of individual shouts as such,' says Jim Craig, of playing before that crowd, 'but on the big occasion, like the Vojvodina game, the noise can be a tremendous advantage. I never ever think it is frightening, but if you're a competitor there must be nothing worse than playing in front of deadly silence.'

Jock Stein was as aware as anyone of the effect of a Parkhead crowd, with the adrenalin pumping, on a March night, in a vital European tie. In his programme notes, Stein played his final card in the war of nerves, with a direct appeal to the supporters. It's hardly *Henry V* but as football programme notes go, it was positively Churchillian.

'We have had wonderful support all season, but I am now calling for a special effort from our faithful following,' Stein began. 'Celtic had a far from warm welcome from the Yugoslav crowd a week ago, and I want our supporters to show Vojvodina how we can welcome a team from overseas. But once the first whistle blows, I want every Celtic supporter to join with the team in defeating the opposition.

'There need be no bounds to the methods used to defeat Vojvodina, as long as they are fair,' he continued. 'The Celtic players have had it drummed into them that their professionalism and their common sense will be severely tested tonight.

'On this night, more than most, I shall not stand for anyone not giving of his best. I may excuse mistakes, but I shall never pardon lack of enthusiasm or real Celtic effort.'

Boskov's final statements were much less dramatic. 'We have all our plans ready for tonight, and they are not all concerned with defence,' he said. 'We will do plenty of attacking, and we expect to win over ninety minutes tonight.'

The fans took Stein's exhortation to heart, and when the teams came out in earnest the roar could be heard for miles. There were surprises, too, for the Celtic fans when the objects of their adoration took the field. Chalmers was there as had been expected, playing as one of two mobile strikers, with Lennox.

Hughes was there, too, to try to get some mileage out of running at the Yugoslavians in soft going. But Charlie Gallagher was also there in place of the injured Auld.

Gallagher was one of the best distributors of a ball in Scottish football, but he and Stein never saw eye to eye. Stein made him nervous and couldn't, or wouldn't, see that the bluff *badinage* that worked with the rest of the team would not work with Gallagher. Whereas others, like Gemmell or Auld, could deal with Stein's training ground hectoring – like water off a duck's back – Gallagher took it all to heart. He was one of the few players at Parkhead who did not thrive under Stein's managerial style, but it wasn't for lack of talent.

'Charlie didn't have the biggest heart in the world,' says Tommy Gemmell. 'But what a passer of the ball. If it hadn't been Bobby Murdoch and Bertie Auld in the midfield, then it would have been Charlie Gallagher. But I think the reason Bobby and Bertie played so often in there was because they were that bit harder. A bit more dig,' he continues, using the all-encompassing footballer's term for heart, will, self-belief, call it what you will. 'They could win the ball and use it and support front players – and score goals. Charlie was a tremendous passer of the ball, and he could land it on a tanner from sixty yards. But he just lacked that wee bit of dig.'

The fans shared Gemmell's view. Joe Connelly, who had been supporting Celtic since the thirties, recalls Gallagher as being a marvellous player of suspect temperament. 'When the crowd got on to Charlie, you could see his head go down,' he remembers. 'But he was a great passer of a ball!.'

The second leg against Vojvodina was undoubtedly going to be a bruising encounter and, doubtless, a fit Auld would have been first choice. But given that Celtic needed to score two goals, it would be nice to think that Stein realised that a little craft and guile might also be needed to crack open a formidable defence. Whatever the thinking, Gallagher's contribution to the game became almost irrelevant as the Yugoslavs, initially, looked the more likely to score.

As Stein had predicted in his Boskov role-playing exercise, they did indeed try to snatch a quick goal. With only five minutes gone, the ball broke to Pusibrik, the man who was returning from suspension. But with no-one to beat but Simpson, he shot past from only six yards. He did the same again in the second half, which must have made Stanic look awfully appealing to Boskov.

Despite the let-offs, Celtic were making no impression. A minder had been put on Chalmers, who found himself charged to the ground every time he went forward. Lennox was getting no change out of the Vojvodina defence either, and Gallagher was also failing to make any impression. The teams went in at half time at 0–0, with only Johnstone having emerged with any real credit.

Johnstone and Hughes appeared to have been playing under orders in the first 45 minutes and were giving every impression of deliberately holding back. But in the second half the gloves were off, and Celtic poured forward realising they were now only 45 minutes away from going out of the tournament. Celtic virtually camped out in the Yugoslavian half for the whole of the second half as wave after wave of attacks crashed in against the Vojvodina defence. The deadlock was broken in the 58th minute. Boskov had been inordinately proud of his goalkeeper Pantelic. He rated him as the greatest goalkeeper in Europe, and Pantelic had proved it, on occasion, so far in these two games. Ironically, it was Pantelic who let him down on the night. Clark had sent Gemmell down the left with a pinpoint pass, and as the defender whipped the ball across the face of the goal, Pantelic threw himself at it, but fumbled the cross. The ball dropped to Steve Chalmers who was able to smack it into the empty net.

The crowd went wild, and no-one was more delighted than Bobby Lennox who had been combing his hair rather gingerly after Pantelic's attempt to scalp him the week before.

'If you look at the photos of us after Stevie scored that goal, you'll see all the boys turning away to celebrate,' Lennox recalls. 'You'll also see me, right in front of Pantelic, giving him what for because he had dropped the ball. I don't dislike people normally, but he really got to me.'

For Lennox, of course, the best revenge would have been sticking the ball past Pantelic himself, and it started to look more and more probable after the first goal. Celtic were revitalised by the goal. They attacked with renewed energy, but still could not make any impression on the Vojvodina defence. Pantelic made up for his error with a couple of fine saves, and the Yugoslavians defended resolutely. McNeill, as he had in the first game, had a rare shot on goal, but could only watch in frustration as it careened off a defender and finished up on the top of the net.

Still there was no breakthrough, and with 89 minutes on the clock it looked as though the tie would have to be decided by a play-off in Rotterdam.

'I didn't know it was that close to the end,' says Tommy Gemmell. 'All I knew was that we were having a right go at them. That was our style. We just went forward. If we could go forward for ninety minutes, then we would. We always knew we could wear teams down with skill and constant pressure.'

Then, the Celtic fairy tale took hold again and, once again, McNeill was at the centre of it. With 40 seconds of the game left, Johnstone burst through on the right and won a corner. Gallagher, who had been fairly anonymous for much of the game, stepped forward to take it – just as he had against Dunfermline in the Scottish Cup eighteen months previously. And, just as he had done that day too, McNeill rose magnificently to meet the ball and head it past the despairing Pantelic.

The referee blew for full time almost as soon as Vojvodina had centred the ball after McNeill's goal. The final whistle was almost drowned in the cauldron of noise which had erupted when the ball had gone in. Anyone dropping in on the game at that moment would have thought that Celtic had won the European Cup instead of just qualifying for the semi-finals.

Gemmell's defensive partner Jim Craig was equally confident of the right result. He, too, had no idea of how close they were to the whistle when the corner was won.

'That sort of thing doesn't bother me,' he says. 'I never bothered asking the time because I learned from experience that it's the wrong thing to do. If somebody tells you there's only two minutes to go, then you find yourself in two minds – do I just sit on this or do I try to make something happen – and invariably you make the wrong choice. So I prefer not to know.

'I knew we were close, but to be honest, as far as I can recall,

I wasn't too bothered. It only meant that we were going to finish 1–1 on the night and we would go to another game. When we got another corner it was just another chance to score as far as I was concerned, but Charlie took a great corner.

'Billy was never great on the ground, but in the air he was magnificent. The thing that you have to credit Billy with is the number of times he got his head to a ball when he was marked. It was quite amazing. There was always a guy standing in front of him to block his run. It's very easy for Billy to run backwards and forwards, but to time his run with a ball coming in from the side is much, much harder. The number of times he got to those balls was incredible. But that one was exceptional. It was a great corner and a great header.'

Boskov was furious. He claimed that McNeill had fouled Pantelic going for the ball. He never got the free kick, and the goal stood. But perhaps it should have been disallowed because Pantelic was fouled – but not by McNeill.

'I fouled the goalkeeper,' says Stevie Chalmers, 30 years after the event. 'I didn't hit him or kick him or anything like that, but I could see what was going to happen. I could see that he was going to challenge Billy, so when he started to move, I just stepped in front of him – just half a stride, but I obstructed him all the same. He never got to Billy, but Billy got to the ball. When you look at pictures now, everyone assumes that the man on the line, as Billy heads into the net, is actually Pantelic. It's not. It's a defender. Pantelic couldn't get there because I stepped in front of him.'

As McNeill said himself, with elegant understatement, of his winning goal against Dunfermline in the 1965 Cup final, 'some things you never forget.' This goal against Vojvodina was another one of those.

'I knew it was late in the game,' he remembers. 'I always liked Charlie Gallagher taking corner kicks because Charlie used to fire them at you, and it was just a matter of getting your timing right. If I got my timing right, and Charlie threw the ball in there, then you always had a chance. The big thing that helped us was their goalkeeper, Pantelic. It was a wee distance out, and the goalkeeper came, and he got mixed up. Stevie stepped across his line, which was part and parcel of the game – people used to do that to me all the time to baulk my runs. Anyway, the goalkeeper was too adventurous, and he made it relatively easy for me. My belief is that, in a situation like that, you always put the ball back to the post from where the ball has come. The interesting thing is that they had put the smallest player in their team on that post, to defend it. He just wasn't big enough to do anything about it to be honest with you.'

The atmosphere on the pitch was incredible. Celtic knew there was no way that Vojvodina could come back from a body-blow like that. But most teams are at their slackest defensively when they have just scored, so McNeill ran back urging his players to tighten up and keep their discipline. Television footage shows him having an animated discussion with his defensive partner, John Clark, as they head back to their own half of the pitch.

'I knew it was late in the game, but I didn't know exactly how late,' McNeill continues. 'I remember running back down the pitch and saying to John Clark, "Right, come one. Don't lose a goal now," and he looked at me as if I was daft. "The game's finished, big man," he said. And I said, "I don't care if it's finished or not, we're not losing a goal at this stage." And he just looked at me. But the referee centred the ball, blew his whistle to re-start the game, they passed once, and then he blew for time up. Luggy just looked at me and said, "What did I tell you." '

On the terracing and in the stand an atmosphere of unconfined pandemonium reigned.

'Vojvodina were a big team and a good team, and I thought we were never going to score,' recalls John McCabe. 'It was well into the second half before we equalised, and then came that header from McNeill. It was a beautifully flighted corner kick, and he met it perfectly. Funnily enough, I remember that at that time he wasn't getting his international cap. Ronnie McKinnon of Rangers was being preferred for Scotland. The man next to me was delirious, and I can still remember him shouting: "Not bad for McKinnon's understudy."

'There are three Celtic goals that I remember. Neilly Mochan's 30-yard shot which won the Coronation Cup in 1953, Billy McNeill's header against Dunfermline in the 1965 Scottish Cup final, and that goal against Vojvodina. It was as if the moment was frozen in time. You could almost hear the thud of the brow of his head meeting the ball.'

Two-nil to Celtic on the night. Two-one on aggregate. Celtic were through to the semi-finals of the European Cup at the first time of asking.

Chapter 13

ONE PHOTOGRAPH SUMS UP the mood of the Celtic players when the final whistle blew against Vojvodina. Ronnie Simpson, a veteran of many big occasions, including two FA Cup finals – but none as big as this – was caught by the cameras swinging in delight, like a child in a playground, from the crossbar of his goal. He may have been 36 years old, but McNeill's goal had taken years off him.

The players and fans knew that this had been their biggest test. It was a trial by ordeal, and they had passed. While questions could reasonably be asked about the provenance of teams like Zurich and Nantes, there was no doubting the quality of Vojvodina who could, with justification, claim a place as one of the top four sides in Europe. Celtic had beaten them, and shown their character in the process. They had moved up a gear and would be nobody's soft touch in the semi-finals.

But still the players remained largely unaffected by ambition in their quest.

'I know everybody says this, but Vojvodina were definitely the hardest side we played that year,' says Bobby Lennox. 'But I think the guys were just happy with their lives; they just wanted to get on and win the next game. I don't recall anyone saying we can go on and win this, because Inter Milan were still in the tournament at that stage. We were just enjoying ourselves. It was a big, big adventure.

'This sounds stupid I know but, when we were playing in the European Cup, we were just happy to be playing a team from a different country; we just wanted to go somewhere we hadn't

121

been before. We didn't want to play anyone from a country we had already visited. In the early days, when we were in Europe, the chairman used to organise coach trips for us, but Big Jock put a stop to all that.'

Standing on the terracing, as Celtic beat Vojvodina that night, was a 10-year-old boy from Soho Street, in the cradle of the club, the East End of Glasgow. Tommy Burns was a promising schoolboy who was attracting the attention of a number of scouts. He would go on to become one of Celtic's best-loved players, and is currently managing the club for which he lived and breathed.

'European nights in those days were unbelievable,' recalls Burns. 'Thousands and thousands of people were packed into the ground. We always went to the Celtic end, and there were so many people there that you just had to stand at the back of the terracing, you couldn't get any further forward. I hadn't started wearing my glasses yet, and I would come along to Celtic Park with my pals, and sometimes we had to stand so far back that I couldn't see a thing. You always knew when Jimmy Johnstone got the ball, because there was a buzz went round the ground, but I couldn't see it.

'I think that goal is always remembered, not just for Big Billy's header, but for Charlie Gallagher's corner. I think Charlie was a great player who never got the credit he deserved. He had a good brain, and he was a lovely passer of the ball. I remember talking to my pals for weeks afterwards about "what a great ball from Gallagher". But I'm sure Charlie would like to be remembered for something more than taking one corner.

'But it was the sheer frenzy that I remember when that goal was scored. The television cameras were there and, afterwards, my pals and I stood outside the TV vans, watching the re-runs of the goal being scored again and again. But it was just the most joyous occasion. Celtic had a couple of wee bits of luck that night. There were a lot of great things about the Lisbon Lions, but that year they got the wee bits of luck that every great side needs. They worked hard for it, though.'

Up and down the country, Celtic fans were celebrating. David Potter, who had stood on the terracing at Hampden two years previously to watch Celtic win the Scottish Cup was, by this stage, a first year Classics student at St Andrews University. He had been a long-standing Celtic fan who now, because of his straitened financial circumstances as a student, couldn't afford to travel down to Glasgow to see his team as often as he would like. For him, the distinctive radio commentaries of the BBC's David Francie were his link with Celtic's progress in Europe. But not on this occasion.

'I didn't listen to the Vojvodina game on the radio,' he remembers. 'The tension was just unbearable and I just couldn't stand it. I had decided to watch the highlights later that night on Scotsport, and I deliberately avoided knowing the score. When the programme started, Arthur Montford warned that it was going to be a cliff-hanger, but I had no idea. I was watching it in one of the halls of residence, and it was late at night. One of my friends made a formal complaint about me because of the yell I let out when McNeill scored. He said he recognised my yell. I think he probably had a girl in his room, but I'm sure my cry of ecstasy would have been more heartfelt than anything coming from his room.'

The morning after the night before was a time for reflection and contemplation at Parkhead. Everyone knew that they had won, and won well, but they also knew that they had, possibly, been only seconds away from having had to take Vojvodina on for a third time. No-one doubted their ability to beat the Yugoslavians over a third game but, all the same, nobody fancied having to do it. Especially not Jock Stein.

'I was not particularly worried about the result, but we have a lot on our plates at the moment,' he said, the morning after the match. 'We have already played forty-eight games this season and we have at least another dozen to come – nine in the League, two in the European Cup and one in the Scottish Cup. That adds up to at least sixty games before the end of April, and that's enough for any team.'

Stein was also unusually expansive about his tactics in the game – albeit after the event. He was plainly delighted with his side and took pleasure in explaining how they had come of age on the European stage.

'Nobody should underrate this Vojvodina side,' said Stein,

perhaps in a sly aside at some of the gainsayers, especially from the English media. 'They were good – very good – in defence in the first half, and after half an hour I realised that I might have to change our plan in the second half. I knew I was taking a chance, but chances have to be taken when you are a goal down and there are only forty-five minutes to play.'

The half-time situation doubtless appealed to the gambler in Stein. The great managers know when changes have to be made. Stein and Shankly both knew it then, Alex Ferguson knows it now. With 45 minutes left, it was time for Stein to put on his game face and indulge in a little high-stakes bluffing.

'I ordered John Hughes to line up at inside-right after the interval, as a diversion,' says Stein, making it plain that his side had indeed been playing to orders in the first half. 'Having done that, Murdoch, Clark and Gemmell were all ordered to move forward and join the attacks. I'm sure the crowd noticed the difference. In the first half we would attack, and then Vojvodina would attack, and things were fairly even. Once we threw in everything, they were unable to hit back at us, and after we had scored they seemed to tire, and we had more room in which to work. McNeill's winner proved that the change of plan worked.'

Vojvodina flew out of Glasgow the following morning under grey, grumbling skies which matched the mood of the team. The Yugoslavian media were in no doubt that their champions had been deprived of their rightful place in the semi-finals of the world's premier club tournament by bad refereeing. The Yugoslavian news agency *Tasjug* accused Chalmers of interference when McNeill and Pantelic went up for Gallagher's corner.

'Pantelic was pushed by Chalmers, and McNeill headed the winning goal,' said the news agency, in a slightly exaggerated version of what actually happened. 'Referee Carlsson did not react to the obvious foul.'

Yugoslavia's leading sports newspaper *Sport* also blamed Mr Carlsson for a grave mistake which lead to a tragedy. However, it also give the referee credit for having been 'neutral, objective, and authoritative' for the rest of the game.

Alone among the Yugoslavian media, the Belgrade daily newspaper *Borba* was prepared to level the blame at Vojvodina themselves. *Borba* pointed out that although Vojvodina were a well-organised and well-disciplined side, they still lacked the experience and skill which were necessary for a team which wanted to compete at the highest level in Europe. *Borba* went on to praise Celtic, even if it was in the most grudging terms.

'Celtic gained their greatest triumph so far,' said the newspaper, 'but it seemed that this was achieved because the visitors allowed them too much scope, rather than by the exceptional qualities of their own players.'

The Yugoslavian media had presumably taken their lead from the Vojvodina manager Vajudin Boskov, who was still complaining about the goal when his side flew out of Glasgow airport. They flew out a much more chastened bunch than they were when they arrived, but Boskov laid the blame fairly and squarely at Carlsson's door.

'We are convinced Chalmers pushed our goalkeeper, that is why we complained,' said Boskov, explaining why his players had surrounded the referee when the vital goal was awarded.

Nonetheless, Boskov was also forced to acknowledge his respect for Stein's side. Having been beaten, there was no point in maintaining the bravado he had been adopting for the previous week. He singled out Tommy Gemmell, Jimmy Johnstone and John Hughes for individual praise, but he also could not help but concede the advantage that Celtic's 'twelfth man' had given them.

'The crowd made a tremendous difference to Celtic,' said Boskov. 'In Yugoslavia they had only a handful of supporters. Last night they had 75,000, and that made a tremendous difference. Celtic were an excellent team last night, and they must have an excellent chance of going on to win the Cup.'

Two men had let Boskov down on the night. No matter how he dressed it up, Pantelic, his pride and joy, had made two catastrophic errors, and each had cost Vojvodina a goal. The other disappointment for Boskov had to be Pusibrik, the man he had favoured over Stanic, the scorer of the only goal in the first leg. Pusibrik missed two clear first-half chances, either of which could have left Celtic with a mountain to climb, very early in the game. But he, too, was forced to acknowledge the quality of Stein's side.

Pusibrik, who spoke reasonable English, was acting as an unofficial interpreter for Boskov at an impromptu question and answer session with the Scottish press. 'Celtic showed tremendous team spirit,' said the Vojvodina player. 'They will be very hard to beat in this tournament.'

No-one knew that more than Jock Stein. He had brought his side this far, and he must have known they could go further. If he did not allow himself to believe they could win, then he must certainly have believed they could, at least, get to the final. He had lost his dream ticket striking partnership of McBride and Wallace. On the other hand, Celtic had beaten Vojvodina, one of the best sides in the tournament, without either of them. Wallace would be eligible for the semi-final and, with the rub of the green when the draw was made, who knows where Celtic might go? They had been to the semi-finals of a major European tournament the year before, and lost, through naivety, by failing to punish Liverpool. Stein would be determined that there should be no repeat of that kind of behaviour this time round.

He was a classic 'one game at a time' manager but, basking in the glow of victory over the Yugoslavians, he allowed his thoughts to turn to the semi-final. The draw would not be made for another fortnight, but Stein knew who he fancied.

'I am not worried about the next round,' he said confidently. 'We are not afraid of any team left in the European Cup. We will take what comes, but I would much rather meet Inter Milan in the final.'

The Italian champions, who had won the European Cup twice in the past three seasons, were already through to the semi-finals, as were Dukla Prague, the Czechoslovakian champions. The only remaining tie to be decided was the quarter-final between CSKA Sofia and Linfield of Ireland. Only the Italians, Stein believed, would pose any serious threat to his young side – but even they could be beaten.

'Their defensive set-up is so good and so well-organised that they must be the most difficult team to beat on a home and away basis,' Stein reasoned. 'It takes world-class players to score against them in Milan, and their defence in their away matches is even more watertight. But over ninety minutes on neutral ground – in Lisbon for example – they will have to come out and attack all the time. We are an attacking team ourselves, and that would give us all the chance we need.'

Stein allowed that if he was to avoid Inter in the semis, then he felt Celtic would have no problem with Dukla Prague. 'But if I had my choice,' he said slyly, 'I would ask for the winners of the Sofia–Linfield tie.'

Stein now had the problem that every manager loves to have. He had a winning side who were ready to take on all-comers. All he had to do was keep them occupied and stop them going off the boil. The Vojvodina game had been a proving ground for Celtic players and fans alike. But for one it was a bitter-sweet experience.

Joe McBride watched the game from the Celtic Park stand as his team-mates achieved one of the greatest victories in the club's history. Doubtless, he played every kick of the ball in his head.

'What a wonderful incentive to get back into the side as soon as possible,' he said, the morning after. 'The lads played wonderful stuff. I was never so proud to be a Celtic player. When Steve Chalmers scored our first goal, I felt just great. When Billy McNeill got the winner, I almost forgot about my knee.'

McBride was speaking just as he was leaving for hospital. Twenty-four hours later, he would go under the surgeon's knife in an operation which would, thankfully, enable him to play again. But it would be a long time before Joe McBride could forget about his knee again.

Chapter 14

THE PROBLEM OF KEEPING a winning side winning is one which can exercise the best managers in the business. Sides can become complacent or, frequently, they can simply go off the boil as quickly and as inexplicably as they began winning. There was little chance of that with this Celtic side. They had gone so long without success, that they revelled in their own winning ways.

'People talk about good losers, but good losers don't win anything,' says Billy McNeill, voicing a philosophy which would have gladdened the heart of the great NFL coach Vince Lombardi, who once pointed out that winning wasn't everything, it was the only thing.

'You've got to be bad losers,' McNeill continued. 'If you're a professional, then that's what the game is all about. Winning is the essence of the sport, and we had people who would sell their soul to win. It was dead easy to keep them going because we all wanted to win, and we had a common interest in winning. We had no inhibitions and no worries about what other people might do. We maybe should have worried more about ourselves, but we didn't, we just wanted to win, and win for Celtic.'

Stein, however, recognised that if maintaining team morale was not going to be difficult, there was the very real danger of playing too much football. As McNeill points out, winners simply want to keep winning and don't care how many games they have to play, but sixty games in eight months can take its toll on anyone.

'The danger now,' Stein pointed out, after his team had beaten Vojvodina, 'is that some of the boys may go a little stale with so much football. We will be stepping down the training a little. We'll be doing just enough to keep them at their peak mentally and physically.'

Stein's arguments made a lot of sense and are accepted practice in the modern game. By the start of April, players are as fit as they are going to get and – injuries aside – they don't require much in the way of fitness training. By that stage of the season, whether a team is in the hunt for a title or a trophy, or fighting off relegation, it's all about attitude. Celtic's secret weapon in maintaining morale was Seamill Hydro, a genteel hotel on the Ayrshire coast, to which they would take off to prepare for the big games, or to unwind after good results.

'We would win a big game, and the manager would come into the dressing room and say, "Right lads, let's go down to the hydro for a couple of days, and bring your clubs," ' remembers Bobby Lennox. 'The golf clubs didn't suit wee Jimmy and I, because we weren't golfers at that time. I've taken it up since, and play a lot with Stevie Chalmers, but Jimmy still phones me and says, "I can't believe you play golf." But we would go down to the hydro, maybe on the Monday and Tuesday, and then come back to train at Celtic Park on Wednesday.'

Since the football season and the holiday season generally don't coincide, Celtic would have the place to themselves on their retreats to Ayrshire. They could unwind, lark about, do whatever they wanted and generally just be themselves, but away from public scrutiny.

'Seamill was great,' says Lennox, with genuine affection. 'It was the best hotel in the world for footballers. There was a lovely bit of grass out at the front, and we must have played hundreds of five-a-side games on that, and it was just super. There was never anybody about, and we had the place pretty much to ourselves.'

Celtic had been going to Seamill for years, and for Tommy Gemmell, the trips to Ayrshire in that European Cup-winning season were ideal chances to recapture the mood of the American tour. Celtic were one big happy family when they were at the hydro. For Stein, it was a chance to recapture the mood of his own glory days as captain of the 1954 double-winning side. That side had its jokers, like the legendary Charlie Tully, and so too did the 1967 side.

'It was all good clean fun,' says Gemmell. 'Some of the married players would come home, and their wives would be unpacking for them and find a packet of condoms that someone had thrown into their case. That usually took a wee bit of explaining. I've seen me coming back and emptying my bag and finding it full of knives and forks from Seamill Hydro – and in those days they all had "Property of Seamill Hydro" stamped on them.'

The open tube of mustard in the blazer pocket, which had found favour on the American tour, was another Seamill favourite. The chief culprits were generally Lennox and Johnstone, who usually roomed together and took the same innocent and childish delight in tormenting their team-mates for the good of the side.

'The boys would be doing a bit of golfing to relax, and Jimmy and I – because I didn't play in those days – would run around the course throwing the golf balls into bunkers. Another favourite was to get up early and go down to the breakfast room and loosen the tops of all the salt and pepper shakers. The old ones are always the best ones,' says Lennox, with an embarrassed grin.

The two wingers, therefore, became fair game for whatever retaliation, and occasional pre-emptive strikes, their colleagues could inflict. It all seems innocent now, in hindsight, but it's a far cry from dentist's chairs in Singapore and Cathay Pacific flights. And it achieved the very real objective of keeping the team loose and relaxed and not worrying too much about what lay ahead.

After beating Vojvodina, Celtic were in an unprecedented position. They were, of course, in the semi-final of the European Cup. They were also top of the League, and a 5–3 win over Queen's Park on the Saturday after the Vojvodina game had put them in the semi-final of the Scottish Cup. With the League Cup and the Glasgow Cup already in the trophy cabinet, Stein's players were poised for a unique grand slam – they had a real chance of winning every competition they had entered. Uppermost in their minds, of course, would be the European Cup.

'We were still very, very naive,' says Jim Craig. 'I don't think winning was ever discussed in the dressing room. There would always be a buzz and an excitement about the next round. There was always, I think, an assumption that we could go all the way, but it would never be said out loud. I think everyone would be reluctant to say it publicly. It's a natural footballer's superstition. They don't like to say it in case they jinx it and it goes disastrously wrong.'

Stein's wish for the semi-final was a game against Sofia or Linfield. He didn't get what he had been looking for but, on the other hand, he managed to avoid the Italians. Inter Milan were drawn against CSKA Sofia, who had won their quarter-final tie against the Irish side. Celtic had been drawn against the Czechoslovakian champions Dukla Prague, with the first leg at Celtic Park.

There was more than a month between the quarter-finals and semi-finals of the European Cup. Celtic would have been looking to press ahead and keep their momentum going, and that is exactly what they did, up to a point. There were five League games and three Scottish Cup ties between the Vojvodina and Dukla Prague ties, and Celtic maintained their winning ways. They scored twenty-one goals and conceded only six. Nonetheless, there were some concerns for Stein. Wallace, who had been bought to bring some punch and variety to the attack, had managed only three goals in those eight games. But, more seriously, Celtic had been hit by the closest thing they would have to an injury crisis.

Auld had missed the Vojvodina game through injury, but was also forced to miss two more League games. Wallace may have scored only three goals, but that had a lot to do with an injury to Murdoch, which forced the new striker to take his place in midfield for four games. Although they notched up a 5–0 win against Falkirk, and a 4–1 win against Partick Thistle, they stuttered in the Cup, drawing 0–0 with Clyde, before beating them 2–0 in the replay. In fact, in the eight games between the European Cup quarter-final and semi-final, Stein was able to play the same team on only two consecutive occasions. He was all for changing the side when it suited him, but these were enforced changes and hardly the ideal preparation for their first European Cup semifinal.

Stein and his players knew that Dukla Prague were a very good side. They were the Czechoslovakian army team, and were marshalled on the field by the magnificent Josef Masopust, who had captained his national side to a World Cup final. Even though, at 36, Masopust was in the twilight of his career, they would be a stern test of Celtic's ability. McNeill had played against Masopust on international duty and knew him to be a marvellously gifted player who deserved the utmost respect.

Stein, again, took his players away to Seamill to prepare for the first leg against Dukla. After beating Motherwell 2–0 on the Saturday with goals from Gemmell and Wallace, the squad was off to the Ayrshire coast to get themselves mentally and physically attuned for the match. For some of the Celtic squad there was the additional pressure of having been named by Scotland manager Bobby Brown in the side to face England at Wembley, the Saturday after the game. It is unthinkable, nowadays, that players would be asked to play in their club's biggest European game, and their country's most bitterly-contested international match, within the space of three days, but no-one thought anything of it then.

The England game brought well-deserved international recognition for Ronnie Simpson who was having something of an Indian summer in career terms. Although Stein and Simpson may not always have been on the best of terms throughout their careers, the manager wasted no time in taking his goalkeeper aside, privately, at Seamill, to offer his sincere and heartfelt congratulations. This international, above all, was one that every Scottish player wanted to play in. England had won the World Cup the previous season, and this was Scotland's first encounter with the Auld Enemy since then. The other Celtic players who had been named in Brown's side were Gemmell, Johnstone and Lennox, with Steve Chalmers named as a substitute. McNeill, despite his magnificent performances in Europe, remained out of favour, and McKinnon of Rangers was again preferred in defence. Nonetheless, having five players from one team in a squad of 13 is an indication of the quality of the Celtic side.

For Lennox, his inclusion in the Scotland party was the sugar-coating of a particularly bitter pill. 'John Clark and I went for a walk at Seamill on the Monday,' Lennox remembers. 'John said: "I think you'll play for Scotland on Saturday. Without being rotten, I can't see who else they've got to play at outside-left." I told him I had no chance, in fact, I didn't even think the boss was going to play me against Dukla on Wednesday, so what chance did I have of playing for Scotland on the Saturday?

'The next thing I knew, this big Mercedes drew up beside us, and Jock and Sean Fallon got out. Jock told me I was playing against England on Saturday. I was delighted, but the sting was that I wasn't playing against Dukla. The England game is the biggest game you can play in if you're a Scotland player. If you're a Scotsman, and you had your choice of any game, then it would be against England at Wembley, but,' says Lennox with real regret, 'I would still rather have played in the European Cup semi-final.'

Breaking the bad news about the Dukla game to Lennox in front of team-mate John Clark was an example of Stein's guile when it came to handling players.

'He was very shrewd,' Lennox continues. 'He would come into our bedroom, in the hydro, and Jimmy and I would be lying on our beds and he'd say: "I'm playing you tonight, Bobby, but you're not playing, wee man." So Jimmy is naturally delighted for me but, at the same time, I'm disappointed for him, and that was clever man-management by Jock.'

Having given the Vojvodina game similar billing, Jock Stein now proclaimed that the first game against Dukla Prague was 'the most important match in Celtic history'. In truth, having got to this stage of the tournament, that tag could be applied to every game they played from here on in.

The Czechoslovakians arrived on the Monday, two days before the match, but there was none of the bluff and bluster of previous Celtic opponents. Coach Bohimil Musil was not one for vainglorious statements. He was sensible enough to realise that, by dint of having reached the semis, Celtic were due some respect. Stein, for his part, continued to play his cards close to his chest.

'When we played Vojvodina, they were a good side, but they had no stars,' says Jim Craig. 'But we knew that Prague had Masopust.'

The big plus for Celtic was that Murdoch was back in the side. Stein had reinvented Murdoch as a player. He had taken him out of the forward line and made him a midfielder. It was – along with the creation of a similar role for Bertie Auld – the single most inspired act of his term at Celtic Park. Murdoch took to his new role like a duck to water and became genuinely world class.

'Murdoch was one of the first things you noticed in that side,' said long-time fan David Potter. 'Stein had turned him from a fairly mediocre inside forward – and, to be honest, he never had the speed for that – and made him a world class wing half.'

Glasgow businessman Brian Dempsey is a lifelong Celtic fan who became a director, briefly, in one of the most turbulent periods of the club's history. 'Bobby Murdoch was an amazingly skilful player,' he says, with admiration. 'I still believe that, in modern parlance, Celtic, then, had the best back four in Europe and the best midfield in Europe, and Murdoch was an integral part of that.'

Murdoch, indeed, was so influential that, when he eventually left Celtic for Middlesborough, the then Middlesborough manager Jack Charlton said: 'He was my first signing as a manager, and I may never be so lucky again.'

So, the Czechs had Masopust but Celtic had Murdoch. They also had Willie Wallace back in the forward line where he was supposed to be, as he prepared to make his European debut against Dukla. Jimmy Johnstone was also back to 100 per cent fitness, and Stein's only decision was whether to play Hughes or Lennox opposite him on the left wing. Publicly, he let it be known that he would make his decision based on the conditions. This lead everyone, including Musil presumably, to believe that Lennox would get the nod. Hughes always performed better on softer ground, and the fact that there had been two days of sunshine, and a fine dry night was forecast for the game, prompted the pundits to speculate that Lennox would wear the number eleven jersey.

Stein, of course, had made up his mind at the start of the week that it was Hughes rather than Lennox who would be playing. Nonetheless, there were no leaks from the Celtic camp, and the Czechs would have been forced to come up with two game plans: one to combat the immensely powerful Hughes, and the other to deal with the rapier-like Lennox. Stein also struck one other important psychological blow. Joe McBride was out of hospital after his cartilage operation, and he was pictured resuming light training at Celtic Park on the day of the Dukla game; in fact, while Dukla were training on the pitch, McBride was doing light running on the surrounding track for the benefit of the press. The presence of as potent a striker as McBride would have been an important fillip for the Celtic players and fans alike.

The key to the semi-final was goals. Stein knew that he would need at least a two-goal cushion to take to Prague in a fortnight. One would probably not be enough, two would be about right, and three would be the answer to everyone's prayers. He suspected that the Czechs might be weak on the flanks and hoped that the guile of Johnstone, and the power of Hughes – allied to his ball control – might enable Celtic to get round behind the Dukla defence. Stein was also relying on a fully fit Murdoch spraying balls from midfield to Wallace, and switching play from right to left with his precision passing to keep the Prague defence under pressure.

Celtic started the match with what amounted to an eight-man attack. Only McNeill, Clark and Simpson were there to defend, as Craig, Gemmell, Murdoch and Auld all pushed forward. But, for all that, it was a stuttering start by Celtic, and they had to rely on Simpson to keep them in the game. With only five minutes gone, it was Masopust who was living up to his reputation. He split the Celtic defence with a glorious pass to their outside-left Strunc, who was left with only Simpson to beat. Simpson, happily, was concentrating on what was going on at Celtic Park on Wednesday, rather than what might happen at Wembley on Saturday. He was off his line in a flash to narrow the angle. Strunc was forced to hurry his shot, and Simpson was able to parry it one-handed. Again, Masopust was instrumental in setting up Nedorost after seventeen minutes but, fortunately for Celtic, the forward missed a simple chance.

Celtic, by this stage, had woken up to the possibility that they could very well have been all but out of the tournament within the first quarter of an hour of the match. They finally clicked into gear and managed to get the ball into the Prague goal when Chalmers headed into the net, but the 'goal' was disallowed for offside. It was now Dukla's turn to show some signs of panic as

Celtic poured forward. After 27 minutes, a shot from Wallace was blocked, and the ball flew to Johnstone inside the penalty area. He controlled the ball with his chest before volleying past the onrushing Viktor and hurdling the keeper with delight as the shot hit the back of the net.

The goal had a bizarre effect on both teams. Celtic, with their fans roaring them on in expectation of another two or three goals, inexplicably wilted. Dukla, equally inexplicably, stopped panicking. They slowed their game down and started to play the sort of football you would expect at this level. On the stroke of half time, after three Celtic defenders had tried and failed to clear their lines, Strunc was presented with the easiest of chances, which he took gratefully, to level the score.

The second half began as the first had ended, with Celtic failing to make any significant impression on a well-marshalled and highly skilled Czech defence. This continued for another fifteen minutes, with none of the Celtic forwards making much of an impact. Ultimately, it was Wallace, who had been less than impressive up to now, who turned the game in a six-minute spell. After 59 minutes, Gemmell launched a hopeful punt upfield from the halfway line. The ball bounced over defender Vlocha and, before he could turn, Wallace was onto it, and had whipped it past Viktor to put Celtic ahead.

Six minutes later, Wallace put the game beyond doubt with one of the goals of his career.

Dukla were being run ragged by Celtic and were visibly tiring. They were doing all they could – including handling the ball – to keep Celtic at bay. One handball meant they had conceded a free kick, their fourth in as many minutes, just outside the penalty box and directly in front of goal. As the Czech defenders formed their defensive wall, Bertie Auld stepped forward to take it but, at the last minute, checked his run and made as if to steady the ball. The defenders relaxed, expecting him to step back for another run but, instead, he simply tapped the ball a few feet to the side for Wallace to hit a 20-yard shot which hit the back of the net before Viktor even saw it.

The Czechs had no reply; they were thoroughly beaten. Wallace had repaid his transfer fee with two goals which had made Celtic almost certain of becoming the first British club to reach the European Cup final. All they had to do was survive 90 minutes in Prague in a fortnight.

Certainly, Stein felt that the performance at Parkhead was enough to take his players through to the final and, with characteristic understatement, he announced that he was 'quite happy' with the result. However, he conceded that his side did not play as well as he, or they, might have liked.

'We might easily have played a lot better and not got the goals,' he said pragmatically. 'We said before the game that we would settle for a two-goal lead and we got it, so we are quite happy.

'There's no doubt that Dukla are a good team,' he continued. 'We won't underestimate them in the second leg, but it's possible that Celtic pulled them out a bit last night in front of our own home crowd. They may, of course, play a different game when we go to Prague but, let me repeat, Celtic are quite happy.'

There was more delight for Willie Wallace when, on the day after his triumph over Dukla Prague, he was called into the Scotland party for the game against England. He was there as cover for Johnstone who, despite playing brilliantly against Dukla, had aggravated his injury. Stein said Johnstone's injury was so serious that he was doubtful for Celtic's next League fixture in ten day's time never mind the England game on the Saturday. Wallace was, however, called up before it was known for certain that Johnstone wouldn't play and, in the end, he took his team-mate's place in the side.

The inclusion of Wallace in the Scotland side meant that Celtic had thirteen internationals on their books at that stage in 1967. This equalled Rangers' record of thirteen internationals in their 1932–33 side. Celtic fans had always insisted that the record was theirs by right as only ten of the Rangers' players were Scottish internationals, whereas twelve of theirs – Charlie Gallagher was capped for the Republic of Ireland – turned out for Scotland. The argument became academic later in the year when Jim Craig got his first cap for Scotland in November 1967, giving Celtic fourteen internationals on their books.

The win over Dukla certainly buoyed up the Celtic players in the Scotland camp. 'It was a wonderful result for us,' said Tommy

Gemmell. 'The way we feel now, we are going to hit England as hard as we can.'

Rangers' captain John Greig, who was also the Scotland skipper, was gracious in his acknowledgement of Celtic's achievement. 'Celtic really did Scotland proud last night,' he said, as the team left for London. 'Their fighting display has made us all feel that we owe everything we have to Scotland. We are going into this game knowing that England must be worried.'

Certainly, the four Celtic players in the side – Simpson, Gemmell, Wallace and Lennox – were in ebullient form that Saturday at Wembley. Rangers were also European semi-finalists in the Cup-Winners Cup, so Greig and McKinnon would have felt equally confident. Taken together, that inflamed sense of national pride and the sheer brilliance of Jim Baxter destroyed England that afternoon, as Scotland won 3–2, with Lennox scoring one of the goals.

With characteristic hubris, Scotland proclaimed themselves, and not entirely in jest, world champions for having so thoroughly humbled Alf Ramsey's World Cup winners.

Chapter 15

AFTER BEATING DUKLA PRAGUE 3–1 at Parkhead, Celtic were in the rare position of being able to concentrate almost exclusively on the return leg. Although there was almost a fortnight between the two games, the England–Scotland international meant that Celtic had only one domestic fixture in the intervening period.

That game, a midweek, goalless draw against Aberdeen at Parkhead, gave Celtic another point in their chase for the title. Rangers, meanwhile, were stumbling in their pursuit. They drew 1–1 with Clyde, a few days later, allowing Celtic to open up a gap with only three games left. The Aberdeen game is significant because of the Celtic line-up. The team that day was:

Simpson, Craig, Gemmell, Murdoch, McNeill, Clark, Johnstone, Wallace, Chalmers, Auld, Lennox.

The Lisbon Lions were playing again for only the second time since that game against St Johnstone back in January. Celtic stars of the period such as Steve Chalmers and Bobby Lennox will suggest that Jock Stein had such a wealth of talent available to him that he didn't really know what his best side was. He must, however, have been coming round to the notion that these were the best eleven players available to him.

The process of building a successful football team tends to be evolutionary rather than revolutionary. Going out and spending large amounts of money on handfuls of new players is seldom as successful as allowing a team to grow and develop. The modern game militates against the patient approach but, in 1967, Stein was under no such strictures.

The defence more or less picked itself: Simpson had been in superb form since replacing Fallon; bringing in Craig for O'Neill and switching Gemmell to left back had given Stein two rapacious overlapping full backs, and there was no more solid defensive partnership than McNeill and Clark. Likewise, Murdoch and Auld, playing in midfield, could orchestrate the pace and tempo of every game they played, as well as giving Stein even more attacking options. The forwards, too, for the most part, picked themselves. Johnstone was world class, being the one Celtic player whose reputation extended beyond British shores in 1967. Wallace, who Stein had hand-picked as the final ingredient in his side, was always going to play if he was fit. Likewise, Chalmers, in the absence of the injured McBride, was first-choice centre forward.

Whatever uncertainty Stein had almost certainly revolved around his left wing. Should it go to the physically powerful Hughes, or to the nippy Lennox. Fans tended to judge the pair like racehorses: Hughes favoured the going when it was good to soft, while Lennox's preference was for good to firm. Nonetheless, Stein must have known that he was going to have to make up his mind and do it soon.

There is no doubt that, of the two, Lennox was the more complete player. His unselfish running off the ball was more suited to the style of play Stein wanted Celtic to adopt. Equally, he could convert the faintest of chances into a goal. Hughes was always more effective playing through the middle, but even he would have to concede that Celtic had an embarrassment of riches in that department.

'I don't think John had a very great tactical appreciation of the game, but he was fast, and he was strong,' says Stein's biographer, Bob Crampsey. 'Stein tended to use him wide on the left, but I remember one occasion, at Dundee in the 67–68 season, where he led the line extremely well as a Continental-style centre forward. It was a great game which Celtic won 5–4, and Hughes' display that day, was magnificent.

'I also think that Bertie Auld, who was frequently paired with Gallagher the following season, was happier playing with Charlie Gallagher than with John Hughes. Charlie could usually be relied upon to do the right thing and you could tell what he was going to do – and he would do it. Hughes, on the other hand, was quite capable of getting Auld to run inside, beating two or three men down the wing, and then losing the ball – and that would be the two of them out of it.'

John Hughes' name was one of those on Stein's list for possible transfer after his Scottish Cup-winning triumph in 1965. It's reasonable to assume that he was one of those who was not a Stein favourite. There were others who were not favourites – Steve Chalmers, for example – but Chalmers was much more valuable to the team than Hughes, and a lot less expendable. The final nail in the coffin in terms of Hughes' selection, as Celtic approached the most important series of games in the club's history, was the simple fact that he had not been playing well. Stein had picked him in five of the seven European Cup ties Celtic had played so far, and he had singularly failed to shine. It was time for change, and that meant Lennox would make the outside-left berth his own.

Ironically, the first time Lennox had played at outside-left had been as a replacement for Hughes some two years previously. Stein's preference was, usually, to play him through the middle. That was Lennox's preference too.

'I had never played at outside-left in my life until the day I took over from Yogi, against St Johnstone,' says Lennox. 'But, within two years, I was an international at outside-left; it's funny that. I didn't like playing wide. I always preferred to play next to the centre forward to get the tap-ins. I loved them. Wee Jimmy always tells this story about one of the European games where he goes past the left back and gets a forearm smash. Another guy comes across to cover him and draws his studs down the wee man's legs. He then goes round the goalie, and the goalie smacks him in the stomach. Then, he says, the ball is rolling towards the goal and I jump in and put it into the net. I'm the one turning away to "the jungle", with my arm in the air, and wee Jimmy's the one lying there with blood pouring out of him.

'We actually did play St Johnstone one day – and he scored two goals. Then he beat about three guys and fired in a shot; then I came in and smacked it in. Jimmy never scored a hat-trick in his life. That was his best chance, and I beat him to it.'

That sort of opportunism may appear selfish, but Lennox and his obsession with making sure the ball had crossed the line, no matter who had originally struck it, was exactly what Stein needed in his team. Going into the game against Dukla, Lennox also had one other very important factor in his favour: the Czechs hadn't seen him. Stein had persevered with Hughes, for what turned out to be the last time in Europe that season, for the first leg at Celtic Park. However, he allowed the Czechs, and everyone else, to think that he might play Lennox. His mind, of course, was made up about Hughes on that occasion. Now, he was about to play the same game in reverse.

The game against Dukla was played on Tuesday, 25 April, and Celtic had their last full training session in Prague on the Monday. After that session, Stein was mobbed by about two dozen Czech journalists. This was as big a game for Dukla as it was for Celtic, so media interest in Czechoslovakia was fierce. The one thing they all wanted to know, and the first question they fired at Stein, was about his line-up the following night.

Stein replied without hesitation. 'Same defence as in Glasgow,' he said tersely, 'Simpson, Craig and Gemmell, Murdoch, McNeill and Clark, and five forwards from these six – Johnstone, Wallace, Chalmers, Auld, Hughes and Lennox.'

Stein was trying to induce the same uncertainty in the Prague coach Musil as he had done in Glasgow, but this time no-one was fooled. Czech journalists, Scottish journalists, and Musil himself, must have known that Lennox was going to be preferred. In the first leg, Johnstone had tormented Dukla while Hughes had been all but anonymous. Playing Lennox in place of Hughes, Stein reasoned, would give Celtic a double advantage. In the first instance, he was banking on Musil putting at least two men onto the right to combat the threat of Johnstone, but he was also counting on the fact that Dukla had never seen Lennox. They would have no idea of his blinding speed and deadly accuracy, and this would allow him, in theory, to put pressure on the Czechs down the left flank.

Regardless of team selection, Celtic still had that all-important, two-goal cushion from the game in Glasgow. Stein knew, however, that Dukla, inspired by Masopust, would go all out to get at least one goal back as quickly as possible. Stein knew exactly when the danger periods for his side would be.

'Dukla must attack,' he reasoned. 'They have no alternative. If they don't, then they don't have the faintest chance of pulling back our two-goal lead. They will go all out for a quick goal, something that will give them hope of saving the game. They will want that goal within the first twenty minutes. That is danger spell number one, and we know it.

'I think, though, that their supreme effort will come in the first fifteen minutes of the second half, so we will have to be especially vigilant in both these periods.'

On the other hand, Stein knew that one goal from his team would finish the game. His players were, by this stage, experienced enough to know that they did not have to risk everything in pursuit of that goal. But once the Czech attack had been blunted, then Celtic could open out as they had done in Switzerland and France, and put the game out of reach of the Czechs.

For the normally unflappable Celtic players, there was real tension in this game. They knew that all the previous matches had been big games, but this was their chance to make history. They were only 90 minutes away from becoming the first British side to reach the final of the European Cup.

'I think we were all aware of that, but again, no-one would have said it out loud,' says Jim Craig. 'The feeling was that we had played very well at Celtic Park, and all we had to do was come up with a competent performance, and we would be okay.'

For some of the more experienced players in the side, such as skipper Billy McNeill, their minds would have gone back to other games in similar circumstances.

'We were only one game away from the final,' he says. 'By that stage, we all knew it, but we had gone to a similar situation in

Hungary a few years back and lost there. From that point of view, I think some of us suspected it would be a backs-to-the-wall job.'

The Scottish media were confident that Celtic had to do little more than turn up to make the final, and they were there in force. The English media, by contrast, appeared to expect Dukla to win at least 2–0, and most English newspapers were conspicuous by their absence. Despite the feeling among the press corps, the game still had to be played.

'It was one of the most intimidating games I've ever played in,' says Steve Chalmers. 'There were just masses of army uniforms everywhere. It was a very strange atmosphere.'

The game was played in the Jaliska Stadium in Prague and, although it was only a small ground, it was full to its 22,000 capacity with Dukla supporters, even though most of them appeared to be there under orders.

'Dukla were the army team,' explains Billy McNeill. 'I think Masopust was a major or a colonel but, anyway, he was one of the best players I had ever played against. I think, because they were the army team, they weren't well-liked by the ordinary Czechs, who saw them, maybe, as the Communist oppressors. But there was one whole side of the ground which was just a mass of grey because it was all army uniforms. I thought it was incredible. I don't think I'd ever seen so many soldiers in one place in my life. Eastern European countries were generally very intimidating to travel to at that time because of all the uniforms, but the Dukla Prague game was exceptional. Once the game starts, though, that all disappears, and you just have to get on with the football.'

The game was played on a bitterly cold day with arctic winds swirling around the ground. Celtic won the toss and kicked off with the biting wind at their backs. It was not a day for standing around, but they would soon find more than enough to keep their minds off the temperature.

Despite all the pre-match predictions, it became fairly obvious early on that Celtic had come to Prague to protect their lead. For once, flair and style had given way to pragmatism and results, and Stein had sent his team out under orders to make sure they didn't lose. They started brightly enough, though, with Johnstone and Auld shooting over the bar in the opening minutes, and then Viktor had to save smartly from Lennox who had been sent away by Chalmers. These, however, were merely skirmishes, and before the game was very old Celtic found themselves defending.

Lennox was the one who was supposed to be exploiting Dukla's weaknesses on the left-hand side. Instead he was back in his own defence.

'I stood next to Tommy Gemmell for the whole game,' he laughs. 'For the whole night, it was just up and down the left-hand side. Dukla didn't get to the semi-final by being a bad team. They pushed us back. No matter what people say about us defending in that game – they made us defend. They were a good team, and they forced us back. People tend to think that Big Jock said to us, "Right, we'll all get back, and we'll all defend." But once a good team start to get at you, it's very hard to break out again, and the longer the game goes on the harder it is to break out.

'Stevie was so isolated at times that it just wasn't real. We just had no options. If I'm standing next to Big Tam and there's somebody else standing next to me, what can I do? All you can do is play it forward for Stevie to run for. That was a hard, hard game.'

The defence were finding things no easier. Normally, Gemmell and Craig would be chasing forward and putting pressure on the opposing wingers and turning them into defenders. Against Dukla, they could scarcely get out of their own half.

'We were in the trenches for the whole ninety minutes,' remembers Jim Craig. 'It was hard going because when you got the ball, who were you going to hit it to? It was all in front of you. It was terribly naive because there was no target for us. Poor Stevie was struggling up front on his own. You'd look up and you'd see him, and you'd try to give the man a break by making a run yourself. As soon as you did that you'd hear Big Jock on the touchline shouting, "Get back and defend." What were you supposed to do? The only thing you could do was put it out for a throw-in.'

Stein's plan had been for Auld to sit in the midfield, and for Wallace to drop back and also revert to a midfield role. This would have left Lennox, Johnstone and Chalmers up front. However, the Czechs put them under such pressure, in the early part of the game, that Chalmers was left to plough a lonely furrow in Dukla's half of the field.

'When I got the ball I would just do what I could with it,' Chalmers remembers. 'I'd take it into the corners and try and hold it until the others could get forward, and if that didn't work then I'd run at the defence. It was all I could do.'

The rest of the team were well aware of the difficulty of the role that Chalmers was filling and how well he was doing it.

'Stevie Chalmers was incredible that night,' says Tommy Gemmell admiringly. 'He played up front on his own, and Jock told us just to stick balls to the corner flag on the right and on the left. He said to Stevie, "Just you chase them." He was marvellous.

'But Dukla were a great side,' Gemmell continues. 'They had Masopust, of course, but they also had this big, tall guy Strunc who I played against, and he was very good. They were a right good side, and Ronnie Simpson saved us a couple of times. He played an absolute blinder.'

Simpson and Chalmers were indeed marvellous in Prague that afternoon, but the performance of the match came from Billy McNeill. This was arguably one of his finest games in a Celtic jersey. McNeill organised his defence superbly and, time after time, the Czech attacks foundered on the rock of his aerial prowess. He didn't miss a single thing in the air all night.

'In the early part of the game they just besieged us,' he says, looking back. 'That's what caused everyone on our side to spend their time chasing and sorting things out. Although, I have to say, that we broke the bulk of their attacks. In the first twenty minutes or so they had a couple of shots at Ronnie. I remember one going screaming past me and thinking, God, I hope Ronnie is in the road of that one. And he was. Latterly, we just frustrated them as much as anything. It was a very uncharacteristic performance by us as a team, but it was the nature of the game, and it was dictated by the circumstances.'

In the midst of his own resolute defending, McNeill, too, had time to have sympathy for Celtic's lone striker. 'It was quite frightening for Stevie,' explains McNeill. 'He was the only one of us who was forward consistently, and I remember, at one point, he got himself involved in a wee fracas with them. He was surrounded by about three or four Dukla players and, because he was so far forward, none of us could get up there in time to help him out. He was on his own until the referee sorted things out.

'We knew it was always going to be something of a rearguard action, but it was never quite intended to turn out like that.'

The shot that Simpson, happily, was in the way of, came from Nedorost early in the game, and was probably Dukla's best chance to get back into the tie. When Simpson handled that one comfortably – as well as another from Strunc – his job was just about done. Dukla may have had most of the play, but that was, as McNeill suggests, because Celtic devoted themselves to simply frustrating them after the initial waves had been unsuccessful. Celtic were happy for Dukla to have the ball providing their defence was capable of stopping them from doing anything with it.

Dukla's style of play also proved to be their ultimate undoing. The Czechs were, undoubtedly, skilfully orchestrated by Masopust, but their game was too deliberate and slow to make any impact. While they could put the Celtic defence under pressure, they were not quick enough to penetrate it, and were generally picked off by some ferocious tackling from the Celtic players. When Celtic won the ball, they were willing to hold on to it, and to pass it among themselves in relatively safe areas of the pitch, to further deny the Czechs possession.

As the game wore on, it became more and more obvious that Dukla had run out of ideas. The defensive cordon that Celtic had thrown up around Simpson had done its job, and after those initial probing shots from Nedorost and Strunc, he hardly had to make another save worthy of the name. By the end of the match, even the hostile Czech crowd had come to appreciate the quality of Celtic's defending. When the referee blew the final whistle, McNeill was given a rousing ovation from the Czech fans.

The final whistle prompted scenes of wild delight among the exhausted Celtic players. They were in the final of the European Cup in their first season in the competition. No-one was more delighted than Jock Stein who had almost reached the pinnacle of his success as a manager.

'He ran very nearly the length of the field to find me,' recalls Steve Chalmers. 'When he got to me, he threw his arms around me and thanked me. I was astonished. I was never one of his favourites, but he went out of his way to thank me.'

There was only one sour note at the end of the game. As the players trooped off the field, Masopust refused to shake hands with the Celtic side. Afterwards, he made his peace with the Celtic players by coming into the dressing room and explaining that he had been overcome by emotion. He realised that this had been his last chance to play in a European Cup final, and it had been denied him. The Celtic players, all of whom had the utmost respect for one of the greatest players in Europe, were touched by his gesture.

After the match, Stein admitted that this had been an uncharacteristic performance from his normally buccaneering side. He also admitted that no Celtic side of his would ever play in such a way again. His right back, Jim Craig, believes Stein's tactics on the night were naive, but he also maintains that Stein's pronouncements after the game have been misinterpreted over the years.

'The Prague game was great at Parkhead but disastrous over there,' Craig says now. 'It was a nightmare because we were in action for the whole ninety minutes. I think Jock has often been misquoted about this. He said after the game that he would never do that again, and I think people took from that that he would never defend again. What he meant was that he would never defend as deep as that again. In future, he would meet them on the halfway line where you have fifty yards to recover from a mistake.

'It was Jock's idea to go for sitting on the eighteen-yard line,' Craig continues. 'In hindsight, he admitted he was wrong. It would have been easier to go for a quick goal or meet them on the halfway line. If you do that, and I break up an attack and gather the ball, then I've got something to aim for. I've got a guy to pass to who's maybe only ten yards in front of me. If it's not a perfect pass, and the ball comes back, then it can miss me out, but we still have a chance to recover.'

Naive or not, Stein's tactics had worked. It was not the prettiest performance by a Celtic side, but it had been an effective one, and they were now in the final of the European Cup. The end more than justified the means, and even though chairman Bob Kelly was unhappy with the display, he could not be unhappy with the outcome.

Although Celtic were through, they did not know who they would meet in the final. The other semi-final between CSKA Sofia and Inter Milan was being played the following day. Sofia had held Inter to a fighting 1–1 draw the previous week, but the Italians were 10–1 on favourites to go through in the second leg. Remarkably, the score in the away leg was also 1–1. At 2–2 on aggregate, the away goals would have to be taken into account, but they had both scored the same number of away goals, so a third game was necessary. In the end, Inter Milan won the play-off in Bologna the following week.

Stein had been remarkably prescient when he looked ahead after beating Vojvodina in the quarter-finals. He had believed, quite rightly, that the Italians would be difficult, if not impossible, to beat over two legs. But over ninety minutes in a neck-or-nothing game at a neutral venue such as Lisbon, then anything was possible.

For his players, that was all ahead of them. For the time being, they were basking in the glow of their semi-final success.

'I think our attitude was just that we were glad to be in the final,' says Billy McNeill. 'But we were also a bit excited that we were going to be prominent in a European sense.'

For left back Tommy Gemmell, there was a definite sense of history about their achievement. 'Once we got that result against Dukla, the pressure was off,' he explains. 'We had got to the final, and if we won it, we won it, if we didn't, we didn't. But we were there first, and no-one could take that away from us. We had done something no-one else in Britain had ever done. We had got to the final of the European Cup.'

Chapter 16

S UCH WAS THE DELIGHT and the elation of the Celtic party, that they could have flown back from Prague without the aeroplane. However, their celebrations would have to be cut short because there were pressing domestic concerns that still needed to be attended to.

The game against Dukla had been on the Tuesday but, on that Saturday, Celtic were also in the Scottish Cup final. Their opponents were Aberdeen who had drawn 0–0 with Celtic just the week before they went to Prague. They had also managed to take a point off Celtic with a 1–1 draw earlier in the season, that being the match in which Celtic lost Joe McBride. Under normal circumstances, they might have fancied their chances against Celtic, especially as the Glasgow side were coming back from a long European trip. These, however, were not normal circumstances. Aberdeen had the misfortune to be playing against a Celtic side that had just had its status confirmed as part of Europe's elite.

With no injury worries, Stein had no problems with team selection. This time there would be no dithering over whether it should be Lennox or Hughes. He named the same team which had gone into the history books against Dukla Prague only a few days earlier. Aberdeen, for their part, had to go into the game without their influential manager, Eddie Turnbull. One of the most charismatic figures in the Scottish game at that time, Turnbull had been taken ill only hours before the final.

Aberdeen played as though their thoughts were with their manager, and contributed very little to the game. Celtic, perhaps still feeling the effects of a sapping game in Prague, played well within themselves. Two goals from Willie Wallace – one on either side of the interval – gave Celtic a well-deserved win in front of a crowd of just over 126,000.

Celtic had now added the Scottish Cup to the League Cup and the Glasgow Cup and, within a few days, the League would be won or lost. With only three games to go, Celtic were in front of Rangers, but the Ibrox side, who were also to reach the European Cup-Winners Cup final that year, were clinging on tenaciously. Despite Rangers' draw against Clyde earlier in the month, the gap between the sides was not large, and it was still mathematically possible for Celtic to be caught. More significantly, the postponed New Year fixture between the sides had been re-arranged for the following week, and was shaping up to be the League decider.

In between times, Celtic had another game to play, and they managed to shoot themselves in the foot quite spectacularly in what was expected to be a formality even though Dundee United were the only team to have beaten Celtic in the League that season. The sides were due to meet again on the Wednesday following the Cup final, but the subsequent form of both sides led everyone to believe Celtic would win to virtually wrap up the league. Celtic were obviously overcome with euphoria because they managed to lose 3–2, giving United a unique double.

'They were there to play, and we were just there for a carry on,' was Billy McNeill's rather harsh judgement, 30 years later, suggesting that the Celtic squad may have already had their minds on Lisbon.

The defeat against Dundee United changed the complexion of the League race. Celtic were now going into a game against Rangers which could decide who would be champions. If Rangers won, then there would be another nail-biting finish as the title went down to the last game of the season. A point for Celtic, however, would give them the title. In the end, Celtic went to Ibrox on 6 May and drew 2–2 with a brace of goals from Jimmy Johnstone. The title was theirs and it had been won at the home of their oldest rivals.

'It was a great way to win a League,' said Bobby Lennox afterwards.

Celtic had now won every domestic honour available to them, and having got the final game of the season out of the way – a meaningless 2–0 win over Kilmarnock at Celtic Park – they could concentrate completely on the last and greatest prize of the season – the European Cup.

There are few finer or more loyal fans anywhere than those who follow Celtic. Their loyalty has been tested almost beyond endurance over the years, but they remain resolute and confirmed in their faith in a football club which to them, is more than a football club. They had stayed loyal through thick and thin and, before Stein arrived, it was mostly thin. Now they were preparing to enjoy their finest hour.

Opposing coaches like Vujadin Boskov of Vojvodina had paid tribute to the effect that a Celtic Park crowd could have on the team. They were capable of lifting them to efforts above and beyond their normal standards. It was, after all, the exhortation of the crowd, as much as the sinew-straining efforts of the players on the field, that had beaten the Yugoslavians. The organisers of the European Cup had taken all of this into account years before, and not just because of Celtic fans. The final was to be played at a neutral venue, both teams would have the same numbers of supporters there, and the contest would be decided in footballing terms, and not by whose fans were the most intimidating.

Celtic supporters were having none of this. They would get to Lisbon by hook or by crook and do their best to turn the European Cup final into a home game for Celtic. The Parkhead club has always had a hard core of travelling fans. They were the 500 who flew out to Switzerland to cheer their team on in the dim and distant days of the first-round game against Zurich. As the team grew more successful so, too, did the desire of the fans to follow them. By the time Celtic ran out onto the pitch for their game against Inter Milan, the hard core of 500 had swollen to an army of 20,000.

For some, such as John McCabe, it was a trip which had been in the backs of their minds for some time.

'There were ten of us who used to go to the stand every Saturday,' says John, now head teacher at St Aloysius College junior school in Glasgow. 'We'd been going for years and, at the start of the European campaign, one of our number, I can't remember who, said, "If we get to the final, we'll get a plane for Lisbon." We all said fine, and thought nothing more about it.'

Willie Wallace's two goals against Dukla Prague may have recovered his transfer fee for Celtic, but it left John McCabe with a massive headache.

'Once we had beaten Dukla 3–1 at Parkhead – that seemed to be a good enough sign for us,' John continues. 'So they all turned to me and said, "Right, get a plane. You've got some experience with school trips to the Continent so you can get the plane." '

Chartering a plane these days would be a fairly daunting prospect; in 1967, it was an immense undertaking.

'I tried Aer Lingus first of all, but without success. Then I tried all sorts of other places, but their planes had all been chartered, and there weren't that many planes about to begin with, to be honest. Eventually, I got a company in Amsterdam who were a subsidiary of KLM. They agreed to provide me with a 96-seater plane – it was propeller-driven and not very modern, but they assured me it would get us to Lisbon and back in one piece. So I hired the plane, told the others in our Parkhead group, they told friends, and eventually we found about seventy-five people.'

Chartering the plane cost £3000. The money was advanced by John's mother, who had a pub in Maryhill in Glasgow. He would then get the cash back by charging £35 for a trip which included a return flight, an overnight stay and a ticket to the match. Match tickets were on sale from the Scottish Football Association offices in Glasgow, and ranged from ten shillings (50p) to two pounds seven shillings and sixpence (£2.38). Although £35 seems like nothing now, John McCabe was earning only £18 a week as a teacher, and an unskilled labourer would earn much less than that. The cost of the trip worked out, in real terms, at about three weeks' wages for most of the Celtic supporters.

On that basis, being twenty short on his plane-load would have cost John McCabe a lot of money. He took an advert in his local paper and was absolutely swamped with replies.

'I got six passengers from a travel agent who was actually laying off clients because he was so busy,' he recalls. 'I also got repeated phone calls from a man who was desperate to buy the whole plane from me. He had organised one plane to go, but he desperately needed another one. And then there were the calls that invariably came at three o'clock on a Sunday morning. You'd pick up the phone, hear the noise of a party in full swing, and some drunken voice would yell: "Hey, pal, are you the guy that's got the plane going to Lisbon?"

'In the end, though, we managed to get the plane filled without too much difficulty, and my mother got her money back.'

Pat Monaghan, who was finding it a lot easier to face his Rangers-supporting pals at the fruit market these days, found himself a trip on a plane for £28. But, as he recalls, every Celtic fan worthy of the name was desperate to get to Lisbon for the game.

'Some people were cashing in insurance policies to get there,' he remembers. 'Others were going by car – I think some even contemplated swimming. They were taking tents, they were hitching lifts, they were doing everything and anything.'

For many of the 20,000 fans, it would be the first time they had ever left Glasgow, so that was a problem in itself. It also meant that one of the busiest places in the city was the passport office.

'I went in to get mine,' says Joe Connelly, who was preparing for his greatest day in almost 30 years of supporting Celtic, 'and the poor man behind the counter just looked up and said: "I know what you're here for." '

As the fans' desire to get to Lisbon by whatever means necessary grew, so too did the media interest. John Quinn is now a veteran sports reporter on the *Evening Times* newspaper in Glasgow. In 1967 he was covering Celtic's European Cup final on a news basis, and he was instrumental in arranging the most colourful and bizarre supporters' outing anyone had ever seen.

'It became obvious that there were huge numbers of people going to this game,' says John, taking up the story. 'They were using whatever means they could, but a great many of them were going by road. They were taking cars, buses, coaches, minibuses, motor bikes – you name it. If it had wheels, and it was halfway roadworthy, then it was going to Lisbon.'

It occurred to John Quinn that this was a great story in itself.

He suggested to his editor that the newspaper make the journey to Lisbon by car, as well. His editor agreed – with the proverbial caveat of editors everywhere that he find as cheap a way of doing it as possible. At that time, the now-defunct Rootes car firm was a major employer in the west of Scotland, with a huge assembly line at Linwood, near Paisley. The flagship of the company was the new Hillman Imp which, they hoped, would dominate the small car market.

John Quinn then had a brainwave.

'I phoned a man called Bill Morris who was then the public relations officer at Linwood,' he continues. 'I said to him, basically, "What are the chances of us getting one of your cars to go to Lisbon?" I pointed out they would get all the publicity from the trip, there would be pictures of us leaving in their car, stories and pictures filed *en route*, and the publicity when we came back. Bill actually thought it was a good idea, and he said he would get back to me.'

A few days later, Quinn, who had only been driving for six months, took delivery of a brand new Hillman Imp from Lord Rootes himself.

'It was a green car,' he recalls, 'but when I went to pick it up they had painted white stripes on it to effectively turn it into a Celtic car. They had gone over it and double-checked it to make sure it would stand the trip. Lord Rootes gave me the keys and a back-up tool kit wrapped in lucky white heather. I said to him, "I hope this won't even be opened by the time we come back," and, sure enough, it wasn't. It was a great car and a great advert for the Hillman Imp.'

And so the 'Celticade' – Quinn coined the name as a derivation of 'cavalcade' – was born. The *Evening Times* undertook to organise the mass pilgrimage. That included a series of meetings with the AA who advised the fans on their route, the price of petrol, where they should stay, and everything else they would need on the journey.

The Celticade caught the imagination of the public and the Celtic players alike. When they left George Square in Glasgow for the beginning of their 1750-mile journey to Lisbon, they were waved off by Billy McNeill, who had come along to wish them luck.

'There were so many things that made the final such a wonderful occasion for us, and that was one of them,' says McNeill. 'Looking back, it seemed to be an eternity before the game, and I remember the green and white Hillman Imp leading the convoy away. It would be a big undertaking even now, but car technology being what it was then, it was an incredible journey. I'm convinced to this day that, although they were setting off on this marathon, not one of those people had any idea of what they were letting themselves in for.'

'Billy is absolutely right,' agrees Quinn, with hindsight. 'I was in the lead car, I was a novice driver with six months' experience under my belt, and I really hadn't a clue of what was in front of us. I've no idea how many cars made the journey. It was one of these things where people were catching up with you and dropping back all the time. I do remember we picked up a lot of people as we went down through England.'

The Celticade's journey took them through England and across the Channel, from Dover to Calais. Appropriately, they made the crossing on a ship called the *Celtic Enterprise* which had been decked out in green and white for the occasion. Once they got to Calais, they then drove down through France, across the Pyrenees into Spain, and finally into Portugal, and then on to Lisbon.

'It was great fun going there, and the fans *en route* were hilarious,' recalls Quinn, who has an abiding memory of groups of supporters cleaning their teeth by the roadside of a morning, with vodka. Smirnoff Blue Label appears to have been the drink of choice for travelling fans. 'The reception was terrific everywhere we went,' he continues. 'In a lot of the small towns, they were waiting for us in the market squares, because others, in cars and coaches ahead of us, had told them we were coming. We would often find cheering crowds, and bunting, and streamers, as we passed through.

'On the border between Spain and Portugal, the customs post had a picture of the Celtic team underneath the sign that said, "Have you anything to declare?" More than one of the cars took the opportunity to tell them that the only thing they had to declare was that Celtic were coming back with the European Cup.

'There was a great sense of fun and adventure and camaraderie about the whole trip,' Quinn recalls. 'Everybody helped each other out. If there was a puncture, there was no shortage of people to help change tyres. It was the same with mechanical problems. Their whole attitude to the trip was incredible. They drove across the Pyrenees like they were driving up Maryhill Road.'

The Celtic side, for their part, were treating the final as they would any other important match, and had gone to Seamill. They had gone there for a full week before the game and, after a weekend with their familes, they would return to Seamill, on the Monday before the match, and fly out to Lisbon the following day. But even at Seamill, where they were, ostensibly, in retreat, they could not fail to be aware of their place in the world now.

'The build up to the final was brilliant,' remembers Billy McNeil. 'All of a sudden we had television companies coming from all over the world to see us. I remember the Italians were particularly keen. We went to Seamill, and some of us went golfing at West Kilbride, and we were absolutely surrounded by camera crews. But we loved all that.'

The order of the day at Seamill was to relax; they had done a job and they could now unwind a little before facing the final task ahead of them. On the first Sunday night a few of the squad took Stein's instructions a little too literally and supped not wisely, but perhaps too well.

'There were a few headaches on the Monday morning,' according to Tommy Gemmell. 'Big Jock was annoyed, but we were all good trainers, and we knew that we would have to work our backsides off, and we did. When you were at Seamill you were away from phones, you got away from people chasing you for tickets, and you could just be yourself. It was an unwinding job; you would have thought that we were there for the break more than anything else.'

Gemmell is probably right. Any passing stranger would have thought this was a bunch of mates out for a golfing break, instead of a team preparing for the most important match any British club side had ever been involved in.

'Maybe we were a wee bit naive by doing stuff – like playing golf – before a big game like that,' says Jim Craig. 'I don't think they'd let you do that nowadays. You're using all sorts of different muscles, so there's the risk of a strain; there's also the risk of someone getting hit with a club or a ball and, especially in Scotland, you could end up with a chill after a shower of rain.

'You would never have thought we were in a European final which was only days away.'

Chapter 17

WHILE CELTIC WERE GOLFING and relaxing on the Ayrshire coast, their European Cup final opponents were undergoing preparations of a much more intensive nature. Inter Milan had won the Cup in 1964 and 1965 and were determined to make Celtic their third victims.

They were managed by Helenio Herrera, arguably the most famous club manager in world football at that time. Never one to hide his light under a bushel, Herrera once claimed that his whole career had been a triumph. He was born in poverty in Buenos Aires, in Argentina, and first played his football on the streets of the slums of Casablanca, where he grew up. Although he was Argentinian by birth, he became French by naturalisation, and played twice for France at international level. He was a much-travelled manager, taking charge of two clubs in France, four in Spain, and one in Portugal. Also, he had the rare distinction of managing three international sides – France, Spain and Italy – and at one point in his career, when he was in charge at Roma, he was the highest paid football manager in the world.

Herrera's first notable triumph came in 1961 when he lead Barcelona to the European Cup final, only to see them lose 3–2 to Benfica of Portugal. But it was at Internazionale of Milan that Herrera really made his name. His spell at Barcelona had been characterised by a hectoring style of management which almost brainwashed his players with bizarre pre-game chants and motivational rituals in the dressing room. This was refined at Milan, where he bombarded his team with slogans, and never allowed them to forget that winning was their prime motive for playing football. He reportedly once shouted after his players as they were leaving in the coach after having won a League match: 'Think of the next game.'

Herrera was a brilliant tactician, but his tactics, if they had gone unchecked, would have strangled the life out of the game. He was a master of 'catenaccio', a style of play which derives its name from the Italian word for the bolt of a door. Basically, it is a sweeper system which was devised by Karl Rappan in the 1940s. The idea is that your side marks the opponents man for man, and you play one man behind your back four to cover all the gaps. The formation also requires that you play only one striker. The idea is that the ball is delivered to the striker who holds it for the rest of the forwards to join him in attack. Catenaccio had dominated Italian football since the 1950s, but Herrera's Inter Milan side had refined the process. He had turned it into a dour, dull game of massed defence and quick breakaways to take a lead. Once they went in front, then they simply defended for the rest of the game.

The irony was that Inter Milan had some of the most skilful players in the world in their side. Facchetti, who also captained Italy, was probably the best overlapping full back in the world. His defensive partner Burgnich, too, was world class, as were the midfielders Mazzola and Suarez. Up front, Domenghini, on his game, was a joy to watch, as was the Brazilian Jair. That so much talent could be harnessed to such a dismal style of play almost beggars belief.

There were some similarities between Herrera and Stein. Although the Argentinian was six years older, they were broadly of the same generation. They had both been raised in hard surroundings and had used football as a means of escape, and they were both superb tacticians. They differed profoundly, however, in their approach to the game. Herrera put his faith in defence, Stein put his in attack. Earlier in his career, Stein had made a thorough study of Herrera and his tactics, and had found them wanting. Now he was going to expose their shortcomings in public. The European Cup final of 1967 was not going to be just a football match, it was going to be an eleven-a-side debate on football philosophy.

In the week before the final, Jock Stein took a break from Seamill to head for London. At a ceremony at the Café Royal in Piccadilly, he was named Britain's manager of the year for the second year in succession. It was a rare and heartfelt tribute to the man who had inspired a team to unprecedented heights in British football. But once he had accepted the accolade, Stein was straight back to Ayrshire to rejoin his players.

By this stage, Stein was in no doubt about his best side, though he gave no hint to the media. The players had already been informed, and it was a relaxed Celtic squad of twenty who turned up at Glasgow Airport on the Tuesday morning. The eleven players who got them into the final with the heroic display against Dukla, had been joined by reserve goalkeeper John Fallon, defenders Willie O'Neill, David Cattanach, Ian Young and Jim Brogan, reserve centre-half John Cushley, and forwards Charlie Gallagher and John Hughes. Although he was unfit and would not take any part in the game, Joe McBride also travelled with the Celtic party. Celtic had chartered their own plane, a De Havilland Comet from Dan Air for the trip, and were waved off by a small knot of well-wishers including wives and girlfriends who would fly out the following day.

Before leaving, Stein said he had no fitness worries and his only concern was a minor one. 'I plan to name my team on our arrival in Lisbon, later today. The players already know the team, but I will not name it until I see how they fare on the flight,' Stein told reporters, at the airport. 'Some of them are not the best travellers, and it could be I will delay naming my side if some of them are not too happy about the flight.'

His captain, betraying no hint of nerves, had a brief but stirring message for the airport press pack. 'We hope and expect,' said Billy McNeill, 'to make this game memorable for Celtic and Scotland.'

If Stein was looking relaxed before he flew out, then it might have been something to do with the news from Italy that two of Inter's most influential players would miss the game. Their Spanish international Suarez and their Brazilian international Jair were both, reportedly, carrying injuries and would not be fit for the final. Suarez had a muscle sprain in his right leg, and Jair had damaged his left knee.

'This is a terrible blow,' Inter's suitably grave and sombre-looking spokesman told reporters. 'We are very worried about the Lisbon game. The Celtic players are fast and will be fresh and relaxed, whereas our players have been involved for a very long time in a very tough struggle for the League championship. Without Suarez and Jair, we shall have an all-Italian team in Lisbon.'

The Inter spokesman then went on to name the side which he thought would take the field on Thursday. The first team was:

Sarti; Burgnich and Facchetti; Bedin, Picchi and Guarneri; Domenghini and Mazzola; Cappellini, Bicicli and Corso.

The loss of Suarez, who was the Italians' play maker, would undoubtedly be a serious blow to Inter's chances, if indeed he was injured. Stein was long enough in the tooth to know that this could simply be a bluff from the wily Herrera. But even if Suarez was out, Stein could not fail to note that the 'all-Italian' side named by the Inter spokesman was almost the Italian national team in everything but name.

However, by the time Celtic arrived at their luxury headquarters in Estoril, on the Tuesday afternoon, Stein had confirmation of the Italians' problems. The Inter side had flown in 90 minutes ahead of them, and Suarez was not with them. He had been left behind in Italy to recover for a vital League game on the weekend after the European Cup final.

Celtic wasted no time in heading for the National Stadium for a thorough workout on the surface on which they would play the match 48 hours later. The training session was timed for 5.30 p.m. – the same time as the game would kick off on Thursday – to ensure that conditions were as similar as possible. The National Stadium was a superb ground, and the playing surface was as good as any the Celtic players had seen. Stein, who would occasionally relax from football with a game of bowls, pointed out that it was good enough to play bowls on.

After his players had been put through their paces Stein, as promised, unveiled his team. These were the men who would make footballing history for club and country. These were the Lisbon Lions:

Simpson; Craig and Gemmell; Murdoch, McNeill and Clark; Johnstone, Wallace, Chalmers, Auld and Lennox.

It was a side that had played together five times that season. In those five games they had clinched the League against Rangers, won the Scottish Cup against Aberdeen and reached the final of the European Cup against Dukla Prague. Stein had no doubt that they could go one step further and bring him the greatest trophy in club football. The Italians had not yet confirmed their side. A spokesman said they would reveal the team the following day, but hinted that it would be largely along the lines that had already been suggested.

This European Cup final was as much a battle of wills between Stein and Herrera, as it was a battle between Celtic and Inter Milan. By revealing his team 48 hours before kickoff, and in such a confident manner, Stein was able to strike the first psychological blow. He then turned the screws with press interviews calculated to drive Herrera up the wall. Stein told reporters not only that his side were going to win, but that he was even prepared to let Herrera know how they were going to do it.

'Herrera knows as well as I do that the men who won the Scottish Cup will be given the honour of winning the European Cup – so why keep it a secret?' Stein said, after that training session. 'I am now also going to tell him how Celtic will be the first team to bring the European Cup back to Britain, but it will not help him in any manner, shape or form.

'We are going to play not one, but three types of game at the National Stadium. This is a special match. It is the most important game in Celtic's history and, for the first time, we are going to have to work to win inside ninety minutes. So we are going to attack as we have never attacked before.

'We will also defend when we have to defend, and we are going to keep control of the midfield when we have to keep control of the midfield. We aim to win by teamwork alone.'

Stein finished his press conference with another calculated snub to the Italian players. With Suarez and Jair out, he knew the side that Herrera would play, just as Herrera must have known the side that he would play. The fact that there were so many international, household names in the Inter Milan side didn't bother Stein in the slightest.

'Cups are not won by individuals, no matter how great they are,' said Stein dismissively. 'They are won by men in a team, men who put their club before personal prestige. I am lucky – I have the players who do just that for Celtic.'

The effect of Stein's attack on Herrera and his team is not documented, but there is no doubt that, in the war of words at least, Stein had got his strike in first. He had boosted his players at the expense of the opposition and, as they relaxed in their hotel, the effect would not have been lost on them.

And while Stein was doing his work with the media, the Celtic fans were doing their job with the Portuguese. Despite their success in Europe, Inter Milan's ultra-defensive style of play had not won them many friends, especially among the neutrals. By the time the Celtic fans rolled into town, and the first of them had arrived in Lisbon at the start of the week, they found an eager pool of willing converts.

'The fans had got to Lisbon ahead of us, and they must have prepared the Portuguese for us,' says Billy McNeill. 'It was incredible. The Portuguese were applauding and cheering us everywhere we went. I don't know if our fans turned them, or whether they were just naturally inclined to support the underdog, but it was brilliant. It was like a home game.'

McNeill's comments are worth noting because, despite the air of relaxed optimism, Celtic were very definitely the underdogs in this contest. This was their first final, and they were playing a team who had won the tournament twice, and were now in their third final. You could not find a bookie outside Scotland who would take a bet on Inter, so fancied were they to win.

In Italy, the feeling was that the 'Italian maestros', as the press dubbed them, only had to turn up, and the game would be theirs. On the other hand, they had been 1–10 favourites when they played CSKA in the previous round.

'I was in the land of Philistines when Celtic had their greatest moment,' recalls Brian Dempsey. 'I was working for Alitalia at the time and was in Rome on a training course. The feeling in the Italian press, in the days before the game, was that Inter Milan were almost invincible. As far as they were concerned, Glasgow Celtic was a provincial club with no pedigree and no players of any note. The only player they ever talked about was Johnstone, but they needed to look at some of the others in that side, Murdoch for example, who was one of the best passers of a ball in football at that time, and the full backs, who would be a credit to the game today. But as far as the Italians were concerned, this was a team of nondescripts, they were not big price-tag players, and they had no reputations worth bothering about.'

Certainly, the mood of the Italian media was not duplicated among the Celtic support, nor would you expect it to be. But most of them, hand on heart, did not expect their team to win.

'I always thought the Italians were going to win because of the catenaccio system,' says Joe Connelly. 'I thought that once they got ahead they would just shut up shop and that would be that. But it never entered my head once not to spend the money and go there. This was history, and I wanted to be part of it.'

Another who was not convinced of a Celtic victory was Jim Craig's father, Jimmy. He was a shop manager in Glasgow and had to work every Saturday, so he missed most of the games in that season. His son was determined that he should see the final, and had bought him a plane ticket and a match ticket almost immediately after they had made it to the final. But it took a lot of persuasion to get him there.

'It was very much a last-minute decision for me to go,' says Jimmy. 'I wasn't keen, because I thought they would get beat. I have to admit that I travelled on the plane with a lot of chaps who shared that view; they weren't optimistic about winning either. They were just hoping to have a good time. I think in the end, though, the Italians just took Celtic too cheaply.'

Brian Dempsey was taking a more hopeful approach. 'I think everyone agreed that Celtic had nothing to lose,' he remembers. 'We didn't have anything to prove, we were there, and provided Celtic could go out and enjoy their football, we could achieve anything. But I don't think anyone in their wildest dreams, being totally honest, would have believed that it could have been such an impressive, committed display. I don't think anyone expected that. Those Celtic players showed not one shred of respect for the so-called Italian maestros.

'But then,' he adds, 'Scots have never been logical in the battles we get into. We don't care. We'll take on the world if it's something we believe in.'

Chapter 18

THERE WAS NO DOUBT that Celtic were in the right frame of mind for the biggest game in British club history. Stein had kept them relaxed, kept them mentally attuned, and kept them occupied as the hours ticked away until the kickoff.

Stein's preparation was meticulous. He had billeted his squad in a luxury hotel complex in Estoril, but there was no way anyone would be deflected from the purpose of the trip. Stein was so thorough in his preparations that he even forbade his players to sunbathe. They were allowed half an hour by the pool in the morning, but no-one was allowed out in the sun after noon. Stein was more paranoid about his players being seen to be treating the game as a holiday than anyone getting sunburned or suffering from heat exhaustion. They were there to win the European Cup, and he was determined that nothing should undermine that.

'I find it difficult now to recall exactly what my feelings were before the game, to be honest,' says Billy McNeill, with commendable candour. 'The whole team had an attitude about us that, on our day, we believed we could beat anyone, and as we were here, we might as well take Inter Milan on. But a lot of things happened in those couple of days which were in our favour.'

One of those things was Herrera's attempt to retaliate against Stein in the mind-game department.

Both teams had had a full training session on the Tuesday night, and it was agreed that they would each have another hour on the pitch of the National Stadium for a light workout on the day before the game. The Portuguese Football Association, as the host body, had arranged the training sessions and allocated set times to each side. Inter were to train from ten until eleven, and Celtic would train for an hour immediately afterwards.

It was Stein's intention to surprise the Italians by having his players there early to watch Inter train. But in a fit of games-manship which bordered on the farcical, Herrera had ordered his players up even earlier. By the time Celtic arrived at 9.30, the Italians had completed their training session and were back in their tracksuits waiting to watch Celtic. Stein didn't give them much satisfaction, he only kept his players out in the blistering sunshine for twenty minutes before taking them back.

Herrera had hoped to unsettle the Celtic players but, instead, he had quite the opposite effect.

'It didn't really matter who trained first,' says Billy McNeill. 'But when we turned up, and they were there watching us, we took a wee nip at that. We felt aggrieved and that, I think, gave us a wee bit of an edge going into the game.'

One other thing which was established at that training session was where the allegiance of the neutrals would lie. Inter went through their routine in front of a sparse crowd who were com-pletely unresponsive. But when Celtic were put through their paces, around 400 Portuguese turned out to cheer them on – and this was just for a kick-about.

Afterwards, Stein continued to score points over the uncom-municative Herrera when he patiently answered every question from a group of Portuguese newsmen. They were particularly concerned about how Stein viewed the loss of Suarez to Inter Milan.

'This will not be a death blow for Inter,' Stein said patiently. 'Mr Herrera, like myself, does not depend on any individual player. We ourselves lost Joe McBride at the end of December,' he reminded them, 'but we still made it to the final.'

Stein would not be drawn on the score in the game. He told the Portuguese media that they hoped to win, and to win in a style that would leave the Portuguese public with a good impression of Scottish football. He did, however, suggest that the team which scored first would win the game. Herrera, for his part, sprinkled his conversation with 'no comments' and would only confirm that his starting line-up would be as previously forecast by the club spokesman.

In Glasgow, meanwhile, anticipation about the game was reaching fever pitch. Thousands of fans were preparing to board dozens of chartered planes to get them to Lisbon for the biggest game of their lives. John McCabe, having been in the happy position of being able to sell his twenty spare seats many times over, assembled his party at Glasgow Airport for the five-and-a-half-hour flight.

One man was missing from the plane. Ernie Wilson was a regular at John McCabe's mother's pub in Maryhill, and was a life-long Celtic fan. He was desperate to go to Lisbon but, in the end, could not raise the cash. McCabe kept a seat vacant as long as he could but, finally, he had to let it go. Wilson was upset but understood. However, he was still desperate to be part of the big day, and implored John that if he could not go himself, then at least his Celtic scarf could be there. He gave the scarf to John and urged him to take care of it.

John McCabe, his friends, and Ernie Wilson's scarf were all set for the trip of a lifetime.

'We left Glasgow late on the Wednesday afternoon,' he remembers. 'The Dutch stewardess assured me that she, and her cabin crew, would be able to handle things, and had brought plenty to drink on board. "We did the World Cup last year," she said, to reassure me, but I had to point out that these were very different people. Sure enough, by the time we got to Manchester, they had drunk the plane dry. On reflection that was no bad thing.

'We got to Lisbon in the evening and were taken by coaches to the three different hotels in which we were staying. A lot of these people had no idea of where they were or where they were going. They had just phoned me up, paid their money, and come along. Many of them arrived with an Irish tricolour flag and a passport – nothing else. Some didn't even have jackets, but they were all in great spirits. A lot of them had been imbibing freely by the time we got to Portugal. The poor people at Lisbon airport had never dealt with anything like this in their lives; they had never had to cope with that many people on one day before.

'When we arrived, the harassed officials would tell you something like, "Okay, your flight will be number nineteen going out." Now, I had to remember, because I was in charge, but the state some of these people were in, they might as well have been talking to themselves. On the way back, I was forever being tannoyed to the information desk to identify someone who thought they might be on our plane, but who had forgotten the number of the flight.'

Many Celtic fans sought solace in drink as they flew to Lisbon.

'I went with a pal, and we got a bottle of Smirnoff Blue Label which we did in, on the plane,' remembers Pat Monaghan. 'I also remember that it was a really turbulent flight, and some of the guys weren't great travellers, so there was a priest on board who was actually hearing confessions during the trip.'

The Celticade had also hit town. A very weary John Quinn arrived in the town square at Lisbon at two o'clock on the Wednesday morning. Stiff and sore from a 640-mile last lap from San Sebastian, John Quinn gingerly stepped out of the car to stretch his legs.

'The first thing I heard was a shout of, "Hey, John. John Quinn,"' he recalls. 'It was a guy from the despatch department of the *Evening Times* who'd come out under his own steam. I'd driven more than 1700 miles to a foreign country, and the first person I saw was someone from my own office. It was that kind of trip.'

While the fans were pouring in, in increasing numbers, Stein and his players spent the Wednesday cloistered in their hotel going over the game plan for the following day.

'Big Jock's team talks for a Saturday game were pretty relaxed,' says Bobby Lennox. 'But for a big game like this they could be very detailed. He would have watched the other team a couple of times, and he could sit you down and tell you everything you needed to know. He could tell you who was quick, who would be slow, that sort of thing.'

Stein had been giving the players informal briefings over the past few days, but it was now time to sit down and formalise things.

'We talked a lot about their players,' remembers Tommy Gemmell. 'He was particularly detailed about their markers, Burgnich and Facchetti. Sure enough, just as Jock said he would, the moment the game started Burgnich came across to mark wee Jimmy – or tried to. We'd been told that Suarez would be the play-maker but, of course, he didn't play. Jock also told us that he thought their goalkeeper wasn't up to much.'

Working out how to stop your opponents was more suited to a Herrera team talk. Stein's view was that it was more important to work out how you were going to win the game.

'Jock had studied Inter at some length, and he told me they would play Capellini up, against me, all the time,' recalls Jim Craig. 'The way we were going to play was to put pressure on *them* all the time. Wee Jimmy and Bobby were to spread them wide, and Tommy and I, if we could, were to come forward into the space they had created. I remember thinking that it was going to be awful hot out there, and ninety minutes of driving forward was going to be hard work. With Big Jock in those days it was always "Go on, go on" when you got the ball. Nowadays, they would give you a bit more time on the ball, but things were a bit less sophisticated then.'

Planeloads of fans were continuing to arrive at Lisbon airport. At their peak, they would come in, every fifteen minutes. On the day of the match itself, John McCabe remembers standing in the town square, looking at the day charter flights coming in, and thinking it looked for all the world like an air raid. As more and more fans poured into Lisbon, they headed for the town square which began to look more and more like a little corner of a foreign field that would forever – or at least for the next 36 hours – be Glasgow.

'They were all in very good spirits, and it was a very pleasant day,' remembers John McCabe. 'There were obviously people who had just dropped what they were doing and made their way to the game. There were chaps who had plainly left a Glasgow bus somewhere, because there they were in Lisbon with their uniforms on. Some of the Portuguese misunderstood the bottle-green Glasgow Corporation livery with all the various badges, chains and whistles and assumed they were there in some sort of official capacity with Celtic. There were a couple of other guys there, who were dressed in brown smocks, from McGhee's bakery. I was told that they had left a van of rolls at Glasgow airport and just jumped on a plane.'

Some fans, however, didn't have the most pleasant of experiences. Pat Monaghan was effectively mugged within minutes of setting foot in Lisbon.

'This wide boy got us a taxi when we got off the plane,' he remembers. 'The taxi took us to some cafe and then, when we were inside, this guy got away with my bag and everything else.'

The more legitimate Portuguese were having a field day with their new visitors. Joe Connelly remembers Lisbon as being full of 'beautiful women and handsome men'. He was also struck by the efficiency of the souvenir trade. On almost every street corner there were youngsters selling miniature European Cups.

On the day of the game, planes would be leaving Glasgow Airport from 1.30 in the morning to get the fans there in time for the match. Some 2000 supporters left Glasgow that day, with a similar number flying from Prestwick Airport. The fans had come from all over Scotland, but the youngest making the trip was Paul Miller, a very lucky seven-year-old from Coatbridge who was being taken to the game by two neighbours.

Two lifelong Celtic supporters, James Brady and Fred Hutcheson, both of them 60, almost missed the game because of a travel blunder. They were booked on a chartered flight from Glasgow Airport but, when they went to catch the shuttle coach, they were told that the flight had been switched and would now be leaving from Prestwick. They got on a coach to Prestwick, but once they got there they found, to their horror, that they had been given the wrong information, and the flight was leaving from Glasgow after all. With no time to get back to Glasgow to catch their plane, the 60-year-olds spent an anxious wait at Prestwick. But, at the last minute, a travel operator with two cancellations honoured their tickets, and put them on one of his flights.

The most popular arrivals at Prestwick were the party of sixteen Celtic wives and girlfriends who were flying out to Lisbon. The one who stood out most in the group was Anne Deas, who was then the fiancée of Tommy Gemmell. She was wearing a duster coat with green and white horizontal stripes to go with a matching green dress. 'It wasn't even specially made,' she confided to a fashion-conscious reporter. 'I spotted it in a shop some time ago and decided to save it for the big occasion.'

While Anne Deas and her friends were flying out to watch their husbands and boyfriends attempt to make history, Jock Stein had been making sure that nothing got in the way of their preparations. However, one of his attempts to relax his players could have cost them the game. Stein was keen to make sure that time did not hang heavy on their hands. He wanted them alert to the task ahead of them but not paralysed with anxiety. One of his ploys to help them unwind was to take them to visit a friend the night before the game. Stein had a pal called Brodie Lennox who ran a country club at Estoril. Since they were staying not far away, Lennox invited Stein and the players up to his house on the night before the match.

'We were going up to watch an international that was on television as I recall,' says Jim Craig. 'As you went out of our hotel at Estoril, you would turn left, and then, after a couple of hundred yards, there was a road which stretched off into the country, and Brodie Lennox's house was at the top of that road.

'So we all went up there and watched the match and had a nice time. It was dusk when we left, and we were walking back to the hotel. All we had to do was go back down this country road, cut along the sea front for a few hundred yards, and then we were back at our hotel. It was getting a bit darker by this time, and Neilly Mochan suddenly said, "Hey, there's our hotel over there. It's just on the other side of this field. Let's take a short cut." '

'We could see the lights of the hotel and, to be fair to Neilly, it didn't seem like a dangerous notion to anyone,' Craig continues. 'There we were on the night before the European Cup final, and the whole first team are clambering over a wall, into this field, and across a couple of fences. There could have been anything there. There could have been barbed wire on the wall, there could have been a bull in the field, someone could have broken a leg in a ditch or tripped over a rock. Looking back, it was an absolutely lunatic thing to do. There was no thought or calculation on our part about this being the night before the European Cup final. It was just the quickest way back to our hotel.'

Luckily for Stein – and, more importantly, for trainer Neilly

Mochan – everyone made it across the field without mishap and was safely bedded down for the night. They were under orders to get a good night's sleep and not show their faces before ten o'clock the following day. Stein and his backroom team of Sean Fallon, Bob Rooney and Neilly Mochan had then mapped out every second of the following day until they took the field at 5.30. Then, they were on their own. But they could turn in for the night heartened by Jock Stein's final message to the Scottish press on the eve of the game.

'This is the high point in Celtic history,' said Stein. 'We have every player fighting fit. They all know the responsibilities resting on their shoulders, and we are not going to be foolish enough to do anything that will jeopardise our chances.'

Chapter 19

I T WAS JUST AFTER five o'clock on the afternoon of 25 May
1967. The Celtic and Inter Milan sides were waiting in the
tunnel of the National Stadium in Lisbon before going out
onto the pitch. The National Stadium was more like an amphi-
theatre than a football ground; it was built in a natural hollow and
presented a picturesque sight for those who had the inclination to
appreciate it. No-one in the ground that day felt much like
admiring the scenery. Because of its singular construction, the
tunnel at the National Stadium was not a tunnel as such. The
players actually lined up in the open air underneath the stadium
and would then make their way out onto one end of the pitch.

The Italians were doing their best to psyche out their opponents.
They had been here in this situation before, they had won the
trophy twice, and they did not expect to come away empty-
handed. It was the sort of clash which, on paper, made David and
Goliath seem like a pretty even contest. The Celtic side were on
a basic wage of £40 a week, and the Italians were earning between
£500 and £600 a week. The total annual wage bill for the entire
Celtic staff – players, ground staff and directors – was £28,000.
That wouldn't have paid the wages of even one of the Italian
players.

The Italians were starting to get to the Celtic players, or at least
some of them.

'We're out there in the fresh air, and the Italians are standing
there like gods,' remembers Jim Craig. 'Their black and blue,
vertical-striped shirts made them look taller, whereas our green
and white hoops make you look squat. They've been massaged

and toned up, and they're gleaming with oil. They're looking dead ahead and, basically, treating us with contempt. Then I looked up and down our lot, and there's Ronnie up at the front with no teeth and a receding hairline and everybody else's teeth in his bunnet, and wee Bertie's standing there bow-legged, and there's Jinky grabbing his jersey and shouting to Facchetti: "Hey big man, you and me after the game, swap jerseys, okay?" They must have thought we were mad.'

Craig himself admits to being extremely nervous before the game, and there were others, too, who were stricken with butter-flies, including Johnstone, Celtic's potential match-winner.

'I remember sitting before the game, and wee Jinky was really worried,' Bobby Lennox recalls. 'He was saying, "They've got Facchetti and they've got this one and that one." And I said to him, "But we've got you, and we've got Big Billy and Murdoch." I felt quite confident, I really did. I'm maybe confident by nature, but I thought we could beat most people. I had put my teeth in Faither's bunnet because I thought we were going to win the European Cup, and I wasn't going to have my picture taken without my teeth in. That was the only time I did that.'

The good fortune, which had never been far away when Celtic really needed it, was with them again that day. They were fortu-nate enough to have the only coach driver in Lisbon who didn't know his way to the National Stadium.

'This guy didn't have a clue, and we were all over the place, and we turned up late,' says Craig. 'But that was actually a good thing because we were straight in and changed instead of sitting there worrying for an hour or more. Actually, by that time I was okay, but I remember being very nervous the night before, worrying about all the things that could go wrong.'

Then, as they were leaving the hotel for the game, they received another boost. As the players were sitting on the bus they noticed Stein talking to someone they recognised. A buzz of excitement went round the bus when they realised it was Alfredo Di Stefano of Real Madrid. Di Stefano was probably the most famous foot-baller in the world at that time and Real had asked Celtic to play in his testimonial game the week after the European Cup final. Di Stefano had turned up in person to see them play, to wish them luck, and to thank them for agreeing to take part in his own match. The Celtic players were agog with delight, and Di Stefano's compliment quickened their pulse as they left for the ground.

Now, in the tunnel, they were on their own. They were only minutes away from the game of their lives. Nothing else mattered – not all of their domestic success, not the heroic rearguard action in Prague, not the last-minute excitement of the Vojvodina tie. It was all down to one game. The players settled themselves down and there was a moment of quiet. The stillness was punctuated by a single voice coming from the middle of the Celtic line-up:

'Hail, hail, the Celts are here, what the hell do we care now . . .' the opening lines of 'The Celtic Song'.

'It was wee Bertie who started singing "The Celtic Song" ' says Jim Craig. 'It was absolutely typical of him, and we all joined in. So there we are, going out to play the biggest game of the season, and we're singing. I'm sure the Italians thought they were playing a pub team.'

Auld's singing was a psychological master stroke. 'The Celtic Song', which was written and sung by Glasgow cabaret artist Glen Daly, blasts over the public address system at Celtic Park every match day. The players take the field to it now, but it has never been as important as it was then. The Lisbon Lions went onto the park laughing and joking, and the Italians – brainwashed and conditioned by Herrera's psychobabble – just didn't know what to make of them.

Jock Stein, meanwhile, was delivering the *coup de grâce* in his psychological battle with Herrera. Both teams had been allocated benches at the touchline. Celtic had been given the home bench but, when Stein came out, he saw that Herrera had already claimed it. Herrera was about to find out why Stein was known as 'The Big Man'. The Celtic manager drew himself up to his full height, marched purposefully across to Herrera and told him, in no uncertain terms, he would have to move. Stein reinforced his words by giving reserve centre half John Cushley, who was no shrinking violet himself, instructions to clear the bench of Inter personnel. The bench which Inter should have taken was at the other end of the pitch, and Herrera and his minions had to take a long, lonely walk while trying to recover whatever poise they had left.

The bench-clearing incident took place in full view of the Celtic players. They had seen that their manager had totally dominated Herrera. It was time for them to do the same with his team.

Brian Dempsey had been looking for a safe haven in order to watch the game on television. He had already told the instructor on his Alitalia course that he had every intention of being sick that afternoon. Not wishing to watch with a partisan Italian crowd, and with his own hotel full of the French national squad – who had checked in for an international tournament – Dempsey sought refuge with his countrymen. He headed for the Scots College, a Roman Catholic seminary on the outskirts of Rome.

'I watched the game with a room full of priests and students,' he remembers. He also remembers his heart sinking as he listened to the pre-match analysis on Italian television. They were saying that Herrera had put together a team that could not be beaten. They allowed that Jock Stein had changed Celtic for the better but maintained that the side still had no pedigree in European competitions. They were young lads who, they claimed, had no great personal skills beyond those of Jimmy Johnstone.

'But it was one of the Italian commentators who pointed out something I hadn't realised up till then,' Dempsey continues. 'He remarked on the fact that all of the Celtic forwards that day – Johnstone, Wallace, Chalmers, Auld and Lennox – had played as a winger at one time or another. He was the only one who sounded a note of caution. During the warm-up to the game, he warned that the Italians would have to be careful playing four men square across the back, because any one of those five forwards could do anything. They were all wingers, they were all fast, they were all pacy.

'He said the Italians must not underestimate them because, and I remember this distinctly, he said: "Glaswegians are gutsy people." I sat listening to all of this and thinking that I was glad that the players weren't there to hear it. It was really quite intimidating to hear so many people say they could only see one result.'

Stein had promised that his team would 'attack and keep on attacking until we win this game', and his players were as good as his word. The Italians probed forward delicately from the kick-off, and Simpson was, perhaps, a little fortunate when a shot from Mazzola hit his legs and rebounded away. But, two minutes later, Celtic gave notice of their intentions when Johnstone set off on a run, which tied the Italian defence in knots, before rifling in a fierce shot which Sarti managed to deflect with his arm.

But in seven minutes, Jim Craig tackled Capellini in the Celtic area. The Italian went down as if he had been shot, and Inter were awarded a penalty. Craig can remember one of the defining moments of his career as if it were yesterday.

'I thought I had started the game quite well, and I had got a couple of tackles in, and then came that penalty,' he says. 'Jock had said in the team talk that Capellini would play up, against me, and he did. He also said that he was very good at turning inside so, when he came up, I ran forward to make sure that he couldn't turn inside. If he tried to turn inside, then he was going to run into me, which is exactly what happened. I think very few referees would have given a penalty at that stage of a major final, but I think there was maybe a wee bit of nerves on his part, too. There was no deliberation on my part. There is a deliberation to get in his way and stop him from turning back, but when I see what they get up to nowadays, this seems a minor detail.'

Nonetheless, referee Tsenscher was convinced by the Italians, and Mazzola scored with the penalty. Celtic were a goal down with only seven minutes on the clock.

'I always insist that I just took Big Jock a wee bit too literally when he told us to go out and make a game of it,' laughs Craig. 'I thought, maybe we could give them a goal start. At half time he told me just to forget it, but at full time he told me in no uncertain terms that I had been a bloody idiot. I still don't think it was a penalty. It was a collision, and the referee was as nervous as the rest of us. The Italians were very good at putting pressure on, and he overreacted.

'People always ask me what I was thinking about when I conceded the penalty,' Craig continues. 'I can honestly say, hand on heart, that all I was thinking about at that time was my Dad. I got some stick from some of the players, others told me it was okay, but I was just thinking about what he was thinking. The old man was up there, he hadn't wanted to come, and I had persuaded him to travel all this way – and now I've given them a penalty. He must be pig sick.'

Far from it. Jimmy Craig's emotions as a fan and as a father were completely in harmony. 'In the first place, I didn't think it was a penalty, because the Italian chap was turning away from the goal,' he says. 'He was going across the goal when Jim slid in. I'm inclined to agree that maybe the referee was a wee bit nervous.

'My only other thought was that I was dreading the prospect of Celtic losing 1–0, and Jim being blamed for it. That was the father in me. I hadn't thought that Celtic could win, but I felt that if they lost 1–0, then Jim was going to be the fall guy the same as that poor chap Southgate in Euro '96.

'But I think it was a good thing that it happened when it did, because the Italians were very, very defensive-minded, and when they got a goal in front, they just fell back. That, of course, is when Celtic started to go forward the whole time.'

Celtic had gone into the game with something of a chip on their shoulder because of the spoiling tactics of Herrera and his players over the previous few days. Now they believed they had a genuine grievance.

'We thought, at the time, that we had been done an injustice with that penalty,' says Billy McNeill. 'I think that helped us in many ways. We had nowhere else to go but have a blast at them. After they scored, they fell back and, to be honest, John Clark and I really didn't take any further part in the game; we could have gone and watched it in the stand. The Italians were so intent on defending, that all we did was gather the ball, pass it five or ten yards, and start another attack. They had this catenaccio thing, and I'm convinced that suited us. We had nine players in our side who had all scored goals, and we had 83 minutes left to score them in.

'Where I think they got it wrong was that they underestimated us. They didn't think we had enough skill in our team – like the quality that came from the midfield through Bertie, and Bobby Murdoch. I think other teams had just blunted themselves against them previously, and I don't think they believed we could break them down. We hit the woodwork umpteen times, and we should have had at least one penalty – and Sarti had a magnificent game.'

The Italian catenaccio system is an ugly thing to watch, but there is no doubt that Inter were masters of their craft, and they were proving very difficult to break down. Also, Celtic had to deal with the cynical side of the Italian game, and the Scottish forwards found themselves body-checked and hacked to the ground at every opportunity. To their immense credit, not a single Celtic player reacted to the mindless provocation of the Italians; they simply picked themselves up and got on with the game. They were given no protection from the referee, who had already awarded a penalty for a much less serious offence, but one penalty was plainly his ration for the game. Referee Tsenscher's decisions became, ultimately, so bizarre that he was booed from the field at half time by the 'neutral' Portuguese fans.

Celtic swarmed forward at every opportunity, and shots rained in on the Inter goal. Watching from the terracing, Joe Connelly thought it looked like a playground game of 'three and in' where a goalkeeper stands in single defiance of a host of forwards. Connelly must have feared it was going to be like one of those games he told his mother about, where Celtic were all over the opposition, but still ended up losing.

The average age of the Celtic side that day was 26, this in an era when footballers were believed to reach their peak at the age of 28 or 29. By the standards of the day, they were a young side – only Chalmers and Simpson were over 30 – and they were certainly much younger than the Italians. Inter started to feel the pace as Celtic ran them ragged.

Time after time Sarti – the man identified by Stein as the weak link – was the Italian hero. On one occasion, he defied Gemmell with a save which even those who saw it could scarcely believe. The Celtic defender had blasted one of his trademark screamers which actually appeared to have beaten Sarti. The roar died in the throats of the Celtic fans as the Italian managed to turn in midair and pluck the ball from behind him before it could cross the line. And when Sarti was beaten, then the posts and crossbar came to the aid of the Italians.

'I thought it was going to be one of those days,' says Gemmell. 'We had ninety-five per cent of the ball, but you have days when you have ninety-five per cent of the ball and you just can't get it into the net. It hit the post, it hit the crossbar, it was cleared off the line, and the keeper made some miraculous saves. Through no fault of your own, there are some days when you just don't score any goals, and we thought that day might be one of them.

'Looking back, the best thing that happened to us was that they sat back in their own half and gave us the ball. There wasn't a team in the world, at that time, who could give us so much of the ball for so much of the game, for us not to score. It was just a case of getting the breakthrough.'

At halftime, whether he felt it or not – and his outburst at Craig at the final whistle suggests otherwise – Stein remained calm. He told his players that he was happy enough with the way the game was going and assured them that they could win it in the second half. He made one tactical adjustment. He felt that the crosses and passes from the wings were going too far inwards. What he wanted was for the ball to be cut back; he wanted his forwards to hit the by-line and cut the ball back into the path of oncoming players around the eighteen-yard line.

Celtic went back on to the field with renewed heart. They had more success in cutting the ball back, but Sarti was still in magnificent form and denied them at every turn. By the law of averages even Sarti had to be beaten and, when a Celtic player deviated from the game plan, he finally was.

Although Stein was fond of his attacking full backs, they operated under instructions. Craig and Gemmell could go forward, but not at the same time. One of them should always be back providing cover in the defence. But eighteen minutes into the second half both full backs went forward when Craig picked up the ball.

'I went forward,' says Craig, 'and I could see there was a player between me and the goal – I know I can be accused of being wise after the event, but I was a fairly experienced player at that time,

Above George Connelly
in action against
Hibernian in the Scottish
Cup final, 1972
(Colorsport)

Right Billy McNeill
(Colorsport)

Left Jimmy Johnstone
(Colorsport)

Right Jim Brogan *(Colorsport)*

Below left Bobby Lennox
(Colorsport)

Below right Willie Wallace is
tackled by Jackie Charlton in the
1971 European Cup semi-final
against Leeds United *(Colorsport)*

Above The mighty Jock Stein *(msi)*

Left Jock Stein in training *(msi)*

Left Stein enjoying the fruits of his labours *(Colorsport)*

Right Lou Macari, a product of Jock Stein's excellent youth policy, flies past a tackle against Hibernian in the 1972 Scottish FA Cup final *(Colorsport)*

Left Receiving recognition at the Scottish FA awards *(msi)*

Right Kenny Dalglish, another Celtic youth star, in action in the European Cup *(msi)*

Dalglish of Celtic and John Greig of Rangers in 1976 *(Colorsport)*

and I'm not daft – and he was stopping me having a direct shot. I carried it forward, and there were now two or three between me and the goal, so I was able to cut in and roll the ball into the path of Tommy Gemmell.'

Gemmell picked up the ball a little way beyond the eighteen-yard line and hit a perfectly placed, unstoppable shot which flew past Sarti and into the net.

'About five minutes before that,' recalls Craig, 'I gave an equally good pass to Bobby Murdoch who let it run on to his left foot instead of hitting it with his right. He told me, years later, it was because he had a dead leg. It was a perfect pass, but there was nothing he could do with it. That was the scenario we were playing to; we had been told to cut the ball back, and it worked. I was out of position, or maybe Tommy was, but certainly one of us was.'

'The one that was out of position was me,' admits Gemmell. 'The ball is on the right-hand side so I'm supposed to be pivoting round behind the central defenders on the left-hand side, but the Italians only had one player in our half, and there was nobody for me to mark. Capellini was the only one there, and if Billy McNeill, John Clark and Ronnie Simpson couldn't take care of him between the three of them, then they had no business being on the pitch.

'If you look back at that goal, on the film of the game, you'll see there's an Italian defender who comes out as I'm lining up to shoot. And he stops about two yards away from me and turns his back. If that guy takes one more pace, and he blocks the shot, then no-one has ever heard of me. I'm glad he turned his back, because that was me etched in Celtic history.

'Once we got that breakthrough, I knew that was it,' Gemmell continues. 'I went back to the halfway line for the restart, and I could hear Big Jock shouting from the touchline: "Take it easy, we'll get them in extra time." I thought, To hell with that, it's eighty-five degrees out here, let's finish them now. As soon as we scored, you could see their heads go down; they were beaten men.'

Gemmell's goal came as a massive relief to the thousands of Celtic fans in the National Stadium.

'Sarti had been remarkable,' remembers John McCabe. 'We

were playing exceptionally well, but he was stopping everything. In the second half we had them completely pinned back, but once we scored the equalising goal, we were much more confident. They were shattered. Johnstone and Lennox and Auld and Murdoch were immense, they had so much pace and energy, and they kept on running.'

The scenes of jubilation on the pitch and on the terracing at Lisbon, when Gemmell scored, were matched in millions of homes and pubs across Scotland. In Soho Street, in Glasgow, the young Tommy Burns was watching the game on television with his father.

'Everybody had been building up to this game for weeks, and my outstanding memory is when Tommy Gemmell scored. My father just grabbed me and hoisted me into the air – and being a council house we had a very low ceiling – and he smashed my head off the light. My mother gave us both a terrible row, but we didn't care.'

For the Italians, catenaccio was everything. That was their plan A, and when it went awry, there was no plan B. Even if there had been, they didn't have the energy to implement it. They were out on their feet, and Celtic were heartened by the sight of the Italian backroom staff running the touchline to throw water to the rapidly wilting Italian maestros.

'They were dead on their feet,' says Billy McNeill, looking back on the game. 'I think if we had won 4–1, then that might have been a fair reflection on the play. I was doing a television programme with Bobby Charlton recently, and he said: "You know Billy, I remember you winning, but watching the footage again, I didn't realise how well you had played." I thought that was a very interesting comment, coming from him.

'If we had got our breakthrough earlier, God knows what might have happened. They might have had it in them to have another go at us, but I don't think so. I think they were astounded by the skill of the side, and by the fitness of our team. People didn't really appreciate that that was a good, fit side that could play for ever if it had to. We always exercised patience coupled with concentration because, if you don't lose goals, then one goal – even in the final minute – can win you the game.'

The Italians were despondent, but Celtic were elated. They

attacked and attacked with fresh heart, and could see that Inter were a side there for the taking. The shots continued to rain in on Sarti's goal. He did his best, but from the moment he had conceded one, the result was never in doubt.

Five minutes from the end, Gemmell had gone forward again down the left. Bertie Auld spotted him and stroked a perfect pass to his feet. Gemmell beat two defenders with a wiggle of his hips and cut the ball back, this time to Murdoch. The Celtic midfielder hit a fierce shot which never rose an inch. It seemed destined to fly harmlessly past Sarti's right-hand post but, at the very last second, centre forward Steve Chalmers stepped in to side-foot the ball into the net and give Celtic the lead.

Chalmers, who believes that the Celtic strikers didn't have a particularly good day, maintains he was simply in the right place at the right time. But there was no accident about that goal; it came directly from the training ground.

'I did have a wee bit of luck, because the shot could have gone anywhere,' he admits. 'But Big Jock made us do that kind of thing all the time in training. He'd have all the other players run down the wings and leave me and Bobby, or me and Joe – or a combination of strikers – in the eighteen-yard box. The other players would then fire these diagonal balls across, and we would smack them past the keeper. Big Jock used to come into our group, and he loved to fire it past the keepers. He gave some of our keepers a really hard time. I don't think some of them were ever the same again. I'm not sure how much the other players liked it, but we thought it was great fun, and it paid off when it had to.'

Inter Milan were 2–1 down with five minutes left, and there was nowhere for them to go. Catenaccio had been left in ruins, and the ageing Italians were physical wrecks.

'We had just kept going and running and shooting,' says Bobby Lennox. 'We tried everything we knew, and the longer the game went on the more we knew there was no way they could hold on. We could have scored five or six if it hadn't been for the goalie. When we went 2–1 up, I watched Facchetti as he went back to the halfway line, and I thought: he's exhausted.

'Stevie's goal was the best thing that ever happened to them. If we had gone to extra time and had another half an hour against them, it would have been a much higher score. They would have been completely embarrassed.

'I heard the Italian international Maldini say, a couple of years ago, that they had the best players in Italy, but they were also the hardest trainers in Italy,' says Lennox, with just a hint of disdain at the Italian claims. 'Maldini said they ran everywhere, but let me tell you that what some teams do as a full training session now, we would do as a warm-up in those days. We would have a right good session, and then the ball would come out, and we would play the games. The ball came out a lot, but there wasn't a fitter team around than us.'

The frustration of the Italians was evident near the end when Capellini took a savage kick at Simpson. If it had happened at the other end, it would have started a riot, but Celtic would not be provoked, even then. They played out the remaining five minutes knowing that nothing could stop them from winning.

A few seconds before the end, Stein left his bench and walked towards the tunnel to greet his Lisbon Lions. Behind him, as he made his way down, he heard Kurt Tsenscher blow the final whistle.

The team that was going nowhere, two years ago, were champions of Europe.

Chapter 20

'WHEN THE FINAL WHISTLE went, Luggy Clark and I just jumped into each other's arms and started leaping about,' remembers Bobby Lennox. 'Suddenly, all these people started passing us; there were thousands of them. I thought, My teeth. They were still in the bunnet at the back of Ronnie's goal, so I started running towards them and won the race to get to the goal.

'Luckily, Ronnie's goal was at the end of the ground nearest the tunnel, so I was able to just keep going and head for safety. You're always a bit wary in a situation like that, in case something happens. You just want away. You just want to get into the dressing room.'

Kurt Tsenchser's final whistle had been the signal for a massive pitch invasion. Thousands of Celtic fans poured down from the terracing and the special stands that had been built for the occasion. The only thought in their minds was to embrace their heroes, the men who had won the European Cup for them.

'There was pandemonium at the end of the game,' remembers John Quinn, who was now reporting on the game for the *Evening Times*. 'As soon as the whistle went, and they realised they had won, they just poured onto the pitch. It was mayhem, absolute bedlam. There was a moat round the ground – it was six feet wide and eight feet deep – and it might as well have been a puddle to these people. They just leaped over it as if it wasn't there. They were on their knees, they were kissing the turf, they were dancing around in their kilts. I had never seen anything like it.'

The Celtic players were equally emotional. Ronnie Simpson

was dancing a jig in his goalmouth; he was the elder statesman of the side, and the tears coursed unashamedly down his cheeks as he contemplated their win. But there was now the very real danger of the Celtic players being seriously injured by the sheer exuberance of their own celebrating fans, as they fought their way into the dressing room.

'I was happy to hear the final whistle,' says Tommy Gemmell. 'I felt like I would now if I had just got six numbers up in the lottery. Some of the guys just got off their marks and sprinted for the dressing room when the whistle went. Unfortunately, I was at the wrong end of the ground, and I had to fight my way back the length of the pitch through the crowds. I couldn't get off the field for about forty-five minutes. It was a great day, and you couldn't grudge our fans their celebrations. There were about twenty thousand of them who travelled, and they deserved their moment of glory as well.'

The other goalscorer, Steve Chalmers, was also at the wrong end of the field and was surrounded by people who all wanted to share the moment with him. 'I have never been so frightened in my life,' said Chalmers afterwards. 'I never thought I was going to get off the pitch and into the safety of the dressing room.'

A lot of the players abandoned items of kit in order to delay souvenir-hunting fans, and allow themselves to make good their escape.

'I never felt threatened,' says Jim Craig, 'but I did have only my shorts left when I made it to the dressing room. I lost my shirt, socks and boots going across the pitch.'

The Celtic fans were in high spirits and meant no harm. There was no vandalism of the pitch or tearing down of goalposts or fighting with police, but their pitch invasion meant that the presentation of the trophy, which was to have taken place on the pitch – and the subsequent lap of honour for the victorious team – had to be cancelled. Billy McNeill was going to have to go and collect the European Cup from the Portuguese President, who was up in one of the stands.

'Billy was getting mobbed and making no progress at all,' says John Quinn. 'It was a friend of mine, Don McMillan, who was from Parkhead and one of seven brothers who were all boxers, who went to help. Don boxed at welterweight, and middleweight, and he had fought for the British title. Now, he got himself in front of Billy and acted as a one-man minder until he could get through the crowd.'

The experience for McNeill was so overwhelming that even now he has difficulty bringing it to mind. 'I'm a blank about the end of the game,' he says candidly. 'I remember a scramble with all these people. I remember Ronnie dancing about, and Bobby rushing to get his teeth, but after that I don't remember much until we got back to the dressing room.

'They told me I would have to go and collect the Cup, and Sean Fallon and I had to go right across the pitch and up through the terracing. It was a shame there was no true presentation, because all the others players were entitled to be there, and they were all entitled to parade the Cup. I think the emotions were far too intense to remember. I did have to fight my way across the pitch, but I wish I was doing it all again tomorrow.'

The chaos at the end of the game was such that the rest of the Celtic side were in the dressing room not knowing what had happened. They knew that no-one had seen the European Cup, but no-one had seen the captain either.

'I was back in the dressing rooms by this time,' recalls Bobby Lennox. 'They were H-shaped, and some of us were changing in one part and some in another. Somebody said, "Where's the European Cup?" Then someone else said, "Never mind that, where's Billy?" Nobody knew. That was the only thing that disappointed us that day – we never got to parade the Cup. It was great for the punters who had paid all that money, and I would never take anything away from them, but I really would have liked a lap of honour with that Cup.'

Even with the aid of his unofficial minder, it took McNeill the better part of half an hour to go up and get the European Cup, and even longer to get back to the dressing room.

'The reason it took so long to get back was because of the crowds that were still on the pitch,' explains McNeill. 'There was no question of going back that way with the European Cup. The police were then delegated to take us round to the dressing rooms in a car. Before we could do that, though, it felt like every policeman in Lisbon wanted their picture taken with me and Sean and the Cup.'

It was a remarkable moment for McNeill. Two years previously he hadn't won a single competitive medal and was on the point of leaving Celtic. Now, he was the first British captain to get his hands on the most coveted trophy in club football. Pictures of the time show a dazed and disbelieving McNeill as he receives the trophy. He's the first to appreciate the irony of the situation.

'All I ever wanted to do was play for Celtic and be successful with Celtic. The two go hand in hand for me. I make no bones about it, that moment was like dying and going to heaven as far as I was concerned.'

The emotion on the terracing can best be summed up by Jim Craig's father who stood with his friends, pleased that his club had won and, also, that his son was not going to be anyone's fall guy.

'I was there with Jim's Uncle Phillip,' he remembers. 'This was a man who had been to the Olympics in 1936 and 1948. He had seen Jesse Owens win medals in front of Adolf Hitler, but he stood there, with tears in his eyes, and said that this was definitely the greatest day of his life.'

By the time McNeill and Sean Fallon made it to the dressing room, the celebrations were in full swing. The changing rooms were full of 'grown men crying and singing stupid songs', as Bobby Lennox describes them. There was a huge 'No Entry' sign posted outside, but that didn't stop some newsmen and more than a few fans getting into the players' inner sanctum.

One of those fortunate fans was Pat Monaghan. He had been robbed of most of his possessions on the way to the game and now he was anxious for some souvenirs to take home.

'The guy I was with had got into a wee bit of a squabble with one of the locals about the price of something or other,' he says, taking up the story. 'The game was still going on, and when the final whistle blew, I remember just jumping over the moat. I remember there were guards with guns who tried to order you back, but nothing came of that. My mate Pat got injured, and he was, eventually, carried away on a stretcher, and I went with him.

'We got round to the back of the ground and, who did I see

coming up but Bertie Auld and all the rest of the players, and they were all going into this tiny square with two doors at the end of it. One was the Italian dressing room and one the Celtic dressing room, so I just left Pat on his stretcher and nipped in.

'They were all celebrating, and they were getting showered and everything else. Tommy Gemmell was in the shower so I went right in and gave him a big hug. I had a new suit on but I didn't care. Then I saw Bob Rooney putting all the kit into a hamper, and as fast as he was putting it in, I started taking it out.

'I got a shirt – I don't know whose because there was no number on the back in those days. I got Jimmy Johnstone's socks because I ran after him – and he eventually gave them to me. I was chasing them for everything. Bobby Lennox gave me a Dukla Prague badge off his lapel.'

Pat Monaghan's undoing was when he started to get overconfident and invited others into the dressing room to join the celebrations.

'There were reporters and photographers there, and there was a guy at the door looking for Willie Wallace. I started to get very blasé and said: "You want to get in? Come on. I'll get you in." That was probably a bit too much, and in the end it was big Yogi who threw me out.'

The scenes back in Glasgow were equally chaotic. Bob Crampsey was fronting television coverage for Scottish Television, from their studio in Cowcaddens, in the centre of Glasgow.

'The atmosphere in the city that day was quite remarkable,' Crampsey recalls. 'I think most people who were not Celtic supporters like myself, expected Inter to win and, act one, scene one, they got the penalty. If you watch the game two or three times you can see Celtic trying all sorts of things. They would try this, and when it didn't work they would move on to this, and then this, and then this. But it was obvious when Celtic went ahead that Inter had no other options at all. They had set their stall out for a 1–0 win and they had no other plan.

'I remember going out onto the streets, just after the final whistle, for a breath of air. I stood there at Cowcaddens, and the streets were very quiet just for a few minutes because everyone was indoors, and then it seemed like every door in the city had been thrown open, and people were out on the streets. There was a genuine, across-the-board gladness at the result. All the more so because Rangers were in the European Cup-Winners Cup final the following week, and they were regarded as having a better chance of success than Celtic, so there was a great sense of optimism.'

For David Potter, who was still studying at St Andrew's University, there was no question of listening to this game on the radio. He had to get himself to a television for this one.

'I found a television in our hall of residence, but it broke down just as Inter got the penalty,' he says, frustration still evident in his voice 30 years on. 'There was sound but no picture, so I could hear them say that Mazzola had scored. I had to race around and find another hall of residence with a television. I remember running up the road cursing and swearing in tears of frustration until I found one. The atmosphere inside was electric, and I have to say that, at the student level, everyone – Scots, English, Rangers' fans, whoever – was supporting Celtic that day, and when they won they almost took the roof off.

'I remember the last five minutes as if they were an eternity. I was gripping the sides of the armchair and begging the referee to blow his whistle. My late father actually went and hid in the garden shed after Chalmers had scored, and my mother had to go out later and tell him they had won. He was like me; he could watch while they were losing, even when they drew level, but once they went ahead it was unbearable.'

If the Scots were jubilant then the Italians were inconsolable. Herrera kept his side in the dressing room for an hour after the game, giving them the tongue-lashing of their lives.

'At the start of the game, the Italians could see only one result,' says Brian Dempsey, who had watched the game on Italian television. 'But at the end of the day they had to confront an entirely different result. The tone of the commentators had changed very early in the game, and they started to say that Celtic were a team who were quite obviously not going to lie down. They were not going to show the respect that others had shown to Inter, and they were going to give them a game.

'Nonetheless, they still expected that being a goal in front, Inter would win,' he recalls. 'I have to say they were very gracious at the end of the game and admitted that Celtic had been outstanding. They said that Celtic were a world-class team with world-class players and that Jock Stein, in particular, ranked among the best in the world.'

If it had been an apprehensive Brian Dempsey who had gone out to the Scots College, it was a much cheerier one who came back. Adorned in a Celtic jersey he had been given by one of the seminarians, he walked through the streets of Rome in a one-man victory parade until he was met by a jubilant French side at his hotel.

'Inter were not a well-liked team, and there were very mixed feelings about them in Rome, which is why I got some applause,' he remembers gleefully. 'Rome being Rome, there were guys sitting outside cafes and bars shouting "Forza, Celtic" as I went by. I have to say there were others saying much less complimentary things because, Inter fans or not, they were still Italians. But the French just went crazy; they had never seen anything like this Celtic display.'

The bars and cafes of Lisbon were preparing for a bumper night, with 20,000 Celtic fans out for a good time. John McCabe left the game in something of a daze. He could not believe they had won. He would have been excused for thinking that he was seeing things when the first person he met in the town square was Ernie Wilson, the man whose scarf he had carefully brought to Lisbon.

'I thought you said you couldn't make it,' said McCabe.

'I just decided to sell the house,' said Wilson. 'The wife understood, so I jumped on a plane this morning.'

Having returned the scarf, and still marvelling at the understanding Mrs Wilson, McCabe and his party headed for a celebration of their own.

'We went to a restaurant for a meal, and the only words of English the owner knew were "Merry Christmas". So we celebrated Celtic's win with a Portuguese man yelling "Merry Christmas" at us all night. After that, we had to head back to the airport, and the scene there was utter chaos.

'No-one could remember where they were, or where they were

going, and everyone seemed to have had too much to drink,' he continues. 'Everyone had been given a little stone jug of port as a souvenir which, under the circumstances, was perhaps not the wisest thing to do. I saw this crowd dancing round in a circle and singing at the tops of their voices, then some clown decided it would be a good idea to go the other way. Naturally, half the jugs fell, and the whole place was swimming in port.

'I was called over to deal with one of our party who no longer had his passport – he'd given it to a taxi driver as a souvenir. I vouched for him at Lisbon, and they put him on a plane and, luckily, there was no bother at the other end. Another man, a very respectable Glasgow businessman, had given his good Gannex raincoat to a taxi driver. He was the worse for drink, but he came to on the plane, and when he realised what he'd done, he sat bolt upright with a cry of, "Oh no, my wife will murder me." Another fella, all he could say was: "What a day, what a day, what a day" – and that's what he's been known as ever since.'

While they were sitting at the airport waiting to leave, John McCabe also got a hint of the truly cosmopolitan nature of the Celtic support. 'As we were sitting on our plane waiting to take off, I looked across at another plane on the runway opposite us,' says John. 'It was full of these people with happy black faces, and each one of them was wearing a fez. It turned out they had been brought over from Morocco by an Irish missionary father. He'd been telling them all about Celtic for years and now they had seen them win their greatest game.'

There was further chaos at the airport when their conquering heroes arrived – albeit briefly. The official Celtic party wasn't due to leave Lisbon until the following day, but some of the players had come out to see their wives and girlfriends off at the airport. The fans went wild, which only added to the confusion.

For the players themselves, the post-match period was a major anti-climax.

'There were wild scenes in the dressing room,' says Bobby Lennox, 'but for me it wasn't as good as the celebrations after we won the Scottish Cup against Dunfermline. That was incredible. I think it was probably better then because, that day, we were all together. In Lisbon, some of the players weren't there, and all sorts of people who shouldn't have been, were.'

The after-match celebrations did little to change the mood. There was an official victory banquet, but Inter turned up an hour later after being given a dressing down by Herrera. Celtic, whose impeccable behaviour on the field had won them many friends that day, refused to take this snub for what it was, and applauded their beaten opponents to their tables.

Jock Stein, however, was using the delay created by Inter to good effect. He had been joined by his great friend, Bill Shankly. The Liverpool boss was one of the few who were officially allowed into the Celtic dressing room after the game, and he greeted his friend Stein with the memorable phrase: 'John, you're immortal.'

Now, Shankly could sit back with the rest of the Celtic players and enjoy the sight of Stein settling a few scores.

'I was sitting next to Shankly, and he was waxing lyrical, but Big Jock was having a real go at the English media,' says Tommy Gemmell. 'None of them had come to Prague for the second leg of the semi-final, as they had all written us off. But there they were, after the final, and all of sudden they wanted into the dressing room; they wanted interviews; they wanted into the banquet after the match. Jock didn't miss a single one of them, and he made them feel about that size,' says Gemmell, squeezing finger and thumb together.

For players like McNeill, Craig and Lennox, who felt they had been deprived of their moment of glory with no lap of honour, there was further disappointment in store.

'There wasn't even a presentation of medals,' says Craig. 'The box was just put on the table, passed around, and we all had to help ourselves.'

Celtic had done what no other British team had done. They had won every competition they had entered, including the European Cup. But with no presentation, a victory banquet which had been turned into a farce by the Italians, and no *real* celebration, there was a genuine sense of: 'is that all there is.'

'Bobby Murdoch and I were back at the hotel, and the place was like a mortuary,' says Steve Chalmers. 'There was no-one about. There was a real sense of anti-climax, especially after we had taken the wives to the airport.'

'I remember sitting in the hotel at about two in the morning, wanting to do it all over again,' agrees Jim Craig. 'I wanted to do something, but there was nothing to do. I eventually went out and met a pal of mine who knew where my uncle Pat was, and then we started to celebrate.'

And as the team headed for bed, the Celticade – or at least parts of it – headed for home. 'We had another 1750-mile drive back, but the Celticade was, to all intents and purposes, finished,' explains John Quinn. 'It really finished the minute we got to Lisbon. Once we had got there, and the fans had got to the game, there was no way you could have said: "Right, we're all going to meet up in the town square at such and such a time to drive back." Some of them headed back straight after the game, while others left the following day – but they went back in ones and twos. We were eventually left on our own because I had a story to file to the paper, and we left the following day.

'We managed the trip back, and I was able to hand the Hillman Imp back to Rootes in as good a condition as we got it.

'It was a great adventure,' he says wistfully. 'It was a dream come true for these people. It was the European Cup final in Lisbon and, not only that, but their team had won every competition they entered that season. Then, they face the mighty Inter Milan, go a goal down in seven minutes and then come back to win. It was astonishing.

'But I can confirm one thing,' says Quinn finally. 'The stories that circulated of people flying back to Glasgow, and then realising they had driven to Lisbon, are absolutely true. I know of three cases. They were bunged on a plane in the midst of the chaos to get them out of Lisbon and didn't remember, till they had sobered up in Glasgow, that they had come by car, and the car was still somewhere in Portugal.'

The real celebration for the Celtic players would come the following day when they returned to Glasgow. Stein had appealed to fans, through the media, not to come to the airport. He pointed out that the players were receiving special treatment at the arrivals hall, and the fans wouldn't get close to them. Instead, he suggested that the fans wait for the team at Celtic Park where they would be parading the Cup.

'Big Jock never actually gave us many details about what was happening,' says Steve Chalmers. 'He just said it would be nice to go back to Celtic Park because there were bound to be a few people there who would want to see us.'

A few? There were 40,000 people packed into Celtic Park that Friday night to see the Lisbon Lions and their latest piece of silverware. Thousands more lined the route from the airport.

'The night that Celtic won the European Cup was such a big thing for Glasgow and the West of Scotland,' recalls East End boy Tommy Burns. 'The joy, especially in the East End, was indescribable. The pubs were thronged, and it just never seemed to stop, because they paraded the Cup the following night.'

Burns missed the triumphal procession at Celtic Park on the Friday night because he was playing in a game that night. His wife Rosemary, however, was one of the thousands who turned out to cheer them on.

There was only one group of people who were unhappy to see Celtic coming home with the European Cup – Glasgow's bookmakers. While almost no-one else in the rest of the country would have bet on Celtic, no Celtic fan worth his salt would have bet against them. One chain of Glasgow bookies estimated its losses on the game at around £60,000. Gemmell's goal alone cost around £6000 on payouts to those who had bet on him scoring first for Celtic. Happily, the bookies were not representative of the population of the city at large.

'The bus trip through Glasgow was just amazing,' says Jim Craig. 'There really is nothing to describe the feeling of doing something like that in your native city. I don't know whether Rangers' fans kept out of the way deliberately or not, but everybody seemed to be cheering us. I have to say though that the Rangers' chairman John Lawrence came out to the airport to meet us, and he was one of the first to offer his congratulations when we got to the foot of the steps. He was maligned for doing that by a section of the Rangers' support, but I thought it was a very generous gesture.'

Even in triumph, the rivalry with the other half of the Old Firm couldn't quite be forgotten.

'There was no motorway out to the airport at that time, and the road that we had to come back in on, took us past Ibrox,' says Tommy Gemmell with a smile. 'I think we probably slowed down a wee bit then. I guess our win was a wee bit of a slap in the face for them, but they were in a European final themselves in a couple of days.

'But there was no doubt that we won that Cup for Celtic,' he says with conviction. 'I keep saying it, but we were one big happy family. I'm sure the guys who were left out that day weren't happy being left out, but they were happy being part of Celtic, and we won it together.'

Chapter 21

N O-ONE IS QUITE certain where the term 'Lisbon Lions' came from. It was almost certainly coined by a newspaperman looking for an emotive description of a heroic performance. There have been many great teams over the years but very few that are worthy of nicknames. The eleven men who took the field for Celtic that afternoon in Lisbon earned the right to be called 'Lisbon Lions'.

The right was earned not so much in the winning, as in the manner of their winning. They played with a free-flowing exuberance which had not been seen since the great days of the all-conquering Real Madrid side in the late fifties – the side which won the first five European Cups. There was an honesty and integrity in their play, and they took real joy in the game. Their sheer delight in playing won them friends wherever they went. But they also made a contribution to the game. Had Inter Milan won, then Herrera's tactics would have become pre-eminent in world football. The world would have seen that cynicism would overcome purity, and 'The Beautiful Game' would have descended into an ugly morass of massed defences and endless 1–0 victories.

Stein's tactics, and the men who executed them so superbly, showed that there was hope for the game. They also denied the spurious claims of those who felt that Alf Ramsey's World Cup-winning 'wingless wonders' were the way ahead. Celtic had arrived on the European stage and, in the next few years, would establish themselves as a genuine world footballing power, a team to be feared and admired in all corners of the globe.

Inter Milan, for their part, were effectively finished as a world footballing power. In the 30 years since then, they have failed to make a significant impression on world football. They have been in only one European Cup final since then, and that was in 1972 when they lost 2–0 to Ajax in Rotterdam. When conversation turns to Italian football now, it is the names of Juventus and Internazionale's neighbours, AC Milan, which dominate, rather than Inter.

'The defeat of Inter Milan was a national disaster as far as the Italians were concerned,' says Brian Dempsey who watched the soul-searching and post-mortems that went on in Italy after the game. 'I remember one newspaper headline the day after the game and with it, was a big picture of Billy McNeill holding up the European Cup, and the words were: "Inter Shown Up". They then went on to destroy Inter Milan as a team and Herrera as a manager. They took it very, very badly.

'Catenaccio was completely discredited, and it changed the way we play football,' Dempsey continues. 'There were new influences on the game now. I don't think people give British football enough credit for taking its place in the world after Celtic's win. It wasn't just us, it was Manchester United, and the way they beat Benfica in the final the following year. The emphasis on defensive football, their style, the way they played the game, all had to change.

'Here was a Glasgow team, from a northern European climate, that was not used to heat, and that came out and gave, for ninety minutes, what the Italians would not have been capable of giving. The Italians played to the climate; they played a slow game, with sharp breaks that they could then recuperate from. They were not used to someone coming at them for ninety minutes, and they could not cope physically or mentally.

'The Italian game has always been based on skilled ball control but their athleticism, for me, has always left something to be desired, probably because of the climate. They are prima donnas. They are artists rather than men working at their craft.'

Although they had won the European Cup in style, the season was not yet over for Celtic. There was one more game and, in psychological terms, this may have been even more important than the game against Inter Milan. Ten days after beating the Italians, Celtic were to go to Spain to face the might of Real

Madrid, in the Bernabeu Stadium, for Di Stefano's testimonial game. This was a real battle for the crown of European football. Real saw themselves as the recognised masters of the game in Europe, whereas Celtic were cast in the role of young pretenders.

Celtic have always maintained that they never play friendlies. Every game is as serious as any other for them and, in this case, they found out that Real didn't play friendlies either. The Spanish were really fired up for what was, ostensibly, a salute to the world's best-known footballer.

'The Di Stefano testimonial is really when it started to sink in that we had won the European Cup,' says Bobby Lennox. 'We got to Madrid, and there were banner headlines in the papers which said things like: "We'll prove we are the real champions." There was another that said: "Celtic have our crown and we should have it." That was as tough a match as I've ever played in and, even though it was just over a week after the European Cup final, we were all desperate to play. It was for Di Stefano. This man was our idol, and he had asked us to come and play in this match.'

It's hardly surprising that someone with the skill, guile, and sheer artistry of Di Stefano should have been the hero of so many of that Celtic team. He was the embodiment of everything they aspired to. Celtic had played Real Madrid a few years earlier and been beaten 3–1, and many of the players who played that night were now in the European Cup-winning side.

'I had played against him in 1963,' remembers Billy McNeill. 'The morning after the match me and Mike Jackson were down at the newspaper offices to see if we could find any shots of us in the same frame as Di Stefano. So this game was a special occasion for us. There was also the fact that Real hadn't been beaten at home by foreign opposition for about forty years.'

The game itself lived up to its billing. It was a glorious game which did credit to everyone who took part in it, but none more so than Jimmy Johnstone. The Celtic winger had an inspired game, and the Spanish crowd took him to their hearts.

'We gave them a good going over,' says Tommy Gemmell before correcting himself. 'Actually, Di Stefano did *us* over for about the first twenty minutes, and then he went off. John Fallon was in goal for Ronnie, and he played a blinder. We won 1–0 in front of about a hundred and thirty-five thousand in the Bernabeu, and what a reception they gave us, especially wee Jimmy.'

The Spaniards, always appreciative of artistry in whatever form, realised that Celtic were worthy champions and cheered them to the echo, but none more so than Johnstone.

'Jimmy would go down the wing and the defenders would back off and back off,' says a still-delighted Steve Chalmers. 'Then he'd just dip his shoulders and go past them, and every time he did that the crowd would yell "Ole" and wave imaginary capes.'

The only goal of the game was scored by Bobby Lennox, which brought the season to a symmetrical close. He had scored the first goal against Manchester United in that pre-season friendly, and now he had scored the last one.

Like Camelot, the Lisbon Lions were a brief and shining moment. They played together in only five more games – four League Cup ties at the start of season 1967–68, and the home leg of their preliminary round tie in the European Cup the following season. That tie was lost 3–2 over two legs and Celtic's defence of the European Cup foundered on its first challenge. Having come together in January of 1967, they played their last competitive tie in September of that year. They had played together only eleven times – they had won six, drawn four, and lost one. Ironically, of the three games they played in Europe, the only one they won was the European Cup final – they had drawn in the semi-final against Dukla and lost, the following year, to Dinamo Kiev.

Although he could be a ruthless and occasionally uncaring man, Stein was sentimentally fond of the eleven players who had won the highest honour in the game at club level. He took a calculated decision that they would never play together again.

'When we were back in the hotel after beating Inter, Jock said to me that that side would never play together again,' says Steve Chalmers. 'In fact, he told me that if it had gone to a replay, he would have dropped me for the second game. Given that I had just scored the winner, I didn't think that was the most tactful thing in the world for him to say.'

'I think Big Jock felt that the team that played in Lisbon that day should be protected,' says Billy McNeill who, at that stage, was closer to Stein than any of the players. 'I think his motives were purely sentimental. He never ever wanted to take the risk of that team being beaten in the way Scotland had beaten England in 1967, and then proclaimed themselves world champions. He didn't want that happening to us.'

There were two notable exceptions when the Lions came together again. The first came in a League game against Motherwell in the February of 1968. John Hughes had started the game for Celtic but, in the second half, he was replaced by Steve Chalmers, coming on as a substitute and thus restoring the eleven players who had been on the field in Lisbon, though not in the same formation. That was accidental. The second was quite deliberate.

The final League fixture of the 1970–71 season was against Clyde, at Parkhead. It was completely meaningless since the title was already won. But in a fairly shameless effort to boost the crowd, Stein had promised that the Lisbon Lions would take the field together for the final time. He shamelessly boosted the game like a carnival barker, claiming it was a match you would want to tell your grandchildren about. The Lions did take the field, but they didn't play the game. Ronnie Simpson had already retired after succumbing to a persistent shoulder injury. He came out with the rest of the side and received a well-deserved standing ovation. He also took part in the kick-in and the warm-up, but for the game itself Evan Williams went between the posts. The other ten players were the ones who played in Lisbon, and Clyde were duly routed 6–1 with two goals from Wallace, one from Chalmers, and a hat-trick by Bobby Lennox.

The game against Clyde was indeed a game to tell the grand-children about, but not, perhaps, for the reasons Stein intended. Celtic had changed in the four years since Lisbon and were no longer the side they once were.

The Lions remained the nucleus of Stein's side but, with Simpson giving way to Fallon and then Williams, through injury, and with the use of substitutes now allowed in Europe, more and more players were brought into the fold. Also, Steve Chalmers had broken his leg at St Johnstone in the October of 1969 which, effectively, ended his career with Celtic. With the experience of the other Lions, and the inclusion of new blood like Evan Williams, and youngsters like David Hay and the superbly talented George Connelly, Celtic continued to win. They were in the middle of a record-setting run of nine League titles in a row, and they made it to another European Cup final.

Three years after Lisbon, Celtic were in Milan for another gala occasion. Once again they had confounded the English media by beating Leeds in the semi-final – a tie which everyone felt should have been the final. Celtic were magnificent in both legs, and the pride of Don Revie was duly humbled. In the final, in Milan, they were facing an unknown Dutch side, Feyenoord. Celtic were as hot a favourite to win the game as Inter Milan had been in 1967. Like Inter, they lost. Like Inter, they lost 2–1. Like Inter, they even scored first.

'I remember every minute of the game against Inter Milan, but I couldn't tell you a thing about the Feyenoord game, and nobody really wants to remember that,' says Tommy Gemmell, who scored the opening goal for Celtic that night, too. In many ways it was a better goal than the one he scored in Lisbon, but it is now consigned to the dustbin of history.

'No-one has ever come up to me and said, "What about that goal you scored against Feyenoord," ' says Gemmell now. 'They do come up and say, "That was some goal you scored," and I'll say, "Which one?" and they say, "The one in the European Cup final," and again, I say, "Which one?"

'But it's never the one against Feyenoord.'

Looking back on that match, some Celtic players admit there was a change in their attitude to the game and to their manager. The ones who had been least likely to complain, but had held their tongues, were now more inclined to give vent to their feelings.

'When Jock first came to Celtic Park, there were a lot of players who had been there for some considerable time,' suggests Jim Craig. 'Players aren't daft, and some of them realised that under this man they were going to go places. So from 1965 until about 1968 or 1969, there was a sort of self-imposed moratorium on complaints.

'But from then on, guys got annoyed about getting dropped, they started moaning about things, and Jock suddenly had problems that he hadn't had before. Before that, there was a feeling that you didn't want to do anything wrong in case you got left out, and you were willing to sit on the bench or carry the hampers, or whatever. I think, though, from a certain point around that time, it got to the stage where some of the personnel started to have individual problems with Jock. I say that, not so much as evidence of a team changing, but as an evolution of players and their attitudes,' he adds in mitigation.

Certainly there were external distractions before the 1970 final which were never an issue three years previously. The players certainly had been shamefully ill-used financially for the game in Lisbon. The club had been so slipshod in paying their bonus that, two years later, the players were hit with huge tax bills. This time round they had appointed someone to look after their commercial interests, and the club then let it leak to the media that they were squabbling over money.

'There were other things simmering in the background, too,' suggests Bob Crampsey. 'One of them was that they knew they were going on an American tour at the end of the season, and they didn't especially want to go. Most of them had done it all before anyway and didn't fancy another one.

'Secondly, Jimmy Johnstone, who was a terrible flyer, had been exempted. There was a certain amount of sympathy for the wee man's position, but there was also the feeling that if he didn't go, then some of them were going to have to play more games. So there was a little bit of that, plus the feeling that this tour was not so much a reward for the players as a money-maker for the club.

'They played very badly against Feyenoord that night, even though they did score the first goal. The substitutions were a bit odd, but then the whole side was a bit odd too.'

Celtic had qualified for the final by beating Leeds. The keystone of that victory was the grip that the Celtic midfield of Auld, Murdoch and George Connelly had taken of the game. They had completely negated Leeds' powerful midfield and stopped them from playing. But, for the final, Stein dropped Connelly, one of the most naturally gifted players to grace the Scottish game, and replaced him with Willie Wallace.

'We couldn't believe the team he had chosen that night,' says Tommy Gemmell. But that was only the beginning.

'We couldn't believe the team talk either,' he continues. 'You would have thought that we were playing St Johnstone, or someone like that. He'd been to Holland and seen them twice, but they must have been having a couple of off-days.

'He said: "The guy who plays midfield, he's all left peg, a bit like Jim Baxter, but you won't see him after ten minutes." This was Wim van Hanegem who only got a hundred and ten caps for Holland. He controlled the game from start to finish and, when we went to extra time, he was still pinging 60-yard passes with that left peg. The guy playing up front, through the middle, was Kindvall and, according to Jock, he was one-paced and couldn't really play. It was like trying to catch pigeons trying to catch him.

'It was the exact opposite of Lisbon. We came out of that team talk thinking we only had to turn up. I was rooming with Bertie and I said to him: "If we just turn up there tomorrow, we can win this." And he said: "Well, the Big Man certainly sounds confident enough." '

And Stein's confidence appears to have been sincerely held. Steve Chalmers was in the party, but was not playing because he was still recovering from his broken leg. He asked Stein, conversationally, on the morning of the game, how he thought it would turn out. The manager told him that if Celtic played anything like themselves, they would win 5–0.

Things, initially, went well for Celtic. Gemmell gave them that early lead, but they could not hold on to it, and Feyenoord equalised very quickly. The game went into extra time and, with only minutes left, Kindvall scored the winner. Again, if Celtic could have held on until the final whistle, they would probably have learned from the game and taken Feyenoord in the replay.

'After we went ahead, we didn't consolidate,' says Gemmell. 'They started knocking it about, and we started chasing. We just never played, especially in midfield. We were non-existent in midfield.'

It would be overstating the case to say that the Celtic players lost faith in Stein after the Feyenoord game, but certainly there were cracks starting to appear in the edifice.

'I think maybe he went down a wee bit in our estimation as far as the tactical side was concerned,' says Gemmell. 'It certainly wasn't like him. It was very out of character for him to have a team talk like that.'

Stein's biographer, Bob Crampsey, believes that there were a number of people in the Celtic side who never quite saw Stein the same way again after they had lost to Feyenoord.

'It was this sort of thing which gave Stein such ascendancy over the players,' he explains. 'In 1967 he had told them not only that they would win, but how they would win. He told them: "We'll take the ball down the wing, we'll cut it back, and someone will run on to it. It might be Murdoch, it might be Gemmell." And that is exactly what happened.

'They really ascribed quasi-miraculous powers to Stein, which they never did again after Feyenoord. They felt in their hearts that he had got it quite carelessly wrong.'

There may well have been those who, like Gemmell, felt that Stein had let them down against the Dutch. But there are others, like Bobby Lennox, who put the blame on their own shoulders.

'I would never have a go at Jock Stein,' says Lennox fiercely. 'One or two of the lads might think his team talk wasn't up to much, but if we're in the European Cup final then we should be up for it. It doesn't matter whether it's the best team talk in the world or the worst team talk in the world.

'We got beat in Milan by the better team, and I can honestly say, hand on heart, that Feyenoord were the best team I ever played against. If Jock had told us they were the best team in the world, would that have made us play any better on the night?' he asks rhetorically. 'It was down to us. We didn't play well.

'It's easy to blame someone else, but I don't hear any of the boys saying that it was a great team talk that won it for us when we beat Inter Milan. As for Stein being less than infallible,' Lennox concludes, 'we only went on to win another five Championships under him.'

Chapter 22

THE MATCH AGAINST CLYDE on 1 May 1971, the game you could tell your grandchildren about, was a last hurrah for the Lisbon Lions. Fans had gone along to pay tribute to the greatest side in the club's history. What they didn't expect was that this would be their last chance to see some of their heroes in a Celtic jersey.

Simpson, of course, had already retired through injury, and Chalmers was never the same player again after breaking his leg. Joe McBride, who had been bought by Stein to win the European Cup, never figured in his plans to any great extent after his cartilage operation, and had been sold in 1968. Willie O'Neill, who had started the 1967 campaign as first-choice full back, had also moved on. He had gone to Carlisle in 1969.

Stein had decided, for whatever reason, to break up the remainder of the side. Men like Auld and Gemmell had never been noted for keeping their own counsel and would frequently voice their opinions and engage in the proverbial 'full and frank exchange of views' with their manager. It was hardly surprising, then, that they were among the first ones out the door.

Celtic fans were stunned when, only five days after the game against Clyde, Bertie Auld was given a free transfer. Within a few weeks he was back in a green and white jersey, but this time for Hibs. In December, Gemmell was transferred to Nottingham Forest. In between times, John Clark had gone to Morton as had Steve Chalmers and, in the most surprising move of all, Willie Wallace and John Hughes had been transferred, in a double deal, to Crystal Palace.

In the space of six months, Stein had got rid of more than half the team. If you include Simpson's retiral, then there were only four of the Lisbon Lions left by the middle of the 1971–72 season. Jim Craig emigrated, briefly – to South Africa – at the end of the season, and then returned to sign for Sheffield Wednesday. Bobby Murdoch went to Middlesborough the following year.

The development of the Lisbon Lions was an evolutionary process, but the end of the team smacked of ritual dismemberment.

No-one was more stunned by the transfers than the players themselves.

'I remember when Wispy and Yogi went,' says Billy McNeill. 'Willie and I were good pals, and we were rooming together down at Seamill. He came back in one day because Jock had sent Neilly Mochan to get a hold of him. I was in the room when he came back and said: "I'll need to pack my bags." I asked him why, and he said: "I'm going down to Crystal Palace. I don't know whether I'll sign or not, but I'm going down anyway." It was a real shock, and that was the first sign of the team really breaking up.'

Wallace's treatment seems harsh in retrospect. It would never happen today but, in 1971, players were seen much more as chattels of the club than they are now. They could be bought and sold and have very little say in the matter.

Bobby Lennox, for example, almost went for a British record transfer fee in 1967 and never found out anything about it for years. 'I remember being on tour and watching Bertie Mee of Arsenal being interviewed on television,' he recalls. 'He told the interviewer that, in 1967, he had been prepared to offer a British record transfer fee to bring me to Highbury. When he said that, I remembered that during the Scotland v. England game in 1967, Frank McLintock, the Arsenal captain, had been talking to me about how Mee was looking for a nippy striker. I had been tapped and I didn't even know it. This was years later, and I remember asking Big Jock, who was watching telly with us, if it was true, and he just changed the subject.'

It was inevitable that some changes would have to be made. As Steve Chalmers points out, even when they had won the European Cup, he and Ronnie Simpson were nearing the end of their careers, and replacements would be needed. Jim Craig, for his part, believes that these things go in cycles and, once one player leaves, then nothing is ever the same. For him, the end of the Lions came when Ronnie Simpson had to retire. Nonetheless, the abrupt break-up of the side was an emotional experience for those who were left.

'They were really close friends and it was a bit upsetting to see them go,' says Bobby Lennox. 'We had been through a lot together.'

Lennox, like many others, believes the Lisbon side was broken up far too quickly. But, like McNeill, he believes Stein was acting sentimentally by ensuring that his pride and joy would never be beaten. All the same, there doesn't appear to be a lot of sentiment involved in transferring five players – at least three of them at the peak of their powers – in six months.

'There was a confidence that built and built in that side,' offers Bob Crampsey. 'It was perhaps justified because, for four or five years from 1967 to 1972, Celtic were among the top three or four sides in Europe – there was no question about that. I think an interesting thing happened at the end, because there is always the tendency for a side like that to stay together too long, but I think Stein dismantled it too quickly.

'I talked to him about this, and I told him that I was surprised that he had lost Hughes and Wallace – not so much Bertie Auld, because he had been there a long time – but certainly John Hughes and Willie Wallace and one or two others. His reply surprised me, because he said: "How many of them did anything at the clubs they went to?" '

Stein's reply seems rather harsh and also unfair to men like Wallace, Murdoch, Hughes and Gemmell who went on to enjoy success with other clubs after they had left Celtic.

The one thing that no-one can ever legislate for is ego and, despite his stated desire to protect his stars, Stein may have subconsciously felt that he wasn't getting the credit he deserved.

'Managers might not even realise they are doing this,' suggests Bob Crampsey. 'It might be a deep, subconscious thing. I think there is a desire to let people know who's doing it, who's running the show. One way Jock had was to drop people in turn from the first eleven, in the great ritual that he had called 'freshening up the side.' Again, this would be quite logical, because Celtic had done nothing before he got there, and nothing after he left.

'I suppose he saw, also, that behind the big names there were some marvellous players coming through. There were players like Kenny Dalglish and Lou Macari – he was a remarkable player, and his scoring rate at Celtic was quite extraordinary. I remember coming back from a game one day and claiming that I had seen the Celtic left wing for the next ten years, and it was Vic Davidson and Paul Wilson – but I hadn't. Neither of them thrived, because they were a bit unlucky coming into the team as it was on its way down.'

The remarkable thing about Celtic was that, despite the whole-sale clear-out of the Lions in the latter half of 1971, they had another great season that year. They reached the semi-final of the European Cup and were drawn against their old adversaries, Inter Milan. The Italians took revenge this time, by winning on penalties, but went on to lose in the final to Ajax.

Stein was obviously convinced that what had been done once could be done again, but this time it would have his stamp on it.

'Maybe he wanted to build a side himself,' says Tommy Gemmell, pondering the break-up of the Lions. 'The only player he had brought into the side that won in Lisbon was Willie Wallace; all the rest had been there since he arrived at Parkhead. I think maybe he did try to build one from scratch.'

'He knew he could build another team,' Billy McNeill insists, 'because he had the nucleus, with the likes of George Connelly and David Hay, who were already in the side. He believed that things could happen. It's perfectly feasible that it might have happened because, following Connelly and Hay, he had Dalglish and Danny McGrain and the others. I think his real strategy was that he knew he didn't have to rush them. He knew he could bring them in as and when he wanted.'

There was one player who was untouchable in the dressing room clear-out, and that was McNeill himself. He, too, had found it difficult to watch the men with whom he had been in the trenches in the 1967 campaign disappear out the door. But there was no way he was going with them, for he was the elder statesman, he was Lisbon personified, and he was the rock on which Stein would build this new team.

'I was fortunate, because Jock obviously deemed me to be important to him, and therefore I was special. I was never allowed to go,' says McNeill, looking back. 'I remember in 1972, Tommy Docherty went to be manager of Manchester United. Tommy had brought me back into the international fold – I'd been out of favour for a few years with different people – and I got another three caps with Tommy. But after he had gone to Manchester United, he phoned me one night and asked if I fancied going to Old Trafford because, he said, he desperately needed a centre half.

'I went to Big Jock the following day and told him. He said: "I know, he's been on to me as well, but you can forget it. There's no chance of you leaving." '

So McNeill stayed, as did Lennox, and very soon they found themselves to be veterans in a team of ever-younger players.

'It's easy to look back with hindsight,' says former Celtic director Brian Dempsey. 'I often wonder what Jock Stein would have done today with freedom of contract. Those players would have come back from Lisbon and suddenly realised their potential and their worth, because, in a free-market football economy, they would have been very wealthy men.

'I think Jock Stein prided himself on his youngsters. I used to love going along to Celtic Park to watch the reserve games and see the new faces and the fresh talent suddenly emerge. With the wealth of talent that he had, I think Jock Stein believed that he could re-create and keep the side going. All the same, the European side, at the age they were, could have been good for another three or four years. But I suppose nothing stays the same.'

Celtic's then world-record equalling run of nine League titles in a row came to an end in 1974. The following season, 74–75, they trailed a distant third to Rangers in the League, and it was obvious, as early as the turn of the year, that their challenge had faded. They had gone out of the European Cup in the first round, to Olympiakos of Greece, but they still managed to win the League Cup and the Scottish Cup.

After that Scottish Cup final in the May of 1975, Billy McNeill announced he was retiring from football. Jimmy Johnstone announced he was going off to join the exodus to the USA and play in the newly formed North American Soccer League. That left only Bobby Lennox as the last of the Lions. It was the end of an era.

That summer, Stein was involved in a near-fatal car crash which left him with catastrophic injuries. Sean Fallon was appointed as temporary manager by the board, but the club ended season 75–76 without a single trophy for the first time in twelve years.

Stein was never the same man after the crash. He was in a lot of pain, and it seemed to have affected him psychologically. Close friends say he never had a proper night's sleep again. They also believe that he came back to football far too soon for his own good because of his love of Celtic. This may have been the result of reports from the boardroom where, as early as November 1975, and only four months after the accident, directors were wondering whether Stein was the man he once was.

Stein himself had lost something of his appetite for the game. A re-ordering of his priorities, after such a close brush with death, would not have been surprising. He offered to step aside from first-team duties and assume responsibility for bringing on the youngsters, the job for which he had been brought to Celtic Park twenty years previously. The board turned down his offer but it was obvious that, with Stein's consent, they should look around for a new manager. David McParland, formerly of Partick Thistle, had been acting as Stein's assistant since the car crash but, as far as Stein was concerned, there was only one man who could succeed him as Celtic manager.

Billy McNeill had not been out of the game long. He had enjoyed some modest success in football management, first with Clyde, and then with Aberdeen. When Stein approached him at a football dinner in Glasgow, McNeill didn't hesitate, and in May 1978 he was named as only the fifth manager in Celtic's history. David McParland and Sean Fallon were given golden handshakes, and Stein was to be awarded a testimonial for his long service to the club. In the August of 1978, his great friend Bill Shankly brought his Liverpool side to Glasgow for the game which the Anfield club won 3–2.

With McNeill in the manager's chair, Jock Stein was offered a directorship. The board saw him as having a role in the club's commercial and fund-raising operations. Stein, however, was not interested. The media perception of the new post was, basically, that Stein was there to sell tickets. The former manager may himself have seen parallels with the public relations job that was offered as a sop to Jimmy McGrory when Stein arrived at Parkhead. Whatever the reasons, he did not take the job and, in August of 1978, only days after his testimonial game, he went to Elland Road to manage Leeds United. He stayed at Leeds only 45 days before returning to succeed Ally McLeod as Scotland manager following the debacle in the World Cup in Argentina where Scotland had been humbled by Peru and Iran. Stein remained in charge of the national side until his death.

'I liked Stein as a manager,' says Bob Crampsey, 'and I take the view that the mistake was made in offering the directorship in the first place. I think you should never offer a directorship to a manager, especially a manager as successful as Stein. How could he accept it? And if he does and decides to stay, then you are immediately imposing the task on the next manager to win the League ten times in a row.

'Making Matt Busby a director did Manchester United great harm for about fifteen or twenty years. It did no favours at all for men like Frank O'Farrell and Wilf McGuinness who succeeded him. Not that Matt Busby was in any sense malign, nothing of the sort, it's just that he was such an overwhelming presence. I think Celtic should have said to Jock: "Thanks very much. You've had your testimonial, but you should go now."

'In that last interview we did at Dunfermline, Jock said something to me that night which is the one thing which I carry with me,' Crampsey continues. 'It was a long interview – maybe two and half hours on stage. I asked him if he thought, looking back – and this was about three months before he died – that he had been, in a sense, too loyal to Celtic.

'He told me that it was a mistake to stay anywhere for too long – and this is an interesting turn of phrase – because you're probably still saying the right things, but they've stopped listening.'

Chapter 23

ELTIC'S EUROPEAN CUP WIN in 1967 heralded a remarkable period in the club's fortunes. Twenty-four trophies in all were won under Jock Stein's stewardship, including ten League titles. In those ten seasons in the European Cup, Celtic won it once, were beaten finalists once, and beaten semi-finalists twice. That last semi-final appearance, against Atlético Madrid in 1974, was the last time Celtic would achieve anything of substance in Europe.

Their last League title was in 1988 when Billy McNeill, in his second spell in charge at the club, lead them to a League and Cup double in their centenary year. Proof positive that McNeill and the Celtic fairy tale go hand in hand. That also brought them their most recent appearance in the tournament they had once distinguished, but again they went out in the early stages.

The writing was on the wall for Celtic's European ambitions as early as 1977 when Kenny Dalglish left for Liverpool. Dalglish is one of the most talented footballers ever to play the game and is certainly Celtic's most distinguished and honoured player. Stein fought harder to keep him at Parkhead than any other player before, or since, but the single-minded Dalglish would not be deflected from his purpose. He was going to Liverpool, and one of the reasons for his transfer was that he wanted to achieve European honours.

Since the departure of Dalglish and Stein, Celtic have been in almost terminal decay. At one stage, under the previous administration, it looked as if the club was in irreversible decline. Before the current board took over, the club was facing ruin. On 3 March

1994, the Bank of Scotland informed the board that the club had reached the limit of its £5 million overdraft, and they would have no option but to call in the loan.

Previous attempts to stave off disaster, such as the election to the board of men of finance and vision like Brian Dempsey, failed miserably. Dempsey was the victim of a boardroom coup at the very board meeting which confirmed his appointment a scant five months after he was named to the board. The Kelly and White families continued to concentrate their dynastic control of the club's shares to the detriment of the club, the ground, and the supporters.

In the end, expatriate businessman Fergus McCann – a man who had made his fortune in the United States – stepped in to save the club. It later emerged that when he took over on 4 March, the club was only eight minutes away from failing to meet the bank's deadline and becoming bankrupt.

The attitude at Celtic Park has changed now (1997), and there is no more visible sign of that than the new stadium which will be among the best in Europe when it is completed. Shares have been made available to the fans in a share issue which was many times over-subscribed, and manager Tommy Burns has money to bring high-priced Continental imports to the club. For the first time in years, they are showing signs of being able to mount a significant challenge to their old rivals Rangers.

Throughout the period of decline, the Lisbon Lions have been a permanent reminder of the glory days. Like Banquo's ghost, they hovered in the background. But instead of seeing them as heroes who should serve as an aspirational example to subsequent generations, the club cast them in the role of villains.

No-one has suffered more than Billy McNeill, who was hounded out of Celtic Park in what appeared to be an orchestrated campaign. What else were the fans to make of it when a memo from the then chief executive, outlining ways of sacking McNeill, was leaked to newspapers five weeks before McNeill was eventually dismissed in the May of 1991. The club's most loyal servant – the man who can, without any qualification, be referred to as the greatest living Celt – was unceremoniously shown the door after being made the whipping boy for the club's lack of success.

Other members of the Lisbon side were similarly victimised and ousted from their jobs as 'greeters' for executive box holders at the stadium. It was made clear to them that they were very definitely *persona non grata*.

In 1992 the Lisbon Lions celebrated the 25th anniversary of their landmark victory. The club did not join in the celebrations with any enthusiasm.

'I think the treatment of the Lions in 1992 was shameful,' says McNeill without hesitation. 'It certainly disappointed me and disillusioned me. The chairman of the club at that time, Kevin Kelly, called us mercenaries in a newspaper article. As far as I was concerned, we were entitled to an awful lot more respect and privilege than we ever received.'

Bobby Lennox, the Lion who stayed at Celtic Park longer than any of them, is equally disappointed at the treatment he and his team-mates have received over the years.

'I think, to be honest, the club are embarrassed by our success,' he says thoughtfully. 'I think the old board, in particular, were like that. I think they wanted us out of there because we showed them up for what they used to be. I don't think the new board is like that, but I think the old regime definitely wanted us out.'

'I think there was a measure of embarrassment,' McNeill agrees, 'because people obviously compared what was there at that time to what had gone before. I was always bemused by people who felt embarrassed by our achievements. We should have been one of the great delights of that club. The boys would never have abused or taken advantage of whatever privilege had been offered to them.

'But, to be honest, I think there were people at the club, then, who felt resentful that they had not been involved during the great days, and they took that out on the Lions.'

No British club has ever had a season like the Lisbon Lions of 1967. Not even Manchester United's great 'double-double' winning side, possibly the best team in this country in recent years, has achieved it. None of the successful Liverpool sides, under the dynastic leadership of Bill Shankly or Joe Fagan or Bob Paisley, came close to winning every competition they entered in a single season. It is an awesome achievement and, especially with the hi-jacking of the European Cup by television, it will never be repeated.

How, then, does a club live with a legacy like that? How can it go forward without the achievements of its past dominating its future? The club has undoubtedly been in turmoil. It has had almost as many managers in the last nine years of its history as it has had in the first hundred. And since Jock Stein, every one of those managers has had to live with the legacy of his achievements and those of his team.

Some have coped better than others. Billy McNeill has been in the manager's chair twice at Parkhead and knows the pressures probably better than anyone.

'Celtic's prowess in Europe was always the hardest thing to live up to,' he says frankly. 'It may well have been a handicap in some ways, because you were always compared to what had gone before but, equally, it's not a bad thing to have a target. Having such a historic achievement to emulate has always been a problem.

'I think it took Celtic far too long to come to terms with the fact that the game has changed,' McNeill continues. 'It is no longer feasible for a side to be raised almost totally from youngsters at the club and succeed at the highest level. Football has changed, and freedom of contract has now come in. I think, had freedom of contract existed in those days, the Lisbon Lions might not have been together for any length of time at all.

'That was our one real grievance. We were a team and we produced the goods, but I don't think we ever got the rewards that we should have had. I remember buying a house for £3000, and we put down £400 and borrowed £2600, and Liz and I wondered how we were ever going to repay the rest. In those days, there was a stockbroker, a lawyer and an accountant on the board, and not one of them offered a scrap of advice.

'Loyalty was easy to talk about because, in those days, what loyalty meant was that they kept players on their books for as low a wage as they could,' McNeill argues. 'This wasn't just at Celtic; it was prevalent. All they had to do to retain you at the end of your contract was to offer the minimum wage allowed by the Scottish Football League. If you didn't accept that, then you didn't get paid, and you couldn't go anywhere else because they retained your registration.

'If there had been freedom of contract, I honestly wonder if Celtic would have won nine titles in a row.'

The club, argues McNeill, has also suffered from a period of neglect – benign or otherwise – which was perhaps disguised by the on-field achievements of him and his cohort.

'I don't think the proper investment was ever made in this club, and I know Big Jock thought the same way as well,' he continues. 'In 1967 the gates were massive, they had the resources, and we were as big a club as anyone in Europe; and it was then that the investment should have been made.'

Subsequent Celtic managers have suffered from that lack of investment. David Hay, who managed the club in between McNeill's two spells, also felt strongly that money had been wasted in the good years, and now there were no resources for the lean years.

That has changed to an extent. Tommy Burns has, in theory, more money at his disposal than any other Celtic manager. But it takes more than money to deal with the legacy of the Lions.

'The Lisbon Lions were a good group of players who came together at exactly the right time,' he says unequivocally. 'A lot of clubs have that. Liverpool had it, Manchester United had it, and have it again, and that's the good thing for us. It can come back again if you work hard.

'It might be true that the achievements of the Lisbon Lions are a burden but, equally, it lets everyone know – management, players, the board, the staff – that this is where this club should be, at the pinnacle of Europe.

'I think there was a lot of jealousy about them in the past but, as far as I'm concerned, they are always welcome here. They are a constant reminder of what this club has achieved, but that's not a bad thing for all our young players. It's good to be reminded of the standards you are capable of.'

Burns takes some heart from the players he has brought in, the young players coming through, and the stadium which is going up around him. He knows this is where the challenge lies, but he also knows that the European Cup can never again be won in the way the Lisbon Lions won it. They were not, as myth has it, the first eleven players of the same nationality to win. That distinction went to Real Madrid, who won the Cup the previous year with an all-Spanish side. They are, however, the only essentially 'local' team to have won the Cup. All eleven players were born within 30 miles of Celtic Park.

'I think that situation is unique,' agrees Tommy Burns. 'Football has changed completely now. There are a lot of foreign players moving around now, and there are going to be even more in the future. I think it would be very rare for something like that to happen again.'

Brian Dempsey has supported Celtic through thick and thin. He has had his spell on the board, and he has had his disagreements with Parkhead administrations, past and present. He remains, however, a charismatic and talismanic figure in the eyes of the Parkhead faithful. For him, there is only one direction to go.

'Not having success at the moment means that the easiest thing in the world is to dwell on the past,' he says. 'I always remember reading Dag Hammarskjöld's letter to John Kennedy when Kennedy was inaugurated as President of the United States, and that letter struck me again when I was at Celtic Park.

'Hammarskjöld warned Kennedy: "Don't live in the past. It will not gain you anything, but will upset your memory. Don't daydream about the future, that can achieve nothing for you either. Your future is here and now, so you make the present count."

'When I went to Celtic and this whole sad chapter began and – in my opinion – has still not ended because there is so much hurt to be washed out,' warns Dempsey, 'the problem was that they had started to live in the past. Our only accolade and claim to fame was that 1967 victory and, of course, that was a great achievement for the club.

'But I think the club has had greater achievements. It's had greater achievements because football clubs are about human beings. If you look through the hundred-odd years of Celtic, you will see the number of human beings it has produced with skill and ability; people who have overcome personal dilemmas, or whatever. These people far outweigh lifting trophies of any nature. I think that down the years people are going to remember men like Willie Maley and Jimmy McGrory whose reputations have lasted decades for the gentlemen they were – and which of us is certain to be remembered, after we're gone, as a gentleman? There is the talent and skill of Jimmy Johnstone, the tragedy of someone like Billy McNeill, who is not at Celtic Park now but should be, and the players that we have produced over the years – not only the Kenny Dalglishes but other, perhaps less skilled, individuals.

'Human beings are much more important than silverware, and we have lost our way in that,' says Dempsey.

'The Lisbon Lions were wonderfully committed professional footballers whose inspiration – the club they played for – was the one thing money couldn't buy. The club they played for was not a club of silverware, it was a club of people. It was a club of individuals, of men and women who often spent their unemployment money to see Celtic on a Saturday. It is that which makes Celtic great.

'Because of that, we have to get away from dwelling in the past. It was a great achievement, but we should be working to re-create it tomorrow.'

And there are those who believe it can be done. Players like Bobby Lennox believe not only that it can be done, but that it has to be done. 'It's a hard job,' he concedes, 'but they have to get back and do it. They have to make sure that it will happen again.

'We played Real Madrid in Glasgow four years before we won the European Cup, and they beat us 3–1. The crowd gave us such a reception that night you would have thought we had won the European Cup. But four years later we did win the European Cup, so it's there to be done. No matter what competition you enter someone has to win it,' argues Lennox. 'It might as well be you.'

The last word in this book should go to the man who struggled his way across the pitch of the National Stadium on 25 May 1967 to get his hands on an oversized piece of silverware. Not long afterwards, an English journalist asked Billy McNeill if he and his team-mates had won the European Cup for Britain. The lion-hearted skipper had no hesitation in his reply.

'Certainly not for Britain,' said McNeill. 'For Scotland perhaps. But definitely for Celtic, that's what it was all about.'

Appendix: Celtic in Europe 1966–67

THE LISBON LIONS

Ronnie Simpson (Goalkeeper)
Born: 11.10.30, Glasgow
Signed for Celtic: 3.9.64
Previous clubs: Queens Park, Third Lanark, Newcastle, Hibernian
Debut: 18.11.64 against Barcelona
Retired: 7.5.70
Appearances: 188, Shut-outs: 91
Honours: 5 Scotland caps

After leaving Celtic, Simpson briefly managed Hamilton Accies between October 1971 and September 1972.

Jim Craig (Right back)
Born: 7.5.43, Glasgow
Signed for Celtic: 7.1.65 (after two years as amateur)
Previous clubs: Glasgow University
Debut: 7.10.65 against Go Ahead Deventer
Left Celtic: 6.5.72 (for Hellenic in South Africa)
Appearances: 231, Goals: 6
Honours: 1 Scotland cap

After six months in South Africa, Craig returned for eighteen months at Sheffield Wednesday before retiring as a player in May 1974. He became the manager of the Irish club Waterford for a short time in 1974.

Tommy Gemmell (Left back)
Born: 16.10.43, Craigneuk, Lanarkshire
Signed for Celtic: 25.10.61
Previous clubs: Coltness United
Debut: 5.1.63 against Aberdeen
Left Celtic: 12.12.71 (for Nottingham Forest)
Appearances: 418, Goals: 64
Honours: 18 Scotland caps, 5 Scottish League caps

After leaving Celtic for Nottingham Forest on a free transfer, Gemmell later signed for Miami Toros and then Dundee. He managed Dundee, and has had two spells as manager of Albion Rovers.

Bobby Murdoch (Right half)
Born: 17.8.44, Bothwell, Lanarkshire
Signed for Celtic: 23.10.59
Previous clubs: none
Debut: 11.8.62 against Hearts
Left Celtic: 17.9.73 (for Middlesborough)
Appearances: 484, Goals: 105
Honours: 12 Scotland caps, 5 Scottish League caps, 1 Scotland Under-23 cap

Once Murdoch had retired from playing at Middlesborough, he became club coach and took over as manager between May 1981 and September 1982.

Billy McNeill (Centre half and captain)
Born: 2.3.40, Bellshill, Lanarkshire
Signed for Celtic: 20.8.57
Previous clubs: none
Debut: 23.8.58 against Clyde
Retired: 3.5.75
Appearances: 790, Goals: 34
Honours: 29 Scotland caps, 9 Scottish League caps, 5 Scotland Under-23 caps

McNeill became manager of Clyde in 1977. He followed this with spells in charge of Aberdeen, Celtic, Manchester City, Aston Villa and Celtic again. He was manager in the club's double-winning centenary year but was dismissed in May 1991.

John Clark (Left half)
Born: 13.3.41, Bellshill, Lanarkshire
Signed for Celtic: 8.10.58
Previous clubs: Larkhall Thistle, Birmingham City, Larkhall Thistle
Debut: 3.10.59 against Arbroath
Left Celtic: 12.6.71 (for Morton)
Appearances: 318, Goals: 3
Honours: 4 Scotland caps, 2 Scottish League caps

John Clark returned to Celtic as a coach in 1973 before joining Billy McNeill as assistant at Aberdeen and then at Celtic. He has also been manager of Cowdenbeath, Stranraer and Clyde.

Jimmy Johnstone (Outside right)
Born: 30.9.44, Viewpark, Lanarkshire
Signed for Celtic: 8.11.61
Previous clubs: Blantyre Celtic
Debut: 27.3.63 against Kilmarnock
Left Celtic: 9.6.75 (for Hamilton Accies)
Appearances: 515, Goals: 129
Honours: 23 Scotland caps, 4 Scottish League caps

Johnstone was only at Hamilton a matter of weeks before signing for San Jose Earthquakes in the burgeoning NASL. He later returned for spells with Sheffield United, Dundee, Shelbourne, Elgin City and Blantyre Celtic where he was player-coach for four months in 1980.

Willie Wallace (Inside right)
Born: 23.6.40, Kirkintilloch
Signed for Celtic: 6.12.66

Previous clubs: Kilsyth Rangers, Stenhousemuir, Raith Rovers, Hearts
Debut: 10.12.66 against Motherwell
Left Celtic: 19.10.71 (for Crystal Palace)
Appearances: 234, Goals: 135
Honours: 4 Scotland caps, 4 Scottish League caps

After signing for Crystal Palace, Wallace went on to play for Dumbarton before emigrating to Australia where he played for Apia. He returned to Scotland for brief spells with Ross County and Dundee before going back to Australia.

Steve Chalmers (Centre forward)
Born: 26.12.36, Glasgow
Signed for Celtic: 6.2.59
Previous clubs: Kirkintilloch Rob Roy, Newmarket Town, Ashfield
Debut: 10.3.59 against Airdrie
Left Celtic: 9.9.71 (for Morton)
Appearances: 405, Goals: 228
Honours: 5 Scotland caps, 4 Scottish League caps

Chalmers joined Morton as a player-coach. He then joined Partick Thistle as a player before joining the Celtic coaching staff in 1975.

Bertie Auld (Inside left)
Born: 3.3.38, Glasgow
Signed for Celtic: 2.4.55
Previous clubs: Panmure Thistle, Maryhill Harp
Debut: 1.5.57 against Rangers
Left Celtic: 1.5.61 (for Birmingham City before returning on 14.1.65)
Appearances: 279, Goals: 85
Honours: 3 Scotland caps, 2 Scottish League caps

After returning from Birmingham in 1965, Auld finally left Celtic for Hibernian in May 1971. He became coach at Hibs before managing Partick Thistle and then returning to Easter Road as manager. He also had spells in charge at Hamilton, Partick Thistle for a second time, and Dumbarton.

Bobby Lennox (Outside left)
Born: 30.8.43, Saltcoats, Ayrshire
Signed for Celtic: 5.9.61
Previous clubs: Ardeer Recreation
Debut: 3.3.62 against Dundee
Retired: 8.11.80
Appearances: 571, Goals: 273
Honours: 10 Scotland caps, 3 Scottish League caps

Lennox left Celtic briefly in March of 1978 for a six-month spell with Houston Hurricanes in the NASL, but returned in September of that year. He joined the Parkhead coaching staff after his retirement from playing but was dismissed in 1993.

THE SQUAD MEMBERS

John Fallon (Goalkeeper)
Born: 16.8.40, Blantyre
Signed for Celtic: 11.12.58
Previous clubs: none
Debut: 26.9.59 against Clyde
Left Celtic: 29.2.72 (for Motherwell)
Appearances: 184, Shut-outs: 61
Honours: none

After joining Motherwell, Fallon then signed for Morton and finally Blantyre Celtic, as coach.

David Cattanach (Defender)
Born: 27.6.46, Falkirk
Signed for Celtic: 19.8.63
Previous clubs: Stilring Albion
Debut: 9.4.66 against St Mirren
Left Celtic: 20.1.72 (for Falkirk)
Appearances: 19, Goals: 1
Honours: none

After joining Falkirk, Cattanach was given a free transfer, at his own request, two years later. After a spell as coach of Stirling Albion, he gave up football to concentrate on his thriving business interests.

Willie O'Neill (Defender)
Born: 30.12.40, Glasgow
Signed for Celtic: 12.10.59
Previous clubs: St Anthony's
Debut: 26.4.61 against Dunfermline
Left Celtic: 13.5.69 (for Carlisle)
Appearances: 86, Goals: 0
Honours: none

Willie O'Neill played for Carlisle for two seasons before being forced to retire in 1971 with an ankle injury.

Ian Young (Defender)
Born: 21.5.43, Glasgow
Signed for Celtic: 28.6.61
Previous clubs: Neilston Waverley
Debut: 5.5.62 against Third Lanark
Left Celtic: 1.5.68 (for St Mirren)
Appearances: 164, Goals: 3
Honours: none

After joining St Mirren, Young stayed at Love Street for two years before joining Saltcoats Victoria as a coach.

Jim Brogan (Defender)
Born: 5.6.44, Glasgow
Signed for Celtic: 11.9.62
Previous clubs: St Roch's
Debut: 21.9.63 against Falkirk
Left Celtic: 4.6.75 (for Coventry City)
Appearances: 339, Goals: 9
Honours: 4 Scotland caps, 1 Scottish League cap

Brogan had a spell at Ayr United before retiring on 1 November 1977.

John Cushley (Centre half)
Born: 21.1.43, Hamilton
Signed for Celtic: 7.7.60
Previous clubs: Blantyre Celtic
Debut: 27.3.63 against Kilmarnock
Left Celtic: 17.7.67 (for West Ham)
Appearances: 41, Goals: 0
Honours: none

After joining West Ham, Cushley also had spells with Dunfermline and Dumbarton. He rejoined Celtic as a coach in 1978 before serving as assistant manager at Dumbarton and Clyde.

Celtic

Charlie Gallagher (Inside forward)
Born: 3.11.40, Glasgow
Signed for Celtic: 20.9.58
Previous clubs: Kilmarnock Amateurs, Yoker Athletic
Debut: 22.8.59 against Raith Rovers
Left Celtic: 1.5.70 (for Dumbarton)
Appearances: 171, Goals: 32
Honours: 2 Republic of Ireland caps
Charlie Gallagher spent three seasons at Dumbarton before retiring from football in 1973.

Joe McBride (Centre forward)
Born: 10.6.38, Glasgow
Signed for Celtic: 5.6.65
Previous clubs: Kilmarnock Amateurs, Shettleston Town, Kirkintilloch Rob Roy, Kilmarnock, Wolves, Luton, Partick Thistle, Motherwell
Debut: 21.8.65 against Dundee
Left Celtic: 5.11.68 (for Hibernian)
Appearances: 94, Goals: 86
Honours: 2 Scotland caps, 4 Scottish League caps
After leaving Celtic for Hibs, the much-travelled McBride then went on to play for Dunfermline and Clyde before retiring in 1972.

John Hughes (Forward)
Born: 3.4.43, Coatbridge
Signed for Celtic: 3.10.59
Previous clubs: Shotts Bon Accord
Debut: 13.8.60 against Third Lanark
Left Celtic: 19.10.71 (for Crystal Palace)
Appearances: 416, Goals: 189
Honours: 8 Scotland caps, 6 Scottish League caps

Hughes moved to Crystal Palace in a double transfer deal with Willie Wallace. He then went on to play for Sunderland before moving into junior football management including four years as coach of the Scottish Junior Football Association side.

THE GAMES

28 September 1966 Celtic 2 Zurich 0
Celtic: Simpson, Gemmell, O'Neill, Murdoch, McNeill, Clark, Johnstone, McBride, Chalmers, Auld, Hughes.
Scorers: Gemmell, McBride

5 October 1966 Zurich 0 Celtic 3
Celtic: Simpson, Gemmell, O'Neill, Murdoch, McNeill, Clark, Johnstone, Lennox, Chalmers, Auld, Hughes.
Scorers: Gemmell (2), Chalmers

30 November 1966 Nantes 1 Celtic 3
Celtic: Simpson, Gemmell, O'Neill, Murdoch, McNeill, Clark, Johnstone, Chalmers, McBride, Lennox, Auld.
Scorers: McBride, Lennox, Chalmers

7 December 1966 Celtic 3 Nantes 1
Celtic: Simpson, Gemmell, O'Neill, Murdoch, McNeill, Clark, Johnstone, Gallagher, Chalmers, Auld, Lennox.
Scorers: Johnstone, Chalmers, Lennox

1 March 1967 Vojvodina 1 Celtic 0
Celtic: Simpson, Craig, Gemmell, Murdoch, McNeill, Clark, Johnstone, Lennox, Chalmers, Auld, Hughes.

8 March 1967 Celtic 2 Vojvodina 0
Celtic: Simpson, Craig, Gemmell, Murdoch, McNeill, Clark, Johnstone, Lennox, Chalmers, Gallagher, Hughes.
Scorers: Chalmers, McNeill

12 April 1967 Celtic 3 Dukla Prague 1
Celtic: Simpson, Craig, Gemmell, Murdoch, McNeill, Clark, Johnstone, Wallace, Chalmers, Auld, Hughes.
Scorers: Johnstone, Wallace (2)

25 April 1967 Dukla Prague 0 Celtic 0

Celtic

Celtic: Simpson, Craig, Gemmell, Murdoch, McNeill, Clark, Johnstone, Wallace, Chalmers, Auld, Lennox.

FINAL: 25 May 1967 Celtic 2 Inter Milan 1
Celtic: Simpson, Craig, Gemmell, Murdoch, McNeill, Clark, Johnstone, Wallace, Chalmers, Auld, Lennox.
Scorers Gemmell, Chalmers

EUROPEAN APPEARANCES 1966–67

Ronnie Simpson 9
Tommy Gemmell 9
Willie O'Neill 4 (Zurich h&a, Nantes h&a)
Jim Craig 5 (Vojvodina h&a, Dukla Prague h&a, Inter Milan)

Bobby Murdoch 9
Billy McNeill 9
John Clark 9
Jimmy Johnstone 9
Bobby Lennox 7 (Zurich a, Nantes h&a, Vojvodina h&a, Dukla Prague a, Inter Milan)
Willie Wallace 3 (Dukla Prague h&a, Inter Milan)
Joe McBride 2 (Zurich h, Nantes a)
Steve Chalmers 9
Charlie Gallagher 2 (Nantes h, Vojvodina h)
Bertie Auld 8 (Zurich h&a, Nantes h&a, Vojvodina a, Dukla Prague h&a, Inter Milan)
John Hughes 5 (Zurich h&a, Vojvodina h&a, Dukla Prague h)

Squad members not used: John Fallon, David Cattanach, Ian Young, John Cushley and Jim Brogan.

CELTIC GOALSCORERS IN EUROPE 1966–67

Steve Chalmers   5
Tommy Gemmell   4
Willie Wallace   2
Bobby Lennox   2
Joe McBride   2
Jimmy Johnstone   2
Billy McNeill   1

Goals for 18, Goals against 5

Index

Index

Masopust, Josef 132, 135, 144, 147, 148
Mattinelli (Zurich) 72
Mazzola (Inter Milan) 160, 179
McBride, Joe 60, 230, 233
  signs for Celtic 38
  goal scoring record 38, 84, 110, 234
  knee injury 60, 88, 90–91, 101–2, 110, 127, 134–5
  scores in European Cup 64, 82
  left out at Zurich 70
  forgets his boots 81–2
  technique 92
  transferred 208
McCabe, John 13, 22, 152–4, 169–70, 171, 193, 194
McCann, Fergus 216
McCardle, Eddie 8
McFadden, John 12
McGrain, Danny 96, 211
McGrory, Jimmy 221
  player 17, 33
  manager 5, 7, 8, 14, 17–18, 30, 37
  public relations officer 18
McGrory, Johnny 5
McGuinness, Wilf 214
McKinnon, Ronnie 119, 132
McLintock, Frank 209
McMillan, Don 188–9
McNeill, Billy 'Caesar' 1, 224–5, 233
  early years with Celtic 8–13, 15–16
  appointed team captain 18–19, 25–6, 59
  relationship with Jock Stein 24–5, 26
  scores in Scottish Cup final (1965) 28–9

technique 69
superstitions 78
scores against Vojvodina 117–20, 122
collects European Cup 188–90
stays on at Celtic 211–12
retires 212–13
as manager 213, 215, 218
dismissed 216
McParland, David 213
McStay, Jimmy 17
Mee, Bertie 209
Meyer (Zurich) 63, 72
Milburn, Jackie 21
Miller, Paul 172
Mochan, Neilly 53, 77, 80, 119, 173–4
Monaghan, Pat 30, 154, 170, 172, 190–91
Montford, Arthur 123
Morris, Bill 155
Motherwell 23, 37, 38, 39, 91, 132, 203
MTK Budapest 39, 58
Muller, Gerd 49–50
Murdoch, Bobby 19, 224, 233
  technique 33, 48, 97
  injury 131
  change of position 131, 133–4
  transferred 134, 209
Musil, Bohimil 133, 142

Nantes 75, 78–83, 87–90, 231
Nedorost (Dukla) 135, 147
Neumann (Zurich) 73
New York 55
Newcastle 21
North American tour (1966) 47–55

O'Farrell, Frank 214

Index